NO ONE MAKES YOU SHOP AT WAL-MART

NO ONE MAKES YOU SHOP AT WAL-MART

★

the surprising deceptions of individual choice

TOM SLEE

BETWEEN THE LiNES

TORONTO

No One Makes You Shop at Wal-Mart

First published in Canada in 2006 by
Between the Lines
720 Bathurst Street, Suite #404
Toronto, Ontario M5S 2R4
1-800-718-7201
www.btlbooks.com

Library and Archives Canada Cataloguing in Publication

Slee, Tom, 1959-
     No one makes you shop at Wal-Mart : the surprising deceptions of individual choice / Tom Slee.
Includes bibliographical references and index.
ISBN 1-897071-06-X

1. Social choice. 2. Consumers' preferences. 3. Conservatism. I. Title.
HB846.8.S56 2006   306.1'23   C2006-900685-7

Cover design by Jennifer Tiberio
Page preparation by Steve Izma
Printed in Canada
Second printing, February 2007
Between the Lines gratefully acknowledges assistance for its publishing activities from the Canada Council for the Arts, the Ontario Arts Council, the Government of Ontario through the Ontario Book Publishers Tax Credit program and through the Ontario Book Initiative, and the Government of Canada through the Book Publishing Industry Development Program.

Canada Council   Conseil des Arts
for the Arts   du Canada

Canadä

ONTARIO ARTS COUNCIL
CONSEIL DES ARTS DE L'ONTARIO

To Lynne, Jamie, and Simon

CONTENTS

FIGURES

ACKNOWLEDGEMENTS

WHEN YOU PUBLISH YOUR FIRST BOOK at age 46, a lot of people have influenced whatever thoughts make their way onto the printed page. Here is a partial list, with apologies to those I have overlooked.

The book is largely a popularization of other people's ideas. I am indebted to all those who carry out the rich and detailed academic work that forms the basis for the descriptions contained here. Those whose works I have returned to over and over again include George Akerlof, Robert Axelrod, Jane Jacobs, Rachel Kranton, Paul Krugman, the late Mancur Olson, Anatol Rapoport, Thomas Schelling, Amartya Sen, and Joseph Stiglitz, none of whom bear any responsibility for my mangling of their thoughts.

You can't make an appeal for the virtues of collective action without having some good collective experiences. I am lucky to have had several. Many thanks to those from the following groups for their intelligence, support, friendship, and inspiration at various points in my life: Park Village 13 and National Organization of Labour Students (Sussex), the RFW Bader lab at McMaster University, the Canadian Union of Educational Workers (especially Local 6),

Hamilton Central America Solidarity Committee, Ontario Central America Solidarity Network, Tools For Peace, Action Against Militarism, and colleagues at Sybase Waterloo. Matthew Caunt, Lawrence Welsh, Garry Brennand, Barb MacQuarrie, and Claudio Chuaqui also deserve special mention. Families provide particularly important collective experiences: Frank, Audrey, Jeff, John, and Liz Slee shaped whatever ideas I have now. Lynne, Jamie, and Simon continue to do so.

Many people have commented on drafts of this book. In blatant violation of all notions of self-interested behaviour, Jim Stanford provided an invaluable endorsement to a complete stranger. John Slee and Graeme MacQueen read multiple drafts of this book. They helped to shape the work in its early and middle stages and provided the right mix of encouragement, criticism, and new ideas.

In later stages the staff and readers of Between the Lines helped to turn a manuscript into a book. My thanks to Paul Eprile, Jonathan Barker, Jennifer Tiberio, Steve Izma, and Andrea Kwan for their contributions to different parts of this process, and to Robert Clarke, whose editing has sharpened presentation throughout. Thanks in particular to Gillian Barker, who contributed at all levels by identifying priorities, deepening arguments, and untangling knots throughout the manuscript; her ideas and insights have been invaluable. I am responsible for those confusions and inaccuracies that remain, despite the best efforts of all these people.

Inspiration for this book comes from the example of three admirable women:

- Jacquie Perey (1964–2004), whose continual challenging of those around her was matched only by the challenges she set herself. In her last letter to me, she asked whether I was pursuing any "magical projects" and strongly suggested that, if not, I should start doing so right away. It is difficult to argue that game theory is magical, but this is as magical as I get. Thank you Jacquie.
- Audrey Slee, who has demonstrated by a half-century of continual political activity and civic commitment that real changes can be made to people's lives if you stick to it. Thank you Mum.

- Lynne Supeene, who has provided emotional and intellectual support and companionship over the several-year period during which this book was written. She has been unfailingly helpful in identifying which strands of this book to pursue and which to drop. She knows when to encourage, when to push a little, when to make suggestions, and when not to. Also, by the way in which she has pursued and succeeded at her own writing, Lynne has been an inspiring example. Thank you Lynne.

Tom Slee

chapter one

A WORLD OF CHOICE

WE LIVE IN A WORLD OF CHOICE.

We make choices every day. We choose the clothes we wear, the way we travel, the movies we watch, and the places we shop. From time to time we make bigger choices as well: the neighbourhoods we live in, the jobs or universities or schools we go to, and even the cultures we identify with. These choices give us a measure of control over our lives, and it seems natural to believe that individual choice is, almost by definition, a good thing.

Members of the political right have long believed in its virtues, but now individual choice has also gained a much broader appeal. Individual choice is being promoted, to different degrees, across the political spectrum as a key ingredient in the recipe for economic prosperity and political freedom.

The recipe has an appealing common-sense simplicity. First, let the people choose. Second, let suppliers compete to give us what we want. Finally, let the invisible hand of the free market provide efficiency, innovation, responsiveness, and growth.

What's more, individual choice appears to be on the side of the powerless. No one, after all, makes you eat at McDonald's, drive Ford cars, wear Nike shoes, or shop at Wal-Mart. In our role as consumers, we can choose to walk away from the sales pitches of even the largest multinational corporations. Consumers are sovereign, and multinationals are their subjects.

It sounds so straightforward, and when faced with a less than adequate school or an intransigent bureaucracy even the most cynical might agree that the opportunity to vote with our feet is attractive. Perhaps opening up government and other institutions to choice and "the discipline of the market" will provide the stimulus needed to make those institutions responsive?

Yet individual choice has not delivered on its promise. A reliance on individual choice has not helped the poor or even average-income citizen, but has instead given more power and wealth to those who are already at the top of the heap. Economists Thomas Piketty and Emmanual Saez, in a detailed analysis of trends in U.S. income, found that a "period of falling inequality" during the first half of the 20th century was "succeeded by a very sharp reversal of the trend since the 1970s."[1]

There are any number of ways to describe this reversal. For example, Piketty and Saez compare CEO compensation to that of the average U.S. employee: while the average income increased by just 13 per cent between 1970 and 2003, the average compensation for the top 100 CEOs grew by 1,300 per cent. In 1970 the tenth-ranked CEO would have had to put in a week of work to earn an amount equal to the average annual income. In 2003 he would have had to work only half a day – he could go home by lunchtime on the first day of the year. Other English-speaking countries have also experienced sky-rocketing incomes at the top, although this trend has been seen "not at all in continental Europe countries or Japan." [2]

The usual counterargument to these observations is that the increase in inequality generates increasing wealth: that it is a rising tide that lifts all boats, even if it lifts the luxury boats most. But the evidence for that rising tide has been increasingly hard to find. For example, Piketty and Saez also showed that between 1973 and 2002 those in the top 0.1 per cent of U.S. taxpayers saw their real incomes increase by a healthy 227 per cent, while the average real income of the bottom 90 per cent actually dropped by 9 per cent.[3]

Of course, the details vary depending on the years, groups, and measure of income or wealth that you use, but the broad picture is clear: in the last few decades the earnings growth in the United States, Canada, and United Kingdom has gone disproportionately to the already wealthy, and many people at the middle or the bottom end of the income scale have failed to become any better off over that time.

Somehow, individual choice has turned out to be on the side of the powerful. And somehow we have ended up making choices that make us worse off. What has gone wrong? Why is it that with more choices than any society in history, we do not get what we want? This book is an attempt to answer these questions.

A Short Modern History of Choice

Over the last half-century, the idea of individual choice has moved steadily to the centre of the economic and political stage. At the end of the Second World War, the citizens of the victorious allied countries rightly felt a tremendous sense of collective accomplishment. The war had demonstrated the power of people working together for common goals. Indeed, the success of the war effort was built on a foundation of collective struggle and shared individual sacrifice – a foundation perhaps best expressed in Britain's "spirit of the Blitz."

This sense of the strength of co-operative, collective action found political expression in the years after the war. These were years that saw the expansion of the welfare state, broader access to health care and higher education, new housing programs, a new standard of unemployment insurance and old-age pensions, and the recognition, and growth, of unions as bona fide institutions. These years also delivered a consistent pattern of economic growth and improved living standards for most people in the industrialized world.

The 1970s saw the long years of growth come to an end, a condition highlighted by the oil crisis of 1973. Societies everywhere started to look for new approaches. Choice, as political scientist and commentator Janice Gross Stein points out, is "a luxury of an affluent society,"[4] and it is no surprise that prosperity had brought with it a demand for increased individual choices. Individualistic ideas drove out the postwar communal ideals and found their own conservative political expression at the end of the decade in the elections of Margaret Thatcher in Britain and Ronald Reagan in the United States, with Brian Mulroney of Canada and Helmut Kohl of Germany following not far behind. As they took power, these neo-conservatives needed theoretical guidance and inspiration, and they found it in a group of economists from the University of Chicago, of which Milton Friedman was the most prominent member.

What became known as the Chicago school had been busy attacking the then-dominant Keynesian ideas that government spending could be used to carry economies through recessions and even pull them out of depressions (U.S. president Richard Nixon famously declared in 1971, "We are all Keynesians now"), and the election of conservative parties gave the Chicago school ideas a chance to be put into practice. One weapon that the school used was the idea of "rational choice." It took the idea of self-interested exchange – a theory introduced in the 18th century by Adam Smith – to, and many would say beyond, its logical extreme. The members of the Chicago school insisted that all decisions, including even non-economic ones, could be understood as the product of self-interested rational individual choices, and they therefore announced that the market was the pathway to prosperity and growth.

During the "Me Decade" of the 1980s these ideas found their way out of academic journals and into the public arena. The centrality of the individual and the rejection of community found its voice in Thatcher's famous declaration, "There is no such thing as society. There are individual men and women, and there are families."

The way forward for economies, according to this view, is to privatize and deregulate, a program implemented within the industrialized world and later exported to the rest of the world in the form of the International Monetary Fund's "Washington Consensus." The role of government is to get out of the way and provide space for the energy of the entrepreneurial classes, who are to be amply rewarded for their efforts. Unregulated private industry is the best provider of choice and efficiency.

The 1990s saw the meeting of choice and technology. The new economy of the Internet extended the realm of choice beyond national borders: information that people could use to make better decisions was on the Web, and purchasing choices were now just a click away, apparently ensuring fiercer competition among businesses, to the benefit of consumers.

In the new century choice continues to hold a special place in the heart of conservative parties, and is presented to the public under the down-home guise of common-sense revolutions and the ownership society. But the true success of this favouring of individual choice is reflected in the Third Way – the adoption by social-democratic and liberal parties of "public markets," "public-private partnerships," and other choice-driven and market-driven approaches to solving social problems.

Choice, it seems, is everywhere.

MarketThink

An obvious problem with building a society around individual choice is that self-interested corporations could choose to plunder rather than to drive growth. But in a free-market economy, many would argue, the corporations are not in charge, consumers are. Even the largest multinational corporations are powerless, so they say, in the face of consumer choice and competitive markets. Here, for example, is Sam Walton, founder of the world's biggest company: "There is only one boss. The customer. And he can fire everybody in the company from the chairman on down, simply by spending his money somewhere else."

It is now conventional wisdom that individual choice tames the wild tigers of private industry, and that free markets provide the mechanism for it to do so. Our ability to walk away, to choose not to buy what they are trying to sell, is the ultimate source of power in a free-enterprise society. The economy is a great democracy in which we cast our votes not once every few years, but each and every time we make a purchase. In the face of our choices, companies have no choice but to respond to our demands, or even to óur whims. Adam Smith's "invisible hand" of the market guides them to carry out our bidding. Brand-name companies, for example, are powerless in the face of individual choice. The British business magazine *The Economist* points out that "Brands do not rule consumers; consumers rule brands." According to one corporate consultant the magazine quoted, "When we like a brand we manifest our loyalty in cash. If we don't like it, we walk away. Customers are in charge."[5]

In a later issue of the magazine, writer Clive Crooks argued:

> The point of a liberal market economy is that it civilises the quest for profit, turning it, willy-nilly, into an engine of social progress. If firms have to compete with rivals for customers and workers, then they will indeed worry about their reputation for quality and fair dealing – even if they do not value those things in themselves. Competition will make them behave as if they did. . . .
>
> There is no question that companies would run the world for profit if they could. What stops them is not governments, powerful as they may be, but markets.[6]

The magic combination of individual choice and the market has taken centre stage in today's political conversations. It has moved from rational-choice Chicago school economists to official government economic policies and from there to political discourse. It colours the views of newspaper columnists and TV commentators and, indeed, everyday conversations. It has become a complete worldview. In this book I call this worldview *MarketThink*.

In the world according to MarketThink, the combination of choice and the market is a mechanism for solving problems and improving outcomes in areas as diverse as education (school choice will provide incentives for schools to improve), city growth (individual homebuyers make choices that ensure they get what they want in a city), and culture (individual choice ensures that we get the culture we want).

Most of all, MarketThink is a way of interpreting the world. The success of a company proves that customers like it. If the unemployed want a job badly enough they will find one. Once you adopt the MarketThink worldview, there is no longer a rationale for collective approaches to social and economic problems. Seen through the lens of MarketThink, national content regulations for TV and film limit viewers' choices; compulsory union membership limits workers' choices; city planning limits homebuyers' choices. Affirmative action programs are redundant because companies that fail to hire and promote based on merit will be driven out of business by those that do. Government-imposed standards for rental accommodation get in the way of free exchange between landlords and tenants; employment standards get in the way of free exchange between employers and employees. Such "red tape" only impedes the working of the market. The discipline of the market is the only discipline needed.

A corollary is that, as long as the government gets out of the way, each individual's situation is a result of the choices made by that individual. And once you accept that our situation is the result of our choices, there really is no need for sympathy or solidarity with the poor or disadvantaged. That point might seem extreme, but there are those who do apply MarketThink in such broad strokes, even to entire nations. Here, for example, is *New York Times* columnist and market enthusiast Thomas Friedman:

> Countries, like companies, can now increasingly choose to be prosperous. They don't have to be prisoners of their natural resources, geography or history. . . .
>
> Today there is no more First World, Second World or Third World. There's just the Fast World – the world of the wide-open – and the Slow World – the world of those who either fall by the wayside or choose to live away from the plain in some artificially walled-off plain valley of their own, because they find the Fast World to be too fast, too scary, too homogenizing or too demanding.[7]

My intent is not to set up a straw man: not many people hold to all of the aspects of MarketThink that I've outlined here. But the logic that is common to these arguments can be found liberally sprinkled through most of today's political debate.

In the United Kingdom, for instance, Prime Minister Tony Blair set out the legislative agenda on public services in June 2004:

> I believe people do want choice, in public services as in other services. But anyway choice isn't an end in itself. It is one important mechanism to ensure that citizens can indeed secure good schools and health services in their communities. And choice matters as much within those institutions as between them: better choice of learning options for each pupil within secondary schools; better choice of access routes into the health service. Choice puts the levers in the hands of parents and patients so that they as citizens and consumers can be a driving force for improvement in their public services. And the choice we support is choice open to all on the basis of their equal status as citizens, not on the unequal basis of their wealth.[8]

The political atmosphere in Canada is captured by Janice Gross Stein in her book *The Cult of Efficiency*. Stein asserts that we "talk about choice more now than ever before." She points to the wide appeal of individual choice: those who dislike one side of the choice coin ("our consumer society, its glorification of material pleasures, and its endless stimulation of public wants – wants, not needs – through advertising") may find that the other side appeals ("Distrust of authority leads . . . to an assertion of the right to choice"). She also highlights how choice "is fundamental to the political language of those who look to markets as models for the configuration of public space."[9]

It is here, in the magic combination of individual choice and markets, that ideas of choice have changed most in recent years. Stein argues that choice has moved from being a "freedom" to become a more basic "right." Individual choice has also increasingly been presented as an instrument of individual power; and the right to spend your money somewhere else is the source of this new type of power.

In the United States, here is John Kerry from the third presidential debate on Oct 13, 2004.

> The fact is that my health-care plan, America, is very simple. It gives you the choice. I don't force you to do anything. It's not a government plan. The government doesn't require you to do anything. You choose your doctor. You choose your plan. . . . Here's what I do: We take over Medicaid children from the states so that every child in America is covered. And in exchange, if the states want to – they're not forced to, they can choose to – they cover individuals up to 300 percent of poverty. It's their choice.[10]

George W. Bush's "Ownership Society" is also built on a core of individual choice. The plan calls for "More Access and More Choices in Health Care." When it comes to retirement savings and social security:

> The President's proposal would ensure that workers who have participated in 401(k) plans for three years are given the freedom to choose where to invest their retirement savings. The President has also proposed that choice be a feature of Social Security itself, allowing individuals to voluntarily invest a portion of their Social Security taxes in personal retirement accounts.[11]

In the disputatious world of politics, such a wide spectrum of agreement is rare indeed. With this level of support it would seem that the virtues of individual choice are broadly appreciated. Ironically, many of us seem to have no choice but choice.

Wanted: A Better Way of Thinking about Choices

To understand what is wrong with MarketThink, we need a better understanding of the dynamics of individual choice. And fortunately, while MarketThink has been grabbing the limelight, other ideas have been developing within academic economics, and those ideas present a different message: they show us why individual choice so often fails to give us what we want.

Many of these ideas have achieved recognition within the economics literature, but they have not yet become as widely known outside economics as they deserve to be. There are several reasons for this. One is that, unlike the seductively simple tale of MarketThink, they do not represent a single story. Leo Tolstoy told us, "Happy families are all alike; every unhappy family is unhappy in its own way." Similarly, the idealized markets of MarketThink are all alike, but many real-world markets prove to be not so happy, and in their own ways they fail to match the ideal picture. Instead of a single big idea, they entail a collection of ideas with a similar theme. As a result, not all of the economists who have been busy developing these ideas would agree with each other, or with the slant the ideas are given in this book.

That modern economists cast these ideas in an abstract mathematical language is another barrier to wider familiarity. The economists base their constructions on game theory, a mathematical approach to thinking about interdependent choices that started out 60 years ago and has been growing steadily in sophistication ever since. In its attack on Keynesian economics, the Chicago school represented one of those approaches that moved economics onto a more mathematical track, and game theory was in its bag of tricks. This book, in collecting some of those ideas and presenting them in an accessible manner, attempts to articulate an alternative worldview to MarketThink – a worldview that reaffirms the role of collective action and the need for the disenfranchised in society to act together on their own behalf. It is not a book "for" or "against" individual choice. It argues that choice is useful only if it helps you to get what you want. And the thing is, it often doesn't.

Jack Shops at Wal-Mart

Scattered throughout the book is a collection of stories set in a fictional town that I call – because it has to be called something – Whimsley. It is a deliberately oversimplified and artificial place. The residents of Whimsley make choices in an unrealistic and stylized manner, and the choices put before them are simplistic. Yet despite all these simplifications we will see that the Whimsley tales give rise to surprising outcomes.

The exercise of watching the inhabitants of Whimsley go about their lives has the benefit of making their choices more transparent than are the choices in our own lives, and it provides a starting point for understanding the choices that we ourselves make on a daily basis.

Now, to see what Whimsley has to tell us, let's take our first visit.

Jack lives in Whimsley. Some time ago Jack used to do most of his shopping in the downtown area – of course, he no longer does – and he also used to walk through the downtown before crossing Whimsley Park on his way to work.

Jack shares an eccentric trait with the other inhabitants of Whimsley: he has an odd way of making choices. As he goes about his daily life, when faced with a decision he assigns numerical points to the benefits and costs of the available options, and he chooses the option that gives the most points.

Let's follow Jack's reasoning as he thinks about what life was like when he shopped in the downtown area.

- *Value.* I did much of my shopping at the two downtown department stores. They provided reasonable selection and price. They were worth two satisfaction points per week.
- *Variety.* I liked the variety of the two stores. Sometimes I went to one store, sometimes the other, depending on what I needed, how much time I had, what other errands I had, and so on. The variety of having two stores was worth an additional two points.
- *Atmosphere.* I assigned myself another two points each week from my enjoyment of the thriving downtown as I walked through it on the way to work.

Jack was happy to the tune of six points per week: two for

selection and price, two for the variety of shopping options he had available, and two for the atmosphere of the thriving downtown.

A few years ago Wal-Mart opened a new store on the outer edge of Whimsley. Wal-Mart has huge economies of scale and tremendous bargaining power with its suppliers, and thus is able to offer the lowest prices. Like any consumer, Jack likes low prices. So Jack started shopping mainly at Wal-Mart.

For a while things were pretty good. Jack was happier because of Wal-Mart's arrival in town. Here is his reasoning.

- *Value.* By shopping mainly at Wal-Mart I not only continue to have a reasonable selection but I also get lower prices. So I give myself three points per week for price and selection, instead of the two I used to get by shopping at the downtown stores.
- *Variety.* What's more, Wal-Mart has extended my range of options: I assign myself an additional satisfaction point for the extra variety that Wal-Mart introduces, because on the days I don't feel like trekking out to Wal-Mart I can still visit one of the other stores and get what I need.
- *Atmosphere.* There is no change to the atmosphere of the city, so I still get my two points for atmosphere.

Soon after Wal-Mart arrived, then, Jack was getting eight points per week: three from Wal-Mart's selection and everyday low prices, three from the expanded variety he has available, and, as before, two from walking through the lively downtown to work. Jack was happier than before Wal-Mart built its store.

Of course, Jack was not the only person in Whimsley to be making choices, and that is where his problems started. Like him, many other people started to shop at Wal-Mart. The smaller department stores downtown started to have troubles, and gradually they went out of business.

Wal-Mart became the only department store in Whimsley. Jack had to shop at Wal-Mart all the time, like it or not. As a result, Jack's points for variety moved down to just a single point. Jack wanted more variety, but instead he got less. With the closing of the downtown department stores, Jack was down to six points per week again. He was as happy as before Wal-Mart came, but no happier. That's not too bad. At least Jack was no worse off than he was before.

But Jack's problems did not stop there. Once the downtown department stores closed, the slower customer traffic in the area meant that other stores closed too. Now downtown is not so interesting anymore: a number of shops are boarded up, others have been replaced by dollar stores, and the buildings are shoddy. Jack does not enjoy walking past the rundown area on the way to work. It gives him no pleasure. No points.

Now Jack has only four points per week. He is less happy than he was before Wal-Mart came.

In the beginning Jack made a choice that he believed would make him happier, but now he finds that he is less happy.

Jack is, of course, an archetypal consumer and citizen, and his tale embodies the frustrating predicaments that many of us face. We have the right to make individual choices, and we make them sensibly, like Jack did, and yet that is not enough to lead to a happy outcome. In fact, we shall see that a system of private enterprise and free markets is particularly likely to produce such poor results on a regular basis.

There is no catch to the tale of Jack and Wal-Mart. There is no hidden information or trick that can lead to a happy answer. Instead, Jack's predicament is just one example of what happens when the individual choices made by individual people have a larger impact. Jack's particular choice influenced, in a small way, the outcome for other shoppers, and their choices in turn influenced Jack's happiness.

The moral of the story is simply that individual choice carries no guarantee of a happy ending. Choices are rarely made in isolation. They become quickly and intricately tangled, and their outcome is often not what we intended or hoped for. Stories like this one about Jack and Wal-Mart lie at the heart of many problems with our modern free-market corporate economy.

People who believe firmly in the virtues of individual choice will assert that Jack must be happier now than he used to be, because he has exercised his freedom of choice. If he didn't like Wal-Mart he would not have shopped there. If he valued the lively downtown so much, he would have shopped there to save it. They will assert that, as a consumer, Jack is sovereign and the market always gives him what he wants. Yet in this story there is no individual choice that Jack could have made that would have improved his outcome. Even if Jack had chosen to continue shopping downtown, his minuscule individual contribution to the revenue of the downtown stores would not have stopped them from closing.

People who are more sceptical about the value of individual choice often have difficulty explaining stories such as Jack's. Some will argue that the appearance of choice is deceptive: in some way Jack did not make a free choice. Yet his decision was made for perfectly good reasons. A common alternative is to suggest that Jack was fooled or tricked in some way, perhaps by advertising. Yet Wal-Mart did not offer anything it could not deliver. Jack's story is not a tale of consumer ignorance: he made his choices in a perfectly sensible way, calculated to increase his happiness. Even so, his individual choices made him unhappy.

The source of the problem here is that Jack's choices are *tangled*. His preferences are tangled: he wants many things, from a lively downtown and a pleasant place to walk to cheap prices for the things he buys, but his choices do not satisfy all of these preferences. Jack's actions are tangled with the actions of other citizens of Whimsley: his own outcome is altered by the outcome for others, and their outcomes depend in turn on his choices.

Tangles such as these may seem surprising, but they are not perverse curiosities or obscure dilemmas; they are the stuff of everyday life. Unfortunately, the knotty behaviour of individual choice is not just a technical problem, and recognizing the existence of bad outcomes is not enough to free us from the dilemmas we face. These tangles have much to say about the workings of power in modern societies. In a free-market system the special interests with the resources to do so can encourage tangles to form, to their own benefit. Individual choice becomes a tool that can be used to maintain and extend privilege under an egalitarian and populist guise.

Certainly, with individual choice being offered by so many as the solution for so many problems, we need to become more familiar with how it works. It is time for a guide to individual choice and its consequences.

Most public discussions about individual choice see one of two possibilities. Either we make good choices and are happy with the outcome, or we make bad choices and are unhappy with the outcome. But there is a third possibility, which is that we make good choices and yet are still unhappy with the outcome: that is, individual choice can lead us into traps.

Much of this book is devoted to cataloguing circumstances in which individual choice goes wrong, and to exposing the mechanisms that lead to disappointment. It provides a taxonomy of these circumstances: situations in which good choices lead to bad results for everyone; winner-take-all situations in which good choices lead to inequality with good results for only a few and bad outcome for most; situations in which "the devil you know" is better than the devil you don't, and in which predictability trumps quality.

As a subtext, this book is a call for the reinstatement of collective action into politics. The neo-conservative right has wielded the promise of individual choice very effectively to discredit organized collective action such as that carried out under the umbrella of trade unions or governments, presenting unions and governments as obsolete bodies whose sole purpose is to restrict choices. But if individual choice can lead us into traps, we will need collective action to make our escape.

A thread that runs through the whole book is that we can make sense of the world by making the respectful assumption that people generally make the best choices they can in the circumstances in which they find themselves.[12] There is no need to resort to arguments that people are tricked, or are behaving against their best interests, or are somehow gullible. But contrary to what MarketThink would have us believe, the picture that emerges is not a pretty one: it is one of growing disparity in which wealth leads to influence and influence leads to wealth. Wealth does not "trickle down," and those at the top can plunder the wealth of nations under the guise of individual choice and free markets.

chapter two

GOOD CHOICES AND BAD OUTCOMES

IN THE STORY OF JACK AND WAL-MART, several factors were at work. Jack's preferences were multifaceted, his choices and actions were tangled with those of others, and Wal-Mart's scale and ability to make demands of its suppliers influenced the outcome. This chapter looks at an even simpler case of individual choice gone wrong. Essentially it is the story of the prisoner's dilemma, which has been written about in hundreds of books but is worth telling again, especially because it raises many of the most important issues about individual choice.

Jack and Jill's Ugly Divorce

Let's return to Whimsley. Some years ago, before Wal-Mart came to town, Jack and his then-wife Jill went through a messy divorce. Putting aside the many human issues involved in their separation, we will look solely at the problem of how they divided their property. Indeed, we will look at just one simple choice that Jack and Jill each had to make: should they be conciliatory in their pursuit of the property and avoid a legal battle, or should they be aggressive and pay a lawyer to take the case to court?

| | | JILL | |
		Conciliatory	Aggressive
	Conciliatory	Jack 50, Jill 50	Jack 0, Jill 80
JACK			
	Aggressive	Jack 80, Jill 0	**Jack 30, Jill 30**

FIGURE 1. The possible outcomes of Jack and Jill's divorce. The equilibrium outcome is in bold.

As good inhabitants of Whimsley, Jack and Jill calculate the consequences of their actions numerically. Because they are not talking to each other, and are not in the mood to care much about each other's feelings, they evaluate how they feel about the outcome purely in terms of how much of the property they get.

Here are the options facing Jack and Jill:

- If both Jack and Jill choose to be conciliatory, there are no lawyers involved and they divide the property 50-50.
- In Whimsley, a lawyer gets 20 per cent of the joint property for handling the case. Both of the lawyers they have are good ones, so if Jack is aggressive while Jill is conciliatory, or vice versa, the aggressive partner ends up with all the goods but has to pay the lawyer, and so gets 80 per cent of the goods. The conciliatory partner ends up with nothing.
- If both of them are aggressive, they end up splitting the property evenly but both of them also have to pay the lawyers, so they end up with only 30 per cent each.

The outcome of the divorce can be determined by reading off

the points from a table (see Figure 1). In this table, each cell contains the points for both Jack and Jill. You can read the table by looking at the choices that lead to each cell, and the outcome that follows from those choices. If Jack is conciliatory (top row) and Jill is aggressive (right column), we are in the top right corner of the table. In this case Jack gets nothing (0 points), while Jill gets 80 per cent of the goods in question (80 points), after paying the lawyer 20 per cent of the proceeds. Then again, if Jack is aggressive (bottom row) and Jill is also aggressive (right column), we are in the bottom right corner of the table. In this case, Jack gets 30 per cent of the proceeds, having paid the lawyer 20 per cent, and Jill gets the same.

Now that we know what the possible outcomes of this divorce are, let's turn to strategy. What is the best choice that Jack and Jill can take? As Jill decides how to pursue the divorce proceedings, a couple of thoughts run through her mind.

- If Jack chooses to be conciliatory (the top row), I will do better to be aggressive (the right column, in which case I will get 80 per cent) than to be conciliatory (the left column, in which case I will get only 50 per cent).
- If Jack chooses to be aggressive (bottom row), then again I will do better if I am aggressive (right column, 30 per cent) than if I am conciliatory (left column, nothing).

So no matter what Jack does, Jill realizes that her best choice – the *best reply* to any of Jack's actions – is to be aggressive. Accordingly, she heads out to Main Street and talks to her lawyer.

The problem is, though, Jack has done the same analysis and realized that, no matter what Jill does, his best choice is also to be aggressive. If Jill is conciliatory (left column), Jack does better to be aggressive (bottom row) than to be conciliatory. If Jill is aggressive, Jack still does better to be aggressive than to be conciliatory. So, without knowing what Jill has done, Jack also instructs his lawyer accordingly. The result is that Jack and Jill both end up in the bottom right corner, each getting 30 per cent of the property. Their lawyers share the other 40 per cent.

But here is something odd. Both players chose what we have just shown to be the better of their two options, but they ended up with 30 per cent each. However, if they had both chosen what we have just seen to be the worse of their options, they would have ended up better off, with 50 per cent of the property each (the top left corner). They are not just worse off as a pair, they are each worse off individually than if they had both made the other choice.

In fact, Jack and Jill would be better off if they had no choice at all – if they lived in a town that did not allow litigation of divorces, but summarily divided the property down the middle. The additional choice has made them worse off.

On first encountering this simple scenario, most people find the outcome surprising, and are further surprised that such a counterintuitive outcome can arise in such a trivial setting. The first and most important lesson we can draw from stories like this one of Jack and Jill is that, in circumstances involving more than one person, the ramifications of individual choice are subtler than might be expected.

A second reaction is to search for loopholes through which Jack and Jill can reach a happier outcome. But just as in the story of Jack and Wal-Mart, there is no trick here. There are ways of reaching happier outcomes, but they involve going outside the rules of the story to include agreements between the players, external rewards, or threats of punishment. We will look at some of the ways out of the dilemma later, but for now we must confine ourselves to play by the rules. Just as with Jack and Wal-Mart, the participants in this story are not being stupid: they are not making "the wrong choice," they are not the victims of "false consciousness," and they are not being duped by the authorities. The bad outcome is a consequence of the dilemma, not of the actors themselves.

A third possible reaction is to say that, no matter what the story says, real people do not act according to the self-interested prescriptions of Whimsley. There is some truth to this (and I treat this topic in more depth in chapter 11). People's preferences certainly can and do depend on other people's outcomes, but this tendency can be represented within game theory: we can represent cases in which one player is sympathetic to the other player by adjusting their outcomes to be higher when the other player has a good outcome; and we can represent motives such as vengeance by adjusting the outcome to be higher when the other player has a bad outcome. For now, we just say that the values in the matrix are established after all these adjustments are taken into account.

The matter is not quite so simple, of course, but the important point remains. I am not trying to construct an entirely accurate picture of the world here, but to represent as clearly as possible selected aspects of the world. I am looking at situations that encourage or discourage co-operation. It is a rare person who does not respond to incentives to some degree. We can find ourselves in situations in which co-operation is easy or in which it is difficult. You don't have to be a naïve determinist to think that more co-operation will happen when the situation encourages it than when it does not.

A fourth possible reaction to the Jack and Jill scenario is to conclude that with all these constraints and qualifications we are left with a rather tortuous and perhaps artificial situation. Yet although there are very few situations in which the dilemma holds exactly, there are many situations in the world around us in which these basic forces and choices are at work. Indeed, as we shall see in the next chapter, the same forces are at work in many different situations with many players, and in those cases it is more difficult for the players to extricate themselves from the dilemma. Stories of this kind have a wide applicability.

The Prisoner's Dilemma

The story of Jack and Jill's divorce is the venerable prisoner's dilemma in another guise. The original story shows how the same structure and forces can be at work in very different situations.

The prisoner's dilemma was invented in the 1950s as game theory gained popularity among economists and political scientists. Game theory is the mathematical theory of decisions and strategic behaviour, and it has a central place in any attempt to understand choice. The "game" in game theory is very broad: it can include any situation that lends itself to strategic thinking, and in particular any situation in which each "player's" outcome depends on the choices of all participants.

The original story of the prisoner's dilemma concerns two criminals accused of conspiring in the commission of two crimes. There is proof of both prisoners' guilt in the theft of a car, for which they each face a sentence of three years. The pair are also suspected of a bank robbery, which carries a sentence of eight years, but the evidence is scant and to be successful the prosecution requires a confession from one of the prisoners. The prosecutor keeps the prisoners separate, and offers each of them a deal:

"If you both stay silent, you'll be convicted of the car theft and you'll get sent to jail for three years. But if you confess to the bank robbery and your partner in crime does not, we will drop all charges against you and you will go free, while your partner will go to jail for eight years. If you both confess to the bank robbery, then we don't need your confession to convict your partner but you will get some credit for confessing, and you will both go to jail for five years."

Again we'll use a table (Figure 2) to consider the possible outcomes. Instead of Jack and Jill, the players are a more abstract "A" and "B." Instead of "Conciliatory" and "Aggressive," we use "Stay Silent" and "Confess." The points represent the number of years by which a player's sentence is cut, from the maximum of eight years, so a high score is a good thing.

The question, again, is what should the prisoners do? The logic is exactly the same as for Jack and Jill's divorce. Working through the table shows that no matter what B does, A's best choice is to confess: if B stays silent, 8 is better than 5; if B confesses, 3 is better than 0. Likewise, no matter what A does, B's best choice is to confess. The only reasonable outcome, then, seems to be for both of them to con-

PLAYER B

		Stay Silent	Confess
	Stay Silent	A 5, B 5	A 0, B 8
PLAYER A			
	Confess	A 8, B 0	A 3, B 3

FIGURE 2. The prisoner's dilemma. The equilibrium outcome is in bold.

fess, but just as in the case of Jack and Jill's divorce this outcome proves to be worse for each player than the alternative in which both stay silent and get five years of freedom each.

As summaries of choices, Figures 1 and 2 show essentially the same results – though each represents a completely different story. The virtue of an abstract approach is that, by reducing the problem to one of numbers in a table, we can see how the same logic applies to many different stories. Instead of the table being a convenience to understand the story, the story is a convenience to help understand the table. It is the table that holds the core of the problem, or the "game," as the game theorists say.

Choosing the Right Words

The prisoner's dilemma again shows the complications of choice, and how easy it is to be misled when considering individual choices and their possible outcomes. To think more clearly about individual choice, perhaps we need a better vocabulary.

Externalities

The cause of the bad outcome is the presence of what economists call *externalities*, the impact that one player's choice has on those around him or her (hence "external"). Any one person's outcome is a result not only of a personal choice, but also of the externalities that spill over from the actions of others. Externalities break the link between choice and preference that forms the basis for MarketThink. Only in special circumstances, not coincidentally including the ideal competitive market on which MarketThink builds its worldview, are externalities non-existent.

Preferences and Best Replies

The prisoner's dilemma shows how, as soon as one person's choice alters the outcome for another person, the idea of "preference" is much more complicated than we usually think.

One way of thinking about preference is to see it as the cause of a choice – the grounds on which we make a choice. Another way to think of preference is as the effect or outcome of a choice. These two ways of using the word "preference" seem interchangeable. You can say "I prefer orange juice to apple juice, so I will reach for the orange juice," or you can say "I prefer orange juice to apple juice, so I am happier that I picked up the orange juice than I would have been if I had to drink apple juice," and it means pretty much the same thing.

Once choices are interdependent, these two meanings of "preference" become different. Jack and Jill use their preferences to guide their choices, but the outcome of those choices is not the one that either of them would prefer. Preference in the prisoner's dilemma can correspond to the grounds for the prisoner's choice, or to the prisoner's happiness at the outcome, but it cannot do both. Choices do not reveal preferences, and preference is a misleading way of thinking about choice. In this book, when I use the word "preference" I am referring to the causes of making a choice, not to the outcomes.

Instead of thinking about choices as revealing preferences, it pays to think of choices as "replies" to the actions or likely actions of others. The best choice you can make is the *best reply* to the likely actions of others. This phrase separates the act of choice from the satisfaction with the outcome.

Utility

The numbers in the game theory tables are called the "utility" or "utility payoff," which each person gains or loses as a result of personal choices and the choices of others in the game. Utility is a vague word, but this usage is deliberate because utility can have many different sources depending on the game being played and the person playing it. In the case of Jack and Jill's divorce the utility values were monetary, but the prisoners facing their dilemma "gained utility" from a short prison sentence. The sources of Jack's utility when he was thinking about shopping at Wal-Mart were value, variety, and the atmosphere of the downtown area. When someone is choosing between orange juice and apple juice, utility is a matter of taste. Later in this book we will see examples in which individuals gain or lose utility from pain, stress, affirming or losing their sense of identity, and sympathy with or antipathy towards other players.

An ugly but common way of saying that people make the best choice available to them is to say that they are "maximizing their utility."

Co-operate and Defect

The structure of the prisoner's dilemma is present in many places, and it is helpful to have a way of talking about the choices involved that is independent of the particular situation. Obviously, to say "hire a lawyer" and "don't hire a lawyer" loses some of the generality of the dilemma.

The words that have come to be accepted are *co-operate* and *defect*. To co-operate means co-operation with the other player of the game, so in the case of Jack and Jill's divorce it means not hiring a lawyer. In the case of the prisoners it means to co-operate with the other prisoner (not the police) by staying silent. To defect means breaking the bond of co-operation, either by hiring a lawyer or confessing to the police. Figure 3 shows this game as it appears in its abstract form.

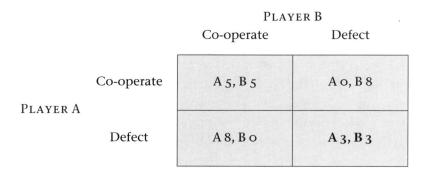

FIGURE 3. The prisoner's dilemma using standard terms. The equilibrium outcome is in bold.

Equilibrium

The prisoner's dilemma demands that we separate the best choice from the best outcome. How, then, do we describe the final outcome of the two dilemmas, in which both convicts confess and both Jack and Jill hire lawyers? The word used in game theory is *equilibrium*, and this is another useful word to keep in mind while thinking about choices.

In the prisoner's dilemma, the best choice for each player is clear, even though its outcome may be disturbing, because defect is the best reply to any of the other players' actions. There are other situations in which the best choice is less obvious, but the idea of equilibrium as the predicted outcome is still useful. We get to make choices, but we do not control what choice others make, so we don't get to select the equilibrium outcome.

An equilibrium outcome is one for which *no one participant can improve their own outcome by their actions alone.* If either prisoner chose to stay silent rather than to confess, they would be rewarded not by the co-operation outcome, but by a long jail term. It requires concerted action by both players to improve the equilibrium outcome.

As long as the actors involved make their best choices, and as long as we stay within the stated rules and constraints of a situation, the equilibrium outcome is the one that game theory predicts will actually happen – but as we have seen, there is no guarantee that the story has a happy ending. We know there is another outcome that leaves each participant better off than the equilibrium outcome, but the players cannot get there without working together, which is not possible in this situation. In the case of Jack and Jill's divorce, the better outcome is the co-operative one of being conciliatory and not hiring a lawyer. But "both be conciliatory" is not an equilibrium, as either player can improve the outcome for themselves by choosing to be aggressive.

We now have a more precise vocabulary that we can use to talk about choice and its dynamics:

1. Preference is a treacherous concept when we are thinking about choices. People do not get to choose what makes them most happy; it is better to think of choice as our *best reply* to the world in which we find ourselves and to the actions of those around us.
2. The lack of alignment between choice and preference comes about because of *externalities*: the effects of one player's action on other players.
3. The end result of the good individual choices is an *equilibrium* outcome, but while an equilibrium outcome cannot be improved by any one individual actor, there is no guarantee that an equilibrium is the happiest outcome for any of the players involved.

Choosing the Right Starting Point

In some cases externalities can be safely ignored; they are cases in which one person's choice has little to do with anyone else. The choice of orange juice over apple juice is such a choice, at least as long as you don't take the last serving in the juice container. In such cases it seems superfluous to talk of a "best reply": there is little in the way of interaction taking place. In the absence of externalities, choice and preference can come into alignment. Such choices are, of course, the staple of MarketThink.

There are other cases in which externalities are everything. You walk along a sidewalk, and another person walks straight towards you. Do you sidestep to the left or the right? You don't make the choice because of any innate preference for one direction or the other; it is all about avoiding a collision with the approaching pedestrian. In these cases choices are tightly coupled to other choices: one person's choice has everything to do with what others choose. Preference is nothing, and "best reply" to the other's action or anticipated action is the only sensible way to think about the decision.

Externalities can be varied in nature. For example, they can be positive or negative: Jill's choice to hire a lawyer imposes a negative externality on Jack, but in other cases our outcome may be improved by some other person's choice – if someone you like goes to the same party, for example. In the case of the prisoner's dilemma the best reply is the same no matter what the other player does, while in the case of passing on the sidewalk the best reply depends very much on what the other person does. In other cases the nature of the choice is more flexible: some people want to blend in with the people around them, while others want to stand out from the crowd.

What's more, externalities are not absolute, but depend on the society we live in. Consider two choices that are, after hundreds of years, suddenly being treated differently in many countries. For centuries smoking was seen as a purely individual choice, and any externalities were treated as secondary, but in the last two decades the externalities associated with smoking – the dangers of second-hand smoke, the inconvenience and unpleasantness of smelly clothes, the health costs of smoking-related diseases – have become paramount, and smoking is being increasingly confined and limited. Gay marriage looks like being a choice that is moving the other way in society's perception. Long portrayed as a corrupting and immoral influence on society, the view of it in many places is changing remarkably quickly to that of a private choice, whose externalities are unimportant. Other choices have moved or may move in the future from being seen predominantly as private choices to being seen as choices laden with externalities. Owning slaves, listening to loud music, driving drunk, wearing fur coats, divorcing one's spouse, eating meat, wearing perfume, having an abortion, reading pornography: all are choices that have been seen both as private and as affecting others, depending on whom you ask.

Amartya Sen, in a famous argument, showed that even the most seemingly private of choices can have externalities associated with them.[1] If you make a choice that I object to, then there is an externality. Sen chose the example of reading *Lady Chatterley's Lover*. If I disapprove of your reading it, then there is an externality to your choice: it affects me. It might seem eccentric of me to be disapproving of such a choice but that is, I could assert, none of your business. Even such a seemingly private and isolated act as reading a book, Sen shows, can lead to tangled choices. And once choices are tangled, things become complicated. If society protects your right to a particular choice, it might be imposing a penalty on me; if society protects me from the consequences of your choice, it imposes a penalty on you. Choice might be everywhere, but externalities are unavoidably everywhere too.

Whenever we try to make sense of what is happening in our society we use simplified pictures of how the world around us works. Choosing the right picture is essential if we want to get realistic and effective answers to the problems that face us. MarketThink is a simplified picture of the world in which choices are independent of each other, and in which the link between choice and outcome is simple. But once we acknowledge that tangled choices are ubiquitous, then it follows that we must use a picture that includes externalities if we are to avoid being misled.

Gases and Liquids

To understand the role of these simplified pictures that we use to make sense of the world around us, it helps to look at an easier problem than human choices: we will look at molecules of a gas bouncing around in a container.

Theories of gases look to explain what happens when you heat, squeeze, or otherwise tamper with a container full of gas. For example, they look at the relationships among the pressure, temperature, and volume of gases.

The simplest theory of gases, taught to high-school and first-year undergraduate students, is called *ideal gas theory*. As the name suggests, an ideal gas is a simplified picture of a real gas, in much the same way economic models are simplified pictures of the real world. An ideal gas is made up of infinitesimally small molecules rather than the very small but still finite molecules that make up real gases. Also, the molecules of an ideal gas do not interact with each other at all, while those of real gases do interact. The molecules of an ideal gas simply bounce around in the container that holds them. The hotter the gas, the faster they move, and that is about it.

From this simple assumption, it turns out that you can say a lot about gases. If you heat gas in a rigid container, the pressure increases because the molecules hit the walls more often and with more energy. If you heat gas in a flexible container, it expands as the force of the molecules hitting the container pushes it outwards. If you squeeze a container while keeping the temperature constant, the molecules hit the wall more often, even if at the same speed, and the pressure increases. What's more, each of these statements not only is a rough statement about directions of change, but also can be made quantitative. They can be collected together in the ideal gas equation, which is that

$$\text{Pressure} \times \text{Volume} = \text{Ideal Gas Constant} \times \text{Temperature}$$
$$\text{or}$$
$$P \times V = R \times T$$

where the Ideal Gas Constant "R" is a number that can be measured. If you remember Boyle's Law and Charles' Law from chemistry or physics lessons, they are both contained in the ideal gas equation.

The ideal gas theory is useful in many practical circumstances, but it is not exact – it is not the truth. If the ideal gas law were true, then as long as the temperature remained the same, the left-hand side of the equation should always be the same. That is, at a fixed temperature, if you measure the pressure of a gas and the volume it takes up, and multiply them together, you should always get the same value. But you don't, quite.

The reason is that the assumptions of ideal gas theory are not entirely true. Molecules of gas are very small, but they are not infinitesimally small, and while they do not interact much, they do interact a little, attracting each other when they are close, but bouncing off each other when they meet.

More accurate theories of gases have more complicated equations to catch the nuances of this behaviour. The simplest correction was made by Johannes van der Waals in the 19th century, and far more elaborate and detailed models are still being developed. But even these theories don't throw away the ideal gas picture: instead they use ideal gas behaviour as a starting point and scrutinize what are called "imperfections," or "deviations" from this ideal. The ideal gas picture is a rough sketch of how gases work; more elaborate work fills in the details.

Modern theories depend on the finest features of the forces between molecules in a gas (so-called "intermolecular forces"). The modern theory of intermolecular forces uses quantum physics and lots of computer CPU cycles to calculate these fine features for molecules in particular gases or mixtures of gases, and it compares how these calculations match reality using ever more accurate and probing experiments.

Returning to the ideal gas law, the main thing about it is not that it is a bit wrong, but that it is mainly right. It is true that if you want to calculate the properties of gases exactly, whether you are trying to understand the evolution of solar systems or design a jet engine, you had better use a more accurate model of how gases behave than the ideal gas law gives. But if you just want a rough idea of "how the world works" you can't do much better than this simplest of all pictures. For many purposes, the molecules of gases can be thought of as infinitesimally small, even though they are not, and they can be thought of as non-interacting, even though they do collide with each other.

The analogy is obvious. The MarketThink picture of the world is rough, not exact. Individuals do not act only to maximize their utility, but it's not a bad starting point. Their choices do interact with each other, but as a rough model it is not too bad to consider the choices as independent, affecting each other only through price. And given that the ideal market has so many good qualities, the role of government would seem to be to minimize the interactions and other imperfections that interfere with its operation, so that we can all benefit.

The analogy may be obvious, but it is wrong. To understand why, we have to return to physics and look at liquids.

The ideal gas law is simple, inexact, and useful. But that does not mean that it is always useful as a starting point for all kinds of behaviour. It does not, for example, have anything whatsoever to say about liquids and solids. This may seem obvious (it is a theory of gases, after all) but it does have consequences that are worth thinking about.

Intermolecular forces, which we have seen are pretty unimportant in gases, are the very things that hold liquids and solids together. A theory of liquids or solids that ignores intermolecular forces would be a complete non-starter. In liquids and solids, far from being a minor "imperfection," interactions are at the heart of the matter. Each molecule of a liquid or a solid is continually bouncing off its neighbours (remember, molecules repel each other at short distances), and then pulling them back in as they move further away (molecules attract at larger distances). Pressure × Volume at constant temperature is nowhere near constant. The predictions of the ideal gas equation are not just a bit wrong, they're completely wrong. You can't make corrections for "imperfections" and "deviations" to get an idea of how liquids and solids behave, you have to start somewhere different. What's more, those starting points are not going to be nearly as simple as the ideal gas law.

Oversimplifying Reality

The real question is not whether the free-market model is true, or exact – it isn't, but that's not important – but whether the world is like a gas, where interactions between the actors may be present, but are important only if you want to get the details right, or whether the world is like a liquid, where neglecting interactions gives a completely false picture of what is going on.

Unfortunately, much political and business discussion today has adopted the MarketThink line that pretty much everything is pretty much like a free market, pretty much all the time. The result is that we get more and more of the simplistic solutions we are familiar with. Schools? Let the market handle it. City planning? Let the market take care of it. In this world the choices we make are like the particles of an ideal gas – they never interact with the choices of others, they travel in nice straight lines and follow nice simple equations (what you choose equals what you get) that lead to nice simple rationalizations (you must like what you have, because you must have chosen it).

But economies and (even more so) other aspects of societies are made of intricately interconnected, constantly interacting, choices. Many of our choices, the outcomes of those choices, and how we feel about those outcomes all depend on the choices of others, whose choices likewise depend on ours. Claiming that the free-market model basically describes how such a world works is not merely a simplification, it is simplistic.

On one hand, the complexity that results from the interactions among the players of games is unfortunate for economists and those who would reduce society to mathematical expressions, for it makes their job fiendishly difficult. On the other hand, at least it gives them job security.

MarketThink takes a model of choice that is totally lacking in externalities and extends it to the whole of our tangled society. It is time to go the other way: to accept that externalities are pervasive and to build a worldview that starts off by acknowledging that fact. A tangled world is inevitably messier and more challenging to understand than the artificially oversimplified vision of MarketThink, but that's the way the world is. Welcome to it.

chapter three

PRIVATE CHOICES AND PUBLIC FAILURES

THE PRISONER'S DILEMMA, although thought-provoking, is a little artificial. Only two players who will never meet again and who have no way of communicating: it hardly seems any more of a model for the world around us than MarketThink does. But the forces at work in the prisoner's dilemma turn out to be at work in more complicated situations too; and co-operation can be even more difficult to achieve in situations involving many actors.

The prisoner's dilemma has a number of key features.

1. Each player has an *unconditional best choice*: Player A's best choice is the same, no matter what choice Player B makes.
2. Each player has an *unconditional preference* regarding the other's choice: Player A wants Player B to make a particular choice, and that choice is the same regardless of the choice that Player A makes for himself.
3. These two preferences go in opposite directions: the choice that A prefers to make is not the choice that she or he prefers B to make.
4. Both players are better off if both make their own unpreferred choices than if both make their own preferred choices.[1]

So we could say that a multi-player prisoner's dilemma occurs when a number of factors are in place.

1. Each player has an *unconditional best choice*: each player has a single preferred choice, no matter what the others do.
2. The best choice is the same for each player.
3. Each player has an *unconditional preference* regarding the others' choice: there is a choice that each player hopes all the others will make, regardless of what choice that player personally makes.
4. These two preferences go in opposite directions: the choice that each player prefers to make is not the choice that the player prefers others to make.
5. If enough people reject their unconditional best choices, and instead choose their unpreferred alternatives, each is better off than if all of them had chosen their own unconditional best choice.

These multi-player prisoner's dilemmas are also called free-rider problems, "tragedies of the commons," and public goods problems.

Jill Drops a Coffee Cup

This story shows the logic of the prisoner's dilemma at work in a setting that involves fifty-one people instead of only two.

It is a sunny morning, and Jill decides to walk to work across Whimsley Park. Before she reaches the park she visits a local coffee shop and picks up a double-double to go. She drinks the coffee as she walks. Halfway across the park Jill drains the last of the coffee. She looks around, but sees no garbage bins in sight. She is left holding the paper cup and has a decision to make, with two choices.

Does she drop the cup in the park, or does she carry it to work and put it in the bin there? As a good resident of Whimsley, Jill takes a methodical approach to her decision-making: she assigns numbers to the costs and benefits that may accrue to her as a result of her decisions.

In the case of Jack and Jill's divorce, it was fairly easy to think of the outcome in terms of numbers, because we were looking at money. In this case no money is involved, but thinking numerically can still help to clarify things. Let's listen in to Jill's thoughts as she wonders what to do with the cup.

- I enjoy walking across the park. It is a meditative time for me, and if the park is clean I get a benefit, say, of 60 points.
- Unfortunately, the presence in my hand of this empty coffee cup disturbs my reflective frame of mind. If I carry the cup out of the park, the irritation will cost me 5 points.
- I enjoy the pleasant surroundings of the tree-lined green park, and my enjoyment of the park would be lessened by the presence of litter. However, just one piece of litter makes very little difference: almost none in fact. So dropping the cup in the park does not make much difference. It cuts into my benefit by just 1 point.

If Jill carries the cup out of the park, she gets 55 points, but if she drops the cup she gets 59 points. So Jill drops the cup and continues her walk. The irritation of the extra litter costs her less than the irritation of carrying the cup to work.

But just as Jack was not the only person to change shopping habits, Jill is not the only person to walk across Whimsley Park. For the sake of simplicity (this is Whimsley after all), let's imagine that 50 other people make the same walk, and that each of them makes the same analysis of their costs and benefits as Jill did. Let's also assume, just to make the arithmetic easier, that the cost imposed by each successive cup dropped is the same: 1 point.

For each person, the "best choice" is the same as Jill's: drop the cup. But where does this leave them? Each of them will have to face 51 cups drifting around the park, while getting the benefit only of dropping their own cup. They now get only a measly 9 points (60 – 51) in crossing the littered parkland, whereas if they had each carried their own cup out of the park they would have enjoyed the walk to the tune of 55 points.

They have all taken a decision that would seem to have left them, individually, better off, yet they are each, individually, worse off than they would have been had they taken the old advice "do as you would be done by." Just as in the case of the divorce, perfectly good choices have become tangled, producing bad outcomes. Choice and preference are out of alignment, and externalities have produced a bad equilibrium.

Just as in Jack and Jill's divorce, not only are the participants worse off as a group, but also each and every one of them is worse off than if all the people involved had made the other choice. Jill and the others crossing the park all have freedom of choice, and each made the best choice under the circumstances, but each individual ends up being unhappy with the outcome.

To show how free-riding works, we can use a graph to indicate Jill's individual benefit, depending on the number of others who are good citizens and carry their cups out of Whimsley Park (see Figure 4).

The two lines on the graph show the different outcomes of choosing to carry the cup or choosing to drop it and litter the park. The left-hand side of the graph shows Jill's points when everyone else drops their cups in the park. The right-hand side shows her points when all others carry their cups out of the park. In the graph, a high number of points is good – it represents a high benefit to Jill. All the way across the graph, the line for dropping the cup is above (preferable to) the line for carrying – indicating that Jill is better off to drop her cup than to carry it out, no matter what percentage of other people carry their cups out. But, as we know, the story does not end there.

The low values on the left-hand side of the graph reveal that Jill will pay a heavy price for the messy park regardless of what she does. The actions of others have cut the enjoyment she gets from the park from 60 points down to only 10. However, if she drops her cup she will lose only 1 more point, leaving her with a benefit of 9 points. If she carries her cup out of the park, she will lose 5 more points, leaving her with only 5 points.

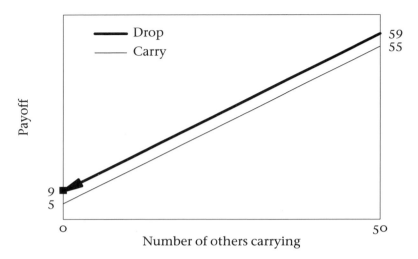

FIGURE 4. Jill's best choice. No matter what others do, Jill's best choice is to drop her cup (bold line). The black square represents the equilibrium outcome.

If everyone else carries their cups out of the park, as the high values on the right-hand side of the graph show, Jill and the others will be pretty happy with the outcome because of the clean park. But, again, Jill can improve her own outcome by littering. If she carries the cup out, she pays a price of 5 points; if she drops the cup, she pays a price of only 1 point; so again her best choice is to litter.

The right side of the graph has higher values than the left side, meaning that the outcome to Jill for carrying along with everyone else (bottom line, right-hand side) is better than the outcome if she and everyone else drop their cups (top line, left-hand side). And this introduces the basic element of the problem with individual choice in such a situation: it leaves everyone worse off.

- Whatever other people are doing, the outcome is always better for Jill if she litters than if she carries. (The drop-cup line is always above the carry-cup line.)
- The more players litter, the worse the outcome for each of them. (Both lines slope down, right to left.)
- The outcome is better, for Jill and for everybody else, if they all

carry, than if they all litter. (The carry line on the right-hand side is above the drop line on the left.)

Littering is an example of free-riding. As in the prisoner's dilemma, the problem arises from how the best choice for each actor alters the outcome for the others. Jill's decision to drop her cup is an individual decision, but it has an unavoidable impact on each of the other people who cross the park: it has an externality.

In the case of Whimsley Park, the bad effect of each individual decision is small. From a selfish point of view, the best thing that any one person can do is to enjoy the scenic park created by other people's good behaviour, but not behave in such a fashion themselves: that is, to get a free ride on others' good behaviour. However, the bad effects of those choices accumulate. The end result is that, as in Jack and Jill's divorce, the bad effects outweigh the good, and there is nothing that any one individual player can do about it. The structure of the problem encourages bad outcomes.

The root of free-riding is that the cost of carrying the cup is *private*, while the cost of dropping the cup is *public*: it is shared among all those who cross the park. For this reason it is also common to refer to free-rider problems as "public goods" problems. A public good does not have to be physical. It can be anything that is, like the litter-free nature of Whimsley Park, inherently shared.

In the free-rider problem any one person's choice has only a small effect on others' outcomes, but because these small effects are shared among everyone, they accumulate and become significant. In the prisoner's dilemma the effects of A's choice on B, and vice versa, are so large that they dominate even though only one other person is playing.

Examples of the free-rider problem are everywhere. Community health provides some of the most familiar examples. It is best for a community if all children are vaccinated against common infectious and dangerous diseases, but there are known risks with some vaccinations, such as the one for whooping cough. The best outcome for any one family would be for everyone else to be vaccinated, so that whooping cough is not a problem, while their own children do not get their shots and so avoid the dangers of a bad reaction. If vaccination were left to individual choice, the most likely outcome is that the level of vaccinated children would be insufficient to keep the infectious diseases out of our communities. As a result, in many countries vaccinations are made compulsory – individual choice is removed – and community health is better as a result.

The use of antibiotics presents a similar problem: overuse leads to the presence of resistant strains of the diseases that antibiotics are meant to fight. Yet when an individual parent is faced with a sick child whose sore throat may be either the result of a bacterial infection treatable by antibiotics or a viral infection against which antibiotics are useless, the wise choice is to request antibiotic treatment immediately rather than force the child to wait through several painful days for test results showing whether the infection is actually bacterial. While the vaccination problem has been resolved by removing individual choice, the problem of antibiotic overuse persists.

Economist and philosopher Amartya Sen makes the same point in the context of malaria prevention in tropical countries:

> I may be willing to pay my share in a social program of malaria eradication, but I cannot buy my part of that protection in the form of a "private good" (like an apple or a shirt). It is a "public good" – malaria-free surroundings – which we have to consume together. Indeed, if I do somehow manage to organize a malaria-free environment where I live, my neighbour too will have that malaria-free environment, without having to "buy" it from anywhere.[2]

The Prisoner's Dilemma as a Graph

Although the graph showing the walk through Whimsley Park (Figure 4) and the table of the prisoner's dilemma (Figure 2) look quite different, they really show the same information.

Figure 5 presents the prisoner's dilemma in graph form. The lines moving across the graph are for clarity only: the only places on this graph that have real meaning are at the left-hand side (where the other person is defecting) or at the right-hand side (where the other person is co-operating). The choice is to co-operate (bottom line) or to defect (top line). The defect line is above the co-operate line at both sides of the graph, showing that defecting has a higher payoff than co-operating no matter what the other person chooses.

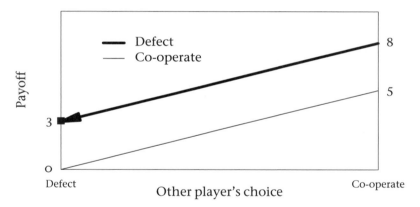

FIGURE 5. The prisoner's dilemma as a graph. The black square is the equilibrium outcome.

If both people defect, the outcome is the top line on the left side. This is the equilibrium, and it is marked by a black square. On the other hand, if both people co-operate, the outcome is a value of 5 points for each person: the lower line on the right-hand side of the graph.

The outcome can be thought of as "sliding down the top line" to the equilibrium. Imagine the players making their choices in sequence. The first player, realizing that the defect line is the best choice no matter what the other player does, chooses to defect. From the point of view of the second player, this has the effect of sliding the decision over to the left side of the graph. The second player also chooses to defect (the top line), fixing the outcome at the equilibrium.

Choosing Our Environment

Some of the clearest examples of free-riding in the real world arise in our treatment or management of the environment – which is not surprising, given that the environment is a shared resource. In this context the problems are often referred to as "the Tragedy of the Commons" after a 1968 article by Garret Hardin in the prestigious magazine *Science*. The public good that is depleted in his illustration is a common grazing ground, and individual villagers have a choice of whether to add an extra head of cattle to the commons. The analysis is identical to that of Whimsley Park – it is to each villager's individual advantage to add cattle, but when all of them do this the commons gets overgrazed, and everyone suffers.

Technological advances mean that large fishing fleets can now catch so many fish that the stocks cannot be naturally replenished. Like many countries, Canada has well-defined fishing boundaries, but the fish know nothing of such boundaries and cross into international waters all the time. Ocean fish stocks are therefore a "commons" or public good accessible to anyone.[3]

In the long run it might be better for all fishing countries to cut back on the amount of fish they catch rather than to deplete the fish stocks by overfishing. But it is better for any given country if everyone else cuts back while that country avoids the private cost of reducing its own catch. The externality is that those who overfish today are running down the stock of fish for other fishers and for future generations, but those who refrain have no reason to believe that the fish they spare will survive the nets of other fleets. For each fishing ship, and for each country, the problem is an exact analogue of Whimsley Park: no matter what others do, their best reply is to collect all the fish they can.

The end result – the equilibrium – is just what we would expect: the depletion of the cod and turbot stocks off Newfoundland has led to international disputes with Spain and the closure of entire fisheries. At the other end of the country the disputes have been with the United States rather than Spain, and the species of fish is the salmon rather than the cod and turbot, but otherwise the story is much the same.

The story has been repeated in many other parts of the world. The Rome Consensus on World Fisheries adopted by the 1995 UN Food and Agriculture Organization (FAO) Ministerial Conference on Fisheries stated that "additional actions are urgently required" to eliminate overfishing and to rebuild and enhance fish stocks. It also stated, "Without such action, further declines will occur in the 70 per cent of the world's fish stocks which are now regarded as fully exploited, over exploited, depleted or recovering."

Realizing how the temptation to free-ride encourages overfishing helps to avoid the good-guy/bad-guy oversimplification of the debate. The fish stocks are not being run down because there are evil people who enjoy driving fish species to extinction, or even necessarily because there are people who selfishly don't care about the long-term sustainability of the fisheries, but because no individual player acting alone can significantly improve the overall outcome. Market-Think would argue that the solution is to establish clear property rights, but fish do not respect such rights and will swim across whatever boundaries are drawn. Even if no one would prefer the fish stocks to be depleted, for each country involved the best reply to the situation is to overfish. The more the country depends on fishing, the stronger the short-term incentive to overfish.

A Selection of Environmental Free-Riders

Littering is, of course, a simple form of pollution, and pollution on a larger scale essentially represents the same problem as dropping a coffee cup in Whimsley Park. The cost of any one company reducing pollution is borne privately, while the benefits of a clean environment are shared by everyone. The problem is made more severe than that of

Whimsley Park because it is not only, or even mainly, companies that bear the cost of a polluted environment, but people in general. Indeed, companies per se do not care about the environment except insofar as it has an impact on their operations. If factories built around a lake need a source of clean water and also put waste into the lake, it might be better for all companies if they treated their waste before expelling it into the lake than for all companies to have to clean the water they take from the lake. But it would be slightly better still for any one company if all the other companies treated their waste while that company avoided the private cost of treating its own.

It is not required that companies be run by evil cigar-smoking industry barons for pollution to take place. One economics textbook describes the issues facing any one company:

> When a firm pollutes a river, it uses some of society's resources just as surely as when it burns coal. However, if the firm pays for the coal but not for the use of clean water, it is to be expected that management will be economical in its use of coal and wasteful in its use of water.

Even well-intentioned companies are put in a position where their best reply to the actions of others is to pollute. It is the structure of the situation that creates the problem, and the structure that must be changed.

Environmental free-rider problems abound. Here are just a few others.

OZONE LAYER. The ozone layer is a "public good" or "commons." It is only to be expected that, if it is left up to individual countries to recognize their long-term interests and refrain from damaging the ozone layer, the result will be a failure – not because countries are too stupid or too short-sighted to act in their own interests, but because any one country contributes only a little to the problem. Each country's own interest is best served if others restrain themselves, while that country continues using the chlorofluorocarbons that damage it. End result: big holes in the ozone layer.

CLIMATE CHANGE. Why should any one country spend the

money to decrease its emissions of carbon dioxide and other "greenhouse gases," when that action will have only a limited effect and other countries may renege? End result: global warming.

ACID RAIN. The bad effects of acid rain are inherently shared, while the benefits of acid-rain-producing technologies are private. End result: dead lakes.

What can be done to get out of the problems of environmental mismanagement?

Odysseus and the Sirens

There are ways of changing the structure of free-rider situations to encourage better outcomes. One of the most obvious is to change the payoffs by penalizing free-rider behaviour or, what amounts to the same thing, rewarding co-operation.

The incentives to free-ride or to co-operate are not determined by the absolute value of the payoffs, but by the differences between the payoffs for free-riding and co-operation. Punishment lowers the payoff for free-riders, while reward raises the payoff for co-operators. Both aim to tip the balance between the choices: to change the structure of the game to favour the co-operative choice over the free-riding choice.

Penalizing those who drop litter is one way of maintaining a clean park. Jill may know that if she is caught dropping her coffee cup she will be fined, or at least embarrassed by a reprimand, and this possibility makes the cost of dropping the cup a bit higher – perhaps high enough to shift the balance and keep the park clean.

Jill may choose to be subject to fines as long as it helps to improve the state of the park: that is, as long as the other coffee drinkers are subject to fines as well. There is no contradiction in this: it makes perfect sense for Jill to drop her cup on the way to work, but also to vote for a bylaw to ban littering and introduce park patrols. Wise people often take steps to eliminate choices that they know will lead to bad outcomes. In Homer's *Odyssey*, Odysseus wanted to hear the song of the sirens and yet knew that he would not be able to resist its lure. His solution was to order himself tied in advance to the mast of his ship so that when he became vulnerable to the song he would be unable to exercise his freedom of choice.

Consider this comment from a hockey player in the times when wearing helmets was not mandatory.

> It's foolish not to wear a helmet. But I don't – because the other guys don't. I know that's silly, but most of the players feel the same way. If the league made us do it, though, we'd all wear them and nobody would mind.[4]

This player is saying that hockey players would be better off if they gave up the choice of wearing helmets by giving an external group (the NHL) the right to make this restriction. Likewise, removing the matter of choice can improve Jill's outcome as long as other people's choices are restricted too, and the cost to her is that she carry her cup out of the park.

Warfare provides an archetypal example of removing choice to improve outcomes in the face of free-riding. Economist David Friedman states:

> In modern warfare, many soldiers don't shoot and many who do shoot don't aim. This is not irrational behaviour – on the contrary. In many situations, the soldier correctly believes that nothing he can do will have much effect on who wins the battle; if he shoots, especially if he takes time to aim, he is more likely to get shot himself. . . .
>
> The problem is not limited to modern warfare. It is a thousand years ago. You are one of a line of men on foot with spears, being charged by a mass of men on horseback, also with spears. If you all stand, you will probably break their charge and only a few of you will die; if you run, most of you will be ridden down and killed. Obviously you should stand.
>
> Obvious – and wrong. You only control you, not the whole line. If the rest of them stand and you run, you run almost no risk of being killed – at least by the enemy. If all of them run, your only chance is to

start running first. So whatever the rest are going to do, you are better off running. Everyone figures that out, everyone runs, and most of you die.[5]

On landing in England in 1066 William the Conqueror is supposed to have burned the boats that brought his army there. This removed the "choice" for his men to flee and ensured that his soldiers would fight harder. End result: military victory and a better chance of survival for each soldier.

Friedman also suggests that one role of the neat geometric formations and bright uniforms of European soldiers in Napoleonic times was to make monitoring of free-rider behaviour easier: individual soldiers found it harder to unobtrusively fall to the rear.

Once this tension is understood, we can see through some of the standard arguments concerning consumer preferences. Journalists sometimes point out that the very people who oppose the building of a Wal-Mart or some other big-box store sometimes end up shopping there after it is built, as if this shows that the protesters changed their minds, or that when it comes down to it they may even like Wal-Mart. Just because they shop at Wal-Mart does not mean that Wal-Mart is "popular" with them, any more than the littered state of Whimsley Park shows that the people passing through it want it to be an unsightly mess. Just as Jill can enjoy a clean park and still drop her coffee cup rather than carry it, so consumers may find it makes sense to shop at Wal-Mart even if they wish it had never been built.

Historically, environmental activists and economists have not always got along particularly well. Generally, economists tend to phrase problems in terms of individual incentives and solutions while environmentalists tend to think that people can move beyond such short-sighted thinking. Oddly enough, however, you can open any economics textbook and find a perfectly good explanation of why "leaving it to the market" leads to bad environmental outcomes.

The belief that markets, as constructed, fail to properly conserve environmental resources was reflected in a 1997 "Economists' Statement on Climate Change" calling for serious measures to limit the emissions of greenhouse gases and signed by no fewer than 2,500 economists. Paul Krugman, a thought-provoking economist and an innovator who has helped to develop new ways of thinking about international trade, was one of the original signatories of the statement. In defence of his profession he points out:

> Economists generally believe that a system of free markets is a pretty efficient way to run an economy, as long as the prices are right – as long, in particular, as people pay the true social costs of their actions. Environmental issues, however, more or less by definition involve situations in which the price is wrong – in which the private costs of an activity fail to reflect its true social costs.[6]

One way of making choices and outcomes align, then, is to require participants to pay for the right to free-ride. If pollution is taxed, firms will be more careful about how much they pollute. An alternative to taxing is for a government to fix a total pollution target and to distribute credits to the members of the industry, an approach inspired by the ideas of Nobel Prize-winning economist Ronald Coase. By letting firms trade these credits rather than trying to impose a uniform limit on all firms, those who have the ability to cut pollution easily have an incentive to cut a lot – the more they cut their pollution, the more they can make by selling their pollution credits to others. Those companies that are less able to cut pollution levels can buy credits from others. As long as pollution can be monitored, and as long as the total target is a realistic one, there is a lot to be said for this approach.

Taxes and credits are not as different as they may seem. Both are an alternative to fixed-limit legislation as a way of tackling the pollution problem. The tax acts like a penalty on the act of pollution (although without the stigma of "breaking the law"), while credits accomplish the same change of incentives by use of the carrot rather than the stick.

Although the concept of pollution credits was originally proposed by Dan Dudek, an environmentalist with the Environmental Defense Fund (EDF) – and other environmental organizations have joined EDF in supporting the plan – some environmentalists have not welcomed the idea. The critics present strong arguments – for example, that monitoring of pollution is so unreliable that enforcement would be difficult, as in the case of the ocean fish stocks. Other arguments are weaker: for example, the contention that credits place a price on pollution and that "buying and selling" pollution is simply wrong. Environmental scientist Barry Commoner, for instance, calls the plan "an abomination." He argues, "It legitimizes the production of pollution." Peg Stevenson of Greenpeace concurs with Commoner's analysis, saying that pollution allowances "create a right to pollute."[7]

Krugman provides another point of view:

> It used to be that the big problem in formulating a sensible environmental policy came from the Left – from people who insisted that since pollution is evil, it is immoral to put a price on it. These days, however, the main problem comes from the Right – from conservatives who, unlike most economists, really do think that the free market is always right – to such an extent that they refuse to believe even the most overwhelming scientific evidence if it seems to suggest a justification for government action.[8]

Just because solutions are based on the market doesn't make them immoral. On the other hand, just because market-based solutions are not immoral, we cannot conclude that all market-based solutions are good. Suspicion of some of the more prominent market-based proposals is well-founded. For example, many participants at the Kyoto environmental summit in 2000 saw the U.S.-sponsored pollution credits initiative as simply a way in which a state could avoid making any significant commitment to reducing pollution, and they were right. But that was because of the particulars of the plan, not because of the very notion of pollution credits.

Pollution credits have some benefits as a way of tackling particular pollution problems. For instance, they may work well for pollutants such as greenhouse gases and ozone-depleting chemicals, which are distributed globally. Because the impact of these gases and chemicals bears little relation to where they are produced, shifting pollution from one site to another does not make the problem better or worse.

But for other kinds of pollution problems the credits fail to deal with the real issues. Liquid industrial effluent travels only down waterways, and heavy waste such as the mercury from coal-fired power stations does not travel far even if it is emitted from smokestacks. In such cases allowing some companies to maintain or even increase their level of emissions if they can buy credits from those who have implemented anti-pollution measures will lead to the creation of highly polluted "hot spots." Despite this, in March 2005 the U.S. Environmental Protection Agency adopted regulations that used pollution credits to tackle the problem of mercury pollution, arguing, "There is similarity in how these emissions are produced, and there should be similarities in how they are controlled."[9] The use of tradeable credits makes life easier for the companies producing the pollution, but does not tackle the damage inflicted by mercury.

Choosing What to Grow

Farmers throughout Canada and other countries are planting more genetically-modified (GM) crops each year, with Monsanto's Roundup Ready strains, first introduced in Canada, being the most widely used. Roundup Ready canola was the first to be developed, Roundup Ready soy and corn are on the market, and Roundup Ready wheat is under development.

Monsanto advertises its product to farmers by claiming that Roundup Ready crops require less herbicide than do "conventional" crops. The canola or other plant is engineered to be resistant to the broad-spectrum herbicide Roundup (made, of course, by Monsanto). Roundup is good at killing weeds, but cannot easily be used on conventional crops because it would kill them too. When farmers plant

Roundup Ready crops, the weed killer kills the weeds and leaves the crop growing healthily. By using Roundup Ready crops, farmers can replace applications of a cocktail of selective pesticides by applications of this single herbicide.

Monsanto puts "Grower success stories" from Canadian farmers on its website to encourage others to adopt the product. For example, Brian Harvey of Durban, Manitoba, reportedly said: "The Roundup did a tremendous job. It wiped out the wild oats and all our other weed problems – wild mustard, wild buckwheat, lambs-quarters, green foxtail and sow thistle. The weed control has been exceptional."[10]

Environmental groups argue that farmers are being forced into dependence on Monsanto by the introduction of GM crops. At first sight there appears to be little basis for this claim: after all, no one makes farmers plant GM crops. But with a closer look the claims of environmental groups become more plausible. Just as with Jill and her coffee cup, the reason is that farmers' actions have externalities: one farmer's choice has an impact on other farmers.

Herbicides are like antibiotics: overuse can degrade their effectiveness as resistant strains develop. Application of a herbicide gives an evolutionary edge to genes that confer immunity to that herbicide. While small amounts of herbicide are unlikely to prompt a shift in the genetic makeup of weeds, large-scale applications can and do, and the move to replace many different pesticides with a single one (Roundup) only makes that shift happen faster.

Widespread application of Roundup promotes the spread of resistance to that herbicide – the spread of what could be called "Roundup Ready weeds." Each field of Roundup Ready canola (with its attendant applications of Roundup) slightly accelerates the appearance and spread of resistant weeds.

But for an individual farmer, choosing not to plant Roundup Ready canola is not necessarily a good alternative. Roundup Ready weeds may harm Roundup Ready crops, but they also harm conventional crops. Fields of conventional canola will then be hurt by both Roundup-resistant weeds and weeds that Roundup can control.

Meanwhile, Roundup Ready fields will be hurt only by the Roundup-resistant weeds. Roundup resistant weeds are a shared form of pollution or "public bad" that cannot be avoided by any one individual. There is no reason for any one farmer to plant conventional crops, because that farmer will get both kinds of weeds on his or her fields.

The testimony on the Monsanto website may well be misleading, then, especially because it comes from early adopters. These farmers are able to drop their cups in the park, but they don't have to face the prospect of a littered park because most other farmers do not yet have the same choice. But this does not mean that, once everyone can make the choice, they will all be better off. Although Roundup Ready crops are sold on the basis that they need fewer herbicides than conventional crops do, and while this claim may be true on an individual basis, widespread Roundup Ready adoption may actually increase the long-term need for herbicides.

The same "perverse logic" was apparent decades earlier in the case of another pesticide, DDT, as Edward Tenner points out in his book *Things Bite Back*: "The more effective a pesticide, and the more widely and intensively farmers apply it, the greater the potential reward for genes that confer immunity to it. In Sweden and elsewhere in Europe and North America, DDT-resistant flies appeared as early as 1947." In 1944 in Naples DDT was applied to over a million residents of Naples in a campaign to get rid of body lice and thus prevent an incipient typhus epidemic; but, according to Tenner, "By the mid-fifties, only ten or fifteen years after the Naples campaign, body lice in many parts of the world were already unaffected by DDT treatment. So were many farm, orchard, and forest insects in the United States."[11]

Reports are already emerging that this is exactly what is happening with the Roundup Ready campaign. One report indicates that total herbicide application on Roundup Ready soy beans in the United States is expanding compared to herbicide use on conventional varieties. As well, according to the report's author, Charles M. Benbrook: "Intense herbicide price competition, triggered by the commercial success of RR soybeans, has reduced the average cost per acre treated with most of today's popular herbicides by close to 50 percent since the introduction of RR soybeans. In response farmers are applying more active ingredients at generally higher rates."[12]

In areas in which Roundup Ready soybeans are in heavy use, according to Benbrook's study, all farmers are using more herbicides than in low Roundup Ready-use areas. An individual farmer cannot avoid the need to apply herbicides by shunning Roundup Ready soybeans. In fact, in areas of high Roundup Ready use and in areas of low Roundup Ready use, farmers using conventional varieties (other than organic farmers) may need to apply more herbicides than are farmers using Roundup Ready varieties.

These trends, then, only increase the risk of resistance and ultimately lead to less reliable and more costly systems.[13] Given the nature of the problem, the response from Bryan Hurley of Monsanto is less than persuasive: "American farmers have planted 60 percent of this year's soybean crop, roughly 40 million acres, with bioengineered Roundup Ready seeds. They would not be selecting these seeds if it was not to their advantage."[14]

But the story does not end with herbicide-resistant weeds. A second free-rider problem is at work here. Roundup Ready crops spread to other fields where they are unwanted, and become weeds themselves ("volunteers").

What is a crop in one field is a weed in another field. Crop plants growing where they are not wanted become litter. While use of Roundup Ready crops was limited to a small number of farmers, this was unlikely to be a big problem for any one farmer, but as the use of Roundup Ready crops grows, so too does the problem. In Canada the problem of volunteers is compounded when more than one kind of herbicide-resistant canola is being widely planted. These different canola "cultivars" can exchange genes, leading to "the unintentional origin of plants with multiple resistance to two, and in some cases three, classes of herbicide," according to a report from the Royal Society of Canada. "Such 'gene stacking' represents a serious development because, to control multiple herbicide-resistant volunteer canola plants, farmers are forced to use older herbicides, some of which are less environmentally benign than newer products."[15]

Of course, the problem will particularly hurt the growers of organic crops, whose ability to sell their product depends in many cases on it being free of, among other things, genetically modified material.

The best outcome for any one farmer may be for every other farmer to not plant Roundup Ready crops, but to take personal advantage of the crop. This is free-rider behaviour, not free-market choice, and the end result is unlikely to be beneficial for farmers as a whole. Farmers are trapped in the prisoner's dilemma. They are likely to find themselves in a spiral of increased herbicide costs and increased dependence on Monsanto, all the while making their own free choices.

Choosing Our Cities

Cities are intricate webs of interconnected systems. Transport, housing, land-zoning, education, public spaces, and services all connect with each other in myriad ways. Externalities are everywhere, and so we should not be surprised if individual choice and the market commonly lead to bad outcomes. In particular, we can expect the free market to value those aspects of city life that are treated as private choices, and to be responsive to those situations in which money changes hands. At the same time, we can expect the market to undervalue public spaces and other non-commercial aspects of cities, where we cannot express our wants through purchases and where free-riding is tempting.

Choosing Urban Sprawl

All of us make tradeoffs in choosing a home, a place to live. Budget, the distance to a workplace or school, and other priorities are all part of this. But within these constraints we do still get to choose the kind of dwelling we live in and the neighbourhoods we move to. As a result, it is common to hear that as long as regulations don't get in the way, cities will evolve to reflect the preferences of their inhabitants:

the market will ensure that we get what we want. Yet there is a deep-seated unhappiness about the shape that our cities are taking – and although some of it is a result of "not in my backyard" thinking, there is much that goes beyond mere selfishness.

Many North American cities are now more suburban than urban, with the perpetual development of new subdivisions on the edge of cities adding ring after ring of new houses. The resulting cityscape has many well-known problems. The diffuse layout makes an effective public transit system impractical and ensures that the city will be car-focused. The same diffuseness makes services expensive and may encroach on valuable surrounding environmental features, including water tables. Hollowed-out cities may lack a viable centre, which can in turn lead to a corresponding lack of public spaces.

But no one made us choose this kind of city, so how does the discontent we see around us fit with the choice made by many people to move into these successive rings of new houses? A professor at the School of Policy, Planning, and Development and Department of Economics at the University of Southern California offers one view of the shape and growth of cities: "The development of neighborhoods by private developers is driven by markets, not by public policy. People are getting the neighborhoods they want. And I trust that competing developers are reading the trade-offs that you and I are willing to make and that those trade-offs include our demand for community."[16]

This is the ubiquitous logic of MarketThink: leave everything to individual choice and the market will ensure that we get what we want. But the coffee cup debacle at Whimsley Park shows what is wrong with this kind of argument, and why individual choice may not leave us all in a happy state of mind.

It is often pointed out that, no matter what people say about urban sprawl, the most popular choice for housing remains so-called "green fields" development: new houses in new subdivisions on the edge of the city. Let's accept that for the moment. But, again, the story of Whimsley Park should tell us that there is always more than one side to a choice, and the decision of where to buy a house is only one of many we make.

By following the trends of home-buying decisions, private developers may be driven by customer choices, but they are also, perhaps, getting a distorted version of what the people want. We all have many different preferences about our cities: in addition to preferences about our houses, we also have a preference for the quality of the air we breathe, the schools we send our children to, the services we get from the city, and the taxes we are prepared to pay to get those services. Perhaps we even have a preference for "green fields" that are actually green and actually fields, or for a city that is small enough to bicycle across. Still, all of these preferences are prone to the principle of free-riding. Jack may like the idea of having both a compact city and a house overlooking green fields, but he cannot choose a compact city by himself so he chooses the house overlooking green fields – and contributes to urban sprawl. Jill might like both low property taxes and a spacious lot, but she cannot by herself keep municipal budgets trim so she chooses the spacious lot – and contributes to a thinly populated city that needs extra school buses and longer sewage pipes. If city councillors rely on house purchases as a measure of our preferences, they will ensure that all those other preferences will vanish into thin air – or, more likely, into thick smog-filled air.

The web of choices can become complicated, and the line between public and private is hard to discern. My new house on the edge of town makes the countryside just a little more difficult for you to reach. If your backyard happens to be close to my balcony, then my "panoramic view" is your loss of privacy. My speedy route to work along a wide road is a dangerous barrier on your child's walk to school. If, to protect your children from my car and from the other cars speeding along the nice wide road, you drive your children to school rather than letting them walk, then you are adding another car on the road and lowering the number of children walking to school. As more children stop walking, we end up with unsafe empty sidewalks and unsafe crowded roads outside the schools. And I still have to drive through a crowded street because of all the extra traffic. All of this is a result of perfectly reasonable individual choices.

To return to the issue of home-buying: we might all be happier if everyone lived in a smaller house with a smaller yard, but it might be slightly better still for an individual family if its members had a big house and a large yard, while everyone else lived in a smaller house. The urban environment is a shared resource, and the free-rider dynamics of individual choice ensure that this environment will not be treated well by individual choice. End result: sprawling subdivisions, and unhappy city dwellers.

There is more to urban sprawl than this, of course, but it is clear from the structure of the situation that if we leave city development to the free market, it will respect those factors that are private, like big houses for those lucky enough to be able to afford them, and will systematically undervalue those that are shared, like interesting, manageable, and compact cities.

Choosing How to Travel

Here is a related urban problem. If everyone took public transit to work, available road space during rush hour in many cities would be increased, allowing everyone to get to and from work more quickly. So why do so many people continue to drive in even the most congested rush-hour traffic? If most people are riding the bus, the best individual choice is to drive your car, because you can move quickly along the empty streets and also avoid the crush and waits of public transit. If most people are driving cars, you would still lose something by riding the bus, because it has to stop to pick up passengers. It is the free-rider problem, and the equilibrium is that everyone takes their car, everyone takes their little piece of the shared resource that is road space at rush hour, the roads become clogged, and everyone takes longer to get to work.

There is more than just transit time to be considered when we choose the freedom and flexibility of car travel as we move around the city. In addition to congested roads, dependence on cars produces bleak parking lots and air pollution. The eyesore of parking lots, like that of litter-strewn parks, is a public "ill" to which everyone is subjected. Pollution is also a shared cost. We can be sure that free individual choice will not get rid of them, even if they are almost universally disliked.

Again, one approach to congestion is to build a system that more clearly focuses drivers' minds on the cost of precious road space by charging them for it. This is precisely what London, England, mayor Ken Livingstone did starting in February 2003, when London began charging motorists £5 to drive in Central London between the hours of seven in the morning and six-thirty in the evening.[17] Every car that drives on a congested street imposes a small cost on all the other road users: a cost that the individual driver is usually not asked to bear, at least alone. Instead the costs are shared among everyone – which means that they add up and, in the end, can easily outweigh the private benefit of driving. They create a trap that catches a lot of unhappy drivers.

With the introduction of a charge, each driver pays a more realistic portion of the cost imposed as a whole on road users. Individual choice remains, but the balance of incentives is tilted to reflect more accurately the true costs and benefits of the decision, including the public costs.

Choosing Where to Shop

The last 20 years have seen the growth of big-box stores in what have become known as "power centres" around the edge of major towns throughout North America. The result has been the erosion of many downtown areas. The power centres have joined an earlier development, the suburban mall, in pulling commerce ever further away from the centre of cities. Companies such as Wal-Mart, Home Depot, Ikea, and Costco are associated with this trend, and established firms such as Sears and Canadian Tire have followed these newer competitors out to the edge of town, paying them the compliment of imitation.

The growth of power centres and the associated hollowing out of cities have been the focus of many arguments. Many cities, although not all, have taken the view that the success of big-box stores is the voice of consumer sovereignty speaking. To prevent the growth of power centres would be to limit choice, to restrict the freedom not only of the companies wanting to build, but also of the consumers wanting to shop there. As the argument goes, the commercial success of power centres is a demonstration of their popularity, because, of course, no one makes you shop at Wal-Mart. Protesters against big-box stores have focused their efforts on preventing the construction of the stores, accepting that once they are built, there is little that can be done.

But, as the story of Jack and Wal-Mart (chapter 1) shows, the success of power centres does not mean what their proponents claim it means. Like Jack, people may shop at them and still end up wishing that they were not built in the first place.

Successful downtowns are public spaces, multiple-use and multiple-owner areas characterized by diversity; and as public spaces, they are vulnerable to free-riding. Jack and the other inhabitants of Whimsley never choose to neglect the downtown area, but once its population slips below a critical point, the whole infrastructure can unravel. City centres are more complex than parks, but we can at least begin to see how a city centre can move from prosperous to decaying without anyone actually wanting it to.

Competition and variety are also public goods: by their nature, neither can be provided by a single store. Jack never explicitly chooses to have a narrower choice of places to shop, and yet he and others like him contribute directly to the problems of the downtown stores.

Of course, individual consumer choices are not the only factors that help to eliminate competition and variety. The story also has a supply-side angle, and that side of the coin is undeniably important. Wal-

Mart is a master at exploiting economies of scale, in its use of technology, its placement of stores, and its purchasing power and leverage with suppliers.

When a major store captures a substantial portion of a particular market, a shift occurs in the balance of power between retailer and suppliers. A huge company like Wal-Mart becomes an essential customer for manufacturers, and essential customers can dictate terms to their suppliers. Wal-Mart is able to demand deep discounts from its suppliers. An essential customer's game of divide and conquer can put suppliers in a prisoner's dilemma, in which their choices are to sell at wafer-thin margins or to miss out on a large market. Wal-Mart will buy from the supplier that offers the lowest prices – and to win in this competition a supplier may have to cut costs, change its way of operating, move jobs to ever-cheaper Third World sweatshops, and still receive only a slim margin from the sale. If all the suppliers hold out, perhaps Wal-Mart would have to back down and the suppliers could get a better deal, but no matter what the other companies do it is in the short-term interests of each of them to take the deal and sell to Wal-Mart rather than to sell nothing. As a result, the suppliers are trapped.

A similar divide-and-conquer aspect exists in the construction of a big-box store. When big-box stores come looking for land to be rezoned so that they can build their power centres, city councils can be placed in a prisoner's dilemma. Power centres are located to take consumers from as wide an area as possible – typically at a location accessible from several urban centres. For each city council, the worst outcome is that a power centre will indeed be established – but in someone else's location. If that happens, the city loses business in its own shops and gains none of the property taxes from the new power centre. It may be best for all cities to prohibit a power centre from going ahead, but it is better for a city to get the power centre than to have it established in a neighbouring area.

While it may also be the case that big-box stores are more economical or efficient than the smaller stores, it is not necessarily so. A recent Canadian example is the construction by Chapters of a large number of big-box bookstores in cities across the country. In bringing about its growth Chapters paid considerable attention to consumer appeal – it brought to Canada the large bookstore model, with in-house coffee shop and comfortable chairs that encouraged customers to linger, not just to buy and go. As a result of its building spree Chapters came to own 70 per cent of the book market in the country.

Book publishers in turn found it essential that Chapters stock their products. In its attempt to dominate the industry from one end to the other Chapters went a step further than even Wal-Mart. It set up its own book distribution service. That branch, Pegasus, distributed books not only to Chapters stores, but also to some of the competitors. Chapters was able to demand, from publishers, deep discounts and favourable policies for returns, and publishers had no alternative but to accept the terms.

Despite these advantages, the reason that Chapters drove so many bookstores out of business was not because the operation was a more successful business model or that economies of scale would sooner or later make bigger stores more efficient and profitable than smaller stores. In fact, in February 2001 Chapters was ignominiously sold to the owners of its major rival, Indigo, following months of rumour and speculation of financial troubles. And by 2004 Indigo itself was moving to devote more of its floor space to goods other than books. Rather, Chapters drove smaller bookstores out of business because its corporate owners had the deep pockets necessary to back investment in the construction of many large new bookstores. It drove publishers such as Stoddart into bankruptcy because they had little choice but to restructure their operations around Chapters' needs.

The animosity between publishers and Chapters was such that, when the Indigo purchase was confirmed, Allan MacDougall, president of B.C.- based Raincoast Distribution, remarked, "I don't know how this business could be in any worse shape and still be called a business. . . . Let's just say the last 18 months have been the worst in the history of publishing in Canada."[18]

The Kind of Problem a City Is

The interconnectedness of choices makes cities what they are, and the MarketThink approach of letting a limited number of individual choices (purchasing decisions) drive the growth of cities is bound to lead to bad outcomes. As Jane Jacobs observed over 40 years ago in *The Death and Life of Great American Cities*, it makes no sense to think of the city as "a collection of separate file drawers" because cities present "situations in which a half-dozen or even several dozen quantities are all varying simultaneously and in subtly interconnected ways."[19]

Jacobs spends the first three chapters of her landmark book on "The Uses of Sidewalks." To focus on sidewalks is itself a novel start for a book on cities: they are exactly those places that most city planners miss. Sidewalks are a physical symbol of the externalities and tangled choices that permeate our cities: "A city sidewalk by itself is nothing. It is an abstraction. It means something only in conjunction with the buildings and other uses that border it, or border other sidewalks very near it." Jacobs does not even talk about what most of us think of as the "purpose" of sidewalks: "Streets in cities serve many purposes besides carrying vehicles, and city sidewalks – the pedestrian parts of the streets – serve many purposes besides carrying pedestrians."[20]

The "uses of sidewalks" that Jacobs investigates are safety, contact, and the assimilation of children into the broader adult society. None of these uses has any significant role to play in a market-based look at cities. Each is a public good: we either have busy, occupied sidewalks or we don't. No one person can buy a bustling city street for themselves. To introduce a market for safety, for example, is to ask for a gated, segmented city. It is in these neglected spaces, at the edge of vision, that the success or failure of cities gets determined. Thinking of cities as a collection of separate problems makes as much sense as trying to understand a liquid by using the ideal gas law (chapter 2). Interactions and tangles are at the heart of the matter; they are not something to be treated as an imperfection or perturbation.

Among her many examples, Jacobs looks at the problem of a

city neighbourhood park.[21] The usage of the park depends on many factors, including the park's own design and who is around to use the park and when. This in turn depends on the uses of the city outside the park itself. Furthermore, the influence of these uses is not just the sum of several independent factors, but depends on the particular combination of uses. These uses near the park and their combinations depend on other factors, including the age and variety of building, and the size of blocks in the vicinity.

We have not, then, chosen the cities that we live in at all, at least in the sense that is usually meant. That is, our cities are not the result of any intrinsic preferences. Instead, we are each making many interconnected choices, and that means we are making choices that depend on those of others. Our decisions of where to live, of how to travel, of where to shop – these are not so much expressions of an intrinsic preference as they are *best replies* to the environment in which we live, shaped by and in turn shaping the actions of others and the future shape of the city. We may not "want" to drive a car to work, but given that most other people do, it is the best alternative available. We may not want to live in a suburban environment, but if that is where good housing is available, at prices we can afford, where people we know are living, and where the new schools are being built, then perhaps it is the best available option. We might not want to avoid the city centre, but if the houses and buildings there are old and rundown, if the streets don't seem as safe, and if businesses are closing, there is no point in going there.

There are no magic solutions for the problems of modern cities. There are, however, preconditions for success, and one of those preconditions is to understand that if we divide the problem of city development into separate compartments, and open each compartment to a market model of "choice," we are most likely to end up in a bad place. MarketThink is guaranteed to erode public space and public goods in the city. If we want to find a favourable equilibrium among the many complex games being played in the city, we cannot hope to do so by avoiding collective decisions regarding the type of city we want.

The lessons that Jacobs draws about cities apply more broadly. There are no simple solutions to the problems of individual choice. But if we think about the problems in the right way, and don't get misled by the false and simplistic promises of MarketThink, we are more likely to find our way to a happy outcome.

chapter four

ARMS RACES AND RED QUEENS

MARKETTHINK PRESENTS INDIVIDUAL CHOICE as the best way in which we as consumers can cast our economic votes and so push the market to provide what we want. One way in which private industry has used individual choice to its own advantage, and against the interests of consumers, has been by luring us into "arms races," a variant of the free-rider problem in which there is no "public good" or "commons" to get overused. The key feature of an arms race is that outcomes depend on the relative position of players in the game. The utility of any one outcome for a particular person is that person's position relative to others.

Getting embroiled in an arms race is an expensive proposition because, like the Red Queen in *Through the Looking Glass and What Alice Found There*, "It takes all the running *you* can do, to keep in the same place."

Status is one common example of a positional outcome. As study after study shows, beyond a certain level people value their relative position in society more than they do their absolute level of income: that is, their utility depends crucially not only on their own income but also on how it compares with that of other people. For example, Andrew Oswald has extensively studied the influence of income on subjective reporting of happiness and concludes that although extra money does make people somewhat happier, the effect is dwarfed by other aspects of their lives. Employment and marriage are two factors that weigh much heavier than income alone.

In his conclusion to a paper entitled "Happiness and Economic Performance," Oswald asks why people strive to make more money when it apparently buys them so little extra well-being. He suggests that what matters is relative income rather than absolute. If this is the case, it explains why intuition misleads us: "Such intuition has been built up by observing how each of us feels as our income rises. Yet, implicitly, that holds others' incomes constant. Hence commonsense may not be a good guide to what happens when a whole society gets richer."[1] Oswald is suggesting that the pursuit of happiness by means of wealth is a competition of status: an arms race. He is not the first to make this observation; Karl Marx said something similar many years ago:

> A house may be large or small; as long as the neighbouring houses are likewise small, it satisfies all social requirement for a residence. But let there arise next to the little house a palace, and the little house shrinks to a hut. The little house now makes it clear that its inmate has no social position at all to maintain, or but a very insignificant one; and however high it may shoot up in the course of civilization, if the neighbouring palace rises in equal or even in greater measure, the occupant of the relatively little house will always find himself more uncomfortable, more dissatisfied, more cramped within his four walls.[2]

Arms races, whether driven by a concern for status or by some other positional consideration – we shall come across others in due course – present opportunities for private industry. If companies can change a market from a commodity market to an arms race, they can change the rules of the game for their customers. They can change it from being a game in which individual choice works to the consumers' benefit because we can walk away from any one company, and turn it into a game in which individual choice works instead to industry's benefit, because it takes all the spending we can do just to remain in the same place.

Jack Keeps up with the Joneses

Jack lives at Number 3 Tiny Close. As its name suggests, Tiny Close is a short street; it has only ten houses. Each house has a single car, and the owner of each car – in this case the owners are all men – is very proud of his possession. On Sundays, the ritual washing and waxing of the cars are interrupted only by the owner looking surreptitiously up and down the street, to see how his car compares to that of his neighbours. For it is not so much the car itself that these people value as it is the status it brings them. Even when they are out walking, the one with the best car has a swing in his step that is a marked contrast with the slouched shuffle of the lowest on the ladder.

Jack is in the middle of the pack, more or less. In his head, he considers that his car is better than the cars at numbers 1, 2, 4, and 8, but worse than those at numbers 5, 6, 7, 9, and 10. But his car is starting to show its age, and Jack has just come into some unexpected money, so he is thinking of getting a new car. In fact, he has done all the necessary research on a rather sporty model that he is contemplating. He just has to decide whether to go and get that car, or whether he should just replace his less fashionable current car with the latest model of the same kind. He thinks in his usual way.

- By the time I have sold my old car and bought the sporty new one, it is going to cost me about $20,000 to buy the new car. I could replace my existing one for about $10,000.
- Getting the sporty new car would move me three places up the social ladder. I would still be below house numbers 5 and 9, but would be ahead of all the others. I value each place on the social ladder at $5,000.
- Replacing my existing model would leave me in the same place I am now. I would gain a more reliable car, but no additional status.

If you do the arithmetic, it is clear that Jack's best decision is to get the sporty car. The overall cost, after the status value is added on, is $5,000, whereas the cost of replacing his existing model is $10,000. So Jack heads off to the dealer and comes back with his sporty new car. He carries his head somewhat higher, walks more confidently, and feels good about his decision.

All is right with Jack's world.

Around him, however, things are not so good. In particular, at houses 6, 7, and 10, the car owners are feeling a little off-colour, as they have slipped down the social ladder one rung.

Over the next year, each of the people on the street buys a new car. Each of them does the same arithmetic (with a few variations for the ones at the top of the social scale), and each comes to the same conclusion: it is time to move up a notch and buy a more prestigious model. As each car owner in turn comes back from his car dealer of choice, each feels the benefit of his decision.

But if we look at the street at the end of the year, we see that each person has stayed in the position in which he started. Each jumped forward as he bought his car, but each was nudged down again when his neighbours leap-frogged him with a new purchase.

Jack looks ruefully back at the notes he made when he bought his car. He realizes that his new car has not bought him the happiness he thought it would. But he also realizes that if he had gone with the cheaper car, he would have slipped down past three other houses and be only one rung from the bottom of the ladder. So he clearly made the best choice he could, but he is not as happy as he hoped.

In a literal arms race, what is important is to have more arms than your opponent has in order to be safe. In less serious arms races, such as the one on Jack's street, it is still position that is important. Arms races are similar in structure to the free-rider and prisoner's dilemma problems. Even though there is no "commons" here to be overgrazed, the structure is the same. Given a choice between continuing the arms race and refraining, no matter what others do, the best choice is to continue the race and attempt to climb the ladder to a higher rank. Arms races lead us into a Looking

Glass world, where we are subject to spiralling costs but do not achieve any real benefit.

The equivalent of the "both co-operate" option in the prisoner's dilemma is an arms-control agreement among the participants in the arms race: an agreement to limit spending and refrain from competition. If an arms-control agreement can be reached and maintained, everyone will be better off; they will keep the same position on the ladder but not have to spend lots of money to do so.

A Selection of Arms Races

Arms races are, like other free-rider variants, surprisingly common. Here are some examples.

REAL ARMS RACES. Game theory and arms races have a long history together. The prisoner's dilemma was, like much else in early game theory, invented at the Rand Corporation in the early 1950s. It quickly rose to prominence partly because it mapped so closely a key event of the Cold War. At that time both the United States and the Soviet Union had a stark strategic decision to make: to build a hydrogen bomb or to refrain from building one.

The decision is a perfect prisoner's dilemma. Unlike most modern international crises, this game was clearly played between two and only two actors. The secrecy of the decision meant that there was little scope for debate within either country, and so the part of each country involved in making the decision – the security and defence establishments – acted in an unusually single-minded way. The actors were driven by the mandates of their own establishments, with no room for soft-hearted or emotional thinking, which made them as close to the self-interested archetype as can be imagined. Although the actors could communicate formally by negotiation, neither were prepared to open up their research laboratories to the kind of inspection that could verify a decision to refrain from building the H-bomb. As a result, the communication was essentially meaningless and neither side could afford to trust the other.

We know the equilibrium of the prisoner's dilemma, and so the outcome of this decision was entirely predictable. Even if both sides might have preferred to be in a world without the H-bomb, the worst possible outcome was that of being in a world in which your opponent had the H-bomb and you didn't. The end result, predictably, was that both countries built the bomb, leaving themselves and the world in a less safe state than before.

Each stage of the escalation of the nuclear arms race was a prisoner's dilemma. The philosophy of "mutually assured destruction" reflected the inability of the two sides to establish any form of trust. The fear of being left behind, and the enticement of establishing a significant advantage drove the military-industrial complexes of each side through successive rounds of the game, past the point at which the idea of advantage or weakness had any connection to the real meaning of those terms. While it may be true that we would all be more secure without nuclear arsenals than with, each country was faced with a choice of being stronger than its opponent or being weaker. The end result: spiralling arms races, a situation that few would "prefer" given other alternatives.

It is possible not only that game theory helps us to understand the dynamics of the arms race, but also that it helped to shape that race itself. The influence of game theory on strategic thinking during the Cold War is hard to estimate, but it was certainly taken seriously. Books such as Thomas Schelling's *The Strategy of Conflict* attempted to apply the theory to real world issues. Anatol Rapoport challenged the strategists on their own ground in his book *Strategy and Conscience*, arguing that the sophistication of game theoretical thinking hid some grievous oversimplifications, and buttressing his arguments by studying how people actually behaved in situations like the prisoner's dilemma.

ARMS RACES ON THE ROAD. Less seriously, but in the same vein, a letter from one Joseph Bernstein, M.D. to *The New York Times* ran as follows.

In "Lives Changed in a Split Second" (Op-Ed, Jan. 10), Charles Wheelan writes about the rollover risk of sport utility vehicles. One could also

write about the countless people whose injuries were prevented or miti-
gated by the heft and improved sight lines that these vehicles offer. In a
crash between a car and an SUV, I would prefer to be in an SUV. In all
such accidents I have witnessed as a trauma surgeon, the occupants of
the car sustained far worse injuries. Mr. Wheelan implies that he is
going back on the road in a car, not an SUV, but for me, rollover risk is a
reasonable price to pay for the other advantages that SUV's offer.[3]

Dr. Bernstein's logic is impeccable. Except, of course, if everyone drives
an SUV they will have no better sightlines than they would if everyone
were driving a car. They get a benefit only if others stay with smaller
cars. If everyone else did choose to drive an SUV, Dr. Bernstein would
be forced to buy a Hummer. After all, the improved sightline is a real
bonus, and in a car crash between a Hummer and an SUV, I would prefer to be in a Hummer. Until everyone else has one, that is.

ARMS RACES IN SPORTS. In the sport of men's tennis it is in the
interests of any one player to get the latest high-technology racket; it
gives that player an edge over the opponents and a better chance of
victory. Yet the technological progress produced by this demand for
an individual edge has made the game of men's tennis less interesting to watch, dominated as it is by power serves and short rallies,
and each professional tennis player has been harmed by the drop in
interest.

ARMS RACES IN NATURE. The giraffe with the longest neck can
reach higher leaves than can its shorter-necked cousins, and so it has
an advantage when it comes to survival. The tallest tree has at least
some of its leaves out of reach of the tallest giraffe, and so has an
advantage when it comes to survival. The end result of this arms race
between giraffes and trees is very tall trees and very long-necked
giraffes.

Such arms races between predators and prey are common. Only
the fastest rabbits survive being caught by the fox, and only the
fastest foxes catch rabbits: end result, fast rabbits and fast foxes. The
equilibrium, however, is not always a good one for the species
involved, as the dictates of an arms race can be so demanding that it

may compromise the fitness of a species in other ways. As one example, trees in a forest compete with each other for access to sunlight. As a result, trees grow taller than their neighbours, which in turn grow taller themselves. The equilibrium is a forest of very tall trees, and yet a forest of tall trees gets no more sunlight than a forest of short trees, while it spends far more resources growing to and sustaining the increased height.

GENETIC ARMS RACES. The possibility of genetically selecting traits in our offspring raises the possibility of dangerous arms races as parents search to enhance qualities that confer status or advantage on their children.

Many parents would be tempted, if the opportunity were available, to have a child who was in the taller half of the population, and yet of course only 50 per cent of the population can ever be taller than the median. The end result is a less happy population, with no better average status but more back problems.[4]

ARMS RACES IN THE WORKPLACE. There is a balance to be found between home and work. Many would say that the balance in North America is tipped too far to the side of work. Newspapers routinely run stories on harried parents and their hectic lives. The pressure to work harder and longer is a status competition: an arms race in which we all have little choice but to work harder because everyone else is also working harder, and in which companies have to press people to work harder because other companies are squeezing more out of their employees. And yet individuals find it very difficult to step out from this race: it will cost them real money when it comes to promotions and bonuses. A reduction in the maximum workweek (legislated, for instance, in France in 1999) would be a step to control this arms race and to allow many people to restore balance in their lives.

Choosing to Be Cool

For people concerned about being stylish, it makes sense to buy fashionable clothes to keep up with other fashionable people. But to do so leaves us running just to remain in the same place. As an individual choice, it is better than the alternative of falling behind in the race, yet it would be better for all if we could avoid the payment, and keep our relative status intact.

All purchases based on coolness, sophistication, or other status-related attributes are arms races in which our choices are inherently tangled. Status is in the eye of the beholder, and this means that you cannot be cool in a vacuum. To be cool requires an audience that agrees on what "cool" is, and on whether your new purchase is it. And as the definition of status is made by other people, the individual consumer caught in a status-based arms race loses independence: if Jack is looking for status when he buys his new car, he can no longer make choices based on his own preferences. He must instead make them based on what he expects others to find appealing. The essence of cool is, of course, to walk the fine line of being distinctive (distinguishable from the uncool) and yet still be recognized by the uncool masses as something to which they might aspire.

The dynamic of cool requires constant change. Being a leader (keeping one step ahead of the crowd) demands that you be a dedicated follower (of fashion). As Joseph Heath and Andrew Potter point out in *The Rebel Sell*:

> Just as not everyone can be upper class and not everyone can have good taste, so not everyone can be cool. This isn't because some people are essentially cooler than others, it's because cool is ultimately a form of distinction . . . in order for some things to be cool, others must suck.[5]

Heath and Potter go on to make a provocative claim: that many of the supposedly anti-capitalist counterculture movements of the last 40 or 50 years have actually done more to promote capitalism than to oppose it. They argue that many on the "countercultural left" have misunderstood the nature of the consumerism they oppose, believing that consumerism is all about conformity ("little boxes made of ticky-tacky and they all look the same") when in fact modern capitalism thrives on selling goods that allow people to distinguish themselves from others: from the Burberry coat to Tommy Hilfiger to Timberlands boots to high fashion, many consumer purchases are about being different from the mainstream.

Rebellion is, argue Heath and Potter, another form of distinction because "not everyone can be a rebel."

> If everyone joins the counterculture, then the counterculture simply becomes the culture. Then the rebel has to invent a new counterculture, in order to re-establish distinction . . . the rebel has to move on to something new. Thus the counterculture must constantly reinvent itself. This is why rebels adopt and discard styles as quickly as fashionistas move through brands.
>
> In this way, countercultural rebellion has become one of the major forces in driving competitive consumption.[6]

Countercultural radicals have thus, according to Heath and Potter, adopted " 'solutions' that in fact exacerbate the very problems they are intended to resolve." The countercultural critique of consumerism plays into this, they say, through its insistence on "analyzing consumer consciousness as a form of manufactured conformity," which means that it "completely overlooks the role that positional goods and the search for distinction play in driving consumer capitalism."

> As a result, the proposed solution – individualistic sartorial and stylistic rebellion – simply feeds the flames, by creating a whole new set of positional goods for these new "rebel consumers" to compete for. The struggle for status is replaced by the quest for cool, but the basic structure of the competition remains unchanged.[7]

From Commodity to Status Symbol

The existence of arms races creates a set of incentives for companies in free-market economies. It encourages companies to do what they can to move markets away from the only structure in which consumers have an influence, which is the competitive market based on price. Marketing, including image-driven advertising and particularly brand development, is the most obvious way in which they seek to effect this change.

There are rich rewards for companies that can successfully turn commodities into status goods. If a handbag is merely a functional container for everyday objects, a good one might last many years; but if a handbag is a fashion accessory, then we may need to buy a new one far more frequently to keep those appreciative looks coming. It is hardly surprising that a massive amount of advertising money is spent trying to turn functional goods into status goods. More money is spent on advertising the attitude of cars than on advertising their specifications. It may not be clear what GM means when it advertises its Pontiac cars as "built for drivers," or what Volkswagen means when it tells us that "on the road of life, there are passengers and there are drivers," but we do know that drivers decide where to go while mere passengers just go along for the ride; that drivers are independent and passengers dependent. And which do you want to be? The same goes for clothes, beer and whisky, and shampoos. The whole purpose of most brand names is to associate some degree of status with a product, and the purpose of visibly displaying a brand logo is to convey the sign to others that the owner of the logo is wearing a high-status product.

To the extent that companies succeed in making this shift from a purely functional item to a conveyer of status, they manage to move the market for their product away from a market of independent choices, in which consumers do have a degree of sovereignty, to an arms race for status, in which individual consumers have the option of paying the entry fee by buying the requisite goods or accepting a position of low status, with the costs that go along with it.

Too many analyses of status-based arms races ignore the real costs of low status, imagining that individuals can avoid paying these costs by simply "not caring" what others think. Yet these costs are often real and are independent of the individual's own taste: job and university interviews, public-speaking, any job that involves gaining the confidence of a customer – in all of these the outcome has as lit-eral a monetary cost as we can imagine, and in all of these the out-come can depend on other people's perceptions of our appearance. To emphasize the real costs that many arms races carry with them, Heath and Potter quote the real estate thesis that to succeed, "one must project an image of success at all times."[8] To step out of arms races is not, from an individual point of view, a good choice.

Again, what we need to improve individual outcomes is some kind of arms-control agreement. Indeed, even an agreement imposed from outside – restricting the individual choice of those engaged in the race – may serve to make everyone better off. An arms race is a trap, and like the other traps of choice, we cannot escape from it through individual choice alone.

The school uniform is a classic example of such an arms-control agreement. The requirement that students wear a common uniform prevents them from engaging in the costly arms race of competing for status on the basis of their clothes. Uniforms do not prevent this com-petition completely, of course – one way or another, students find ways of looking cool or of failing to look cool – but they do put limits on the money that families are pushed into spending. Students may still have to run to stay in the same place, but they (or their parents) don't have to run as fast.

Arms-control agreements inevitably place limits on individual choice – that is the mechanism by which they work – but in many cases this limitation is preferable to the damage we do ourselves when we are caught in an arms race. Whether it is a progressive income tax to stem arms controls in the competition for positional goods or France's legislated 35-hour workweek to stem the competition for sta-tus through work, arms-control agreements can curtail antisocial and destructive competitions, to everyone's benefit.

chapter five

CO-OPERATION AND ITS LIMITS

THE TEMPTATION TO FREE-RIDE makes it difficult for groups, and especially loosely organized large groups, to act collectively. Even if there is a collective goal that is the preferred outcome for each and every member in the group, it is in the short-term self-interest of each member to free-ride: to forego the hard work required, to let others make the effort, and to collect the rewards anyway. End result: a group that fails to reach its goals.

The free-rider problem as it applies to groups is also called the collective action problem. It has not always been recognized as a problem at all – even now, many arguments assume that groups logically act together to achieve goals that are in their common interest. Mancur Olson focused attention on this assumption at the beginning of *The Logic of Collective Action*:

> If the members of some group have a common interest or objective, and if they would all be better off if that objective were achieved, it has been thought to follow logically that the individuals in that group would, if they were rational and self-interested, act to achieve that objective.[1]

Like other instances of free-riding, the collective action problem challenges many commonplace assertions. If shareholders cannot effectively act together, it makes little sense to say that corporate executives are responsible to their shareholders, and if individual employees cannot come together to form a union, we cannot infer that they are opposed to unionization.

Collective action relies on co-operation, and co-operation is as much about circumstances as it is about attitudes: people of good will may fail to co-operate despite themselves, while in other circumstances co-operation may emerge even among those have no interest in each other's welfare.

Enduring Love

The beginning of Ian McEwan's haunting novel *Enduring Love* is a dramatic introduction to the problems of collective action and co-operation. The narrator is looking back to a day when he and his girlfriend, sharing a picnic, were interrupted by a hot-air balloon landing in the field. The pilot of the balloon was in trouble. He must have been halfway out of the passenger basket as it touched the ground and his leg had become entangled in a rope attached to an anchor. As the wind gusted and lifted the balloon towards a nearby escarpment, the pilot was half-dragged, half-carried across the field. In the basket was a child, a boy of about ten.

The narrator and four other people saw the danger, and ran to help. Together with the balloon pilot, they each grabbed hold of a line to try to keep the balloon from rising into the air. Then, amidst much confusion, there was a gust of wind, the pilot lost his grip, and the balloon rose into the air with five people holding on desperately, the young boy still in the basket. For a few seconds they all held on, and then . . .

> I didn't know, nor have I ever discovered, who let go first. I'm not prepared to accept that it was me. But everyone claims not to have been first. What is certain is that if we had not broken ranks, our collective

weight would have brought the balloon to earth a quarter of the way down the slope as the gust subsided a few seconds later.²

As four of the men tumbled to the ground and the balloon surged upwards, one man held on – apparently, for him, the "flame of altruism must have burned a little stronger." As the balloon drifted off he quickly became "a tiny figure, almost black against the sky," hanging from a rope.

Afterwards those who let go knew that, by failing to stick together, they had broken a "covenant, ancient and automatic, written in our nature." Even though "there was no plan, no agreement to be broken," they had come face to face with "morality's ancient, irresolvable dilemma – us, or me. Someone said me, and then there was nothing to be gained by saying us."

McEwan's passage speaks eloquently to the conflict between co-operation and selfishness, between mutual aid and self interest, which is the subject of much of this book. As he says, "A good society is one that makes sense of being good. Suddenly, hanging there below the basket, we were a bad society. Suddenly, the sensible choice was to look out for yourself." It is in the free-rider problem that we see the "ancient, irresolvable dilemma – us, or me" acted out.

The dilemma proved irresolvable for those holding onto the balloon. Like Jack and Jill going to their divorce lawyers or the prisoners in their cells, the men have no chance to communicate: "there was no team, there was no plan, no agreement to be broken." They didn't know what kind of people they were trying to co-operate with, and if others did not hold on too, then being good made no sense. And of course there was no second chance, in which they could learn the lessons from their failure. With all that stacked against them, being good people was not enough: there is more to co-operation than good intentions.

Choosing to Reciprocate

Ian McEwan's story shows how, when circumstances are unfavourable, co-operation fails even among well-intentioned people. At the other end of the spectrum, given the right circumstances, co-operation can be achieved even among selfish players who have no qualms about free-riding and no concern for others' welfare.

We know that the equilibrium of the prisoner's dilemma is an unhappy one in which both players free-ride and consequently fail to achieve the benefits of their co-operation. But things change if the prisoner's dilemma game is played between two players not once, but repeatedly. One "game" is a set of "rounds," with each round being a playing of the prisoner's dilemma. Each round of the game allows the players to send signals to the other about the kind of strategy they are adopting. Each player gets to learn about "what kind of player" the other is and to make use of that knowledge.[3]

Political scientist Robert Axelrod carried out the best-known investigation into effective strategies for the repeated prisoner's dilemma.[4] He invited a group of game theorists and others to participate in a computer-based tournament: each invitee was to submit a strategy – a set of rules for making decisions. Axelrod put these strategies into a computer program and ran them against each other, in a round-robin tournament. Each game in the tournament consisted of 200 rounds of the prisoner's dilemma played between a pair of programs. The points for each round were assigned using the standard prisoner's dilemma table (see Figure 3).

Each of the 14 submitted strategies was played against each of the others in one of these 200-round games, as well as against itself and against a random strategy. The winner was to be the strategy that accumulated the most overall points during the tournament, or equivalently the highest number of points per game.

The conditions for victory do not include "beating" opponents in the game. For example, to avoid being trapped in the bad outcome of mutual defection, a player might take up the strategy of gaining a high score by defecting when the "opponent" co-operates.

Alternatively, a strategy may promote co-operation somehow, so that the games are high-scoring. Just how to balance these incentives was not clear, and contestants took a variety of approaches to the tournament. For example, a strategy that is often called "Grim" would be to co-operate until the other player defected, and then to defect for the remainder of the game. A strategy called "Joss" would involve co-operating most of the time but would make an unprovoked defection every ten moves. Many tried to walk a line between the two extremes of frequent defection and tolerant co-operation, responding with various degrees of sophistication to the actions of the other player.

But sophistication was not the key to success: the winner of the tournament was the simplest strategy. Submitted by Anatol Rapoport, a game theorist at the University of Toronto who had made many studies of the psychology of people playing the prisoner's dilemma, it was the now well-known strategy of Tit-for-Tat:

- On the first move, co-operate.
- On every subsequent move, play what the other player played on the previous move.

If the other player co-operates, then, Tit-for-Tat co-operates on the next move. If the other player defects, Tit-for-Tat defects on the next move. Tit-for-Tat exemplifies *reciprocity*. It successfully encourages, using a mixture of carrot and stick, other strategies to take part in a mutually beneficial co-operation. Overall, it got the most points of any strategy even though, or perhaps even because, it can never do better than any "opponent." Instead, its success at encouraging co-operation means that games in which it plays are high-scoring. In contrast, strategies that are too opportunistic in their attempt to take advantage of the other player may have scored more points than their opponent, but the large number of "defect-defect" rounds made their games, overall, lower-scoring.

Axelrod then held a second, larger tournament. Each entrant was supplied with the results of the first tournament and a complete analysis of how each strategy performed, and why. The result was that

Rapoport again was the only contestant to submit Tit-for-Tat, and again it was the simplest of all strategies submitted, and again it won.

Despite its success in Axelrod's tournaments, Tit-for-Tat is not an equilibrium for the indefinitely repeated prisoner's dilemma. In fact, there is no unambiguous "best strategy" for the game: the best strategy depends on the strategies being played by other players. What's more, investigations since these tournaments have shown that, while the best strategy always depends on the other players playing the game, there are other strategies that, had they been submitted, would have performed as well as, or even better than, Tit-for-Tat. Nevertheless, considerable empirical evidence supports the observation that under a wide range of conditions, Tit-for-Tat and similar strategies are highly successful in games such as the repeated prisoner's dilemma. Most of these successful strategies share similar traits, which Axelrod went on to highlight in his analysis of his tournaments.

BE NICE. Co-operating on the first move gives the opportunity for a mutually beneficial co-operative pattern to become established.

BE UNEXPLOITABLE. By responding to defection with defection, Tit-for-Tat avoids being taken advantage of by strategies looking to exploit generous opponents.

BE FORGIVING. If the other player co-operates even once after a defection, Tit-for-Tat would co-operate again and forget all about the defection. This prevented patterns of mutually destructive defections from becoming established.

BE CLEAR. It is not difficult to see what Tit-for-Tat is doing. Other strategies found it easy to settle into beneficial co-operative patterns.

Axelrod argues that reciprocity, as exemplified by the properties of Tit-for-Tat, is a mechanism for the evolution of co-operation. He confesses that he was surprised by his own results. His initial attitude was that, to promote co-operation, one should be "slow to anger"; but reciprocating strategies are, on the contrary, prompt to respond to defection with a defection of their own. The importance of being unexploitable in order to promote co-operation is a condition that he did not expect.

Of course, strategies embodied in computer programs have no motives. Biologist Maynard Smith had shown how co-operation can evolve even in situations in which no individual has intelligence or foresight, and even when no central body is present to enforce co-operation and punish free-riding. It is not necessary for the participants to understand game theory in order for co-operation to evolve, any more than it is necessary to compute accurate trajectories of projectiles in order to catch a ball.

The picture that Axelrod paints suggests that repetition alone can be enough to move us from the free-rider trap to a co-operative solution that is better for each and every player. As long as the likelihood of repetition – what Axelrod calls "the shadow of the future" – is strong enough to keep us from temptation, we can build up what some call "social capital."[5] It also suggests that chances of co-operation becoming established depends as much on the environment in which the game is played as on the qualities of the people involved. Selfish players can achieve co-operation "when the future is important enough relative to the present. This is because the players can each use the implicit threat of retaliation against the other's defection – if the interaction will last long enough to make the threat effective."[6] The other side of the coin is that selfless players may fail to achieve co-operation in short-term interactions because the lack of a future introduces the fear that to play a co-operative move is not being generous, it is just being a sucker.

One of the most famous examples of reciprocal co-operation among fierce competitors is the case of the trenches in World War I. In the Western front of the war, in northern France and in Belgium, the British and German armies faced each other across a narrow "No Man's Land" for an extended period of time between battles. Battles were fought fiercely, but between battles, instead of taking every chance to inflict damage on the enemy, "live-and-let-live" practices developed in many places along the front. Each army avoided inflicting too much damage on each other, realizing that such damage would merely invite retaliation. As one soldier said, "If the British shelled the Germans, the Germans replied, and the damage was equal: if the Germans bombed an advanced piece of trench and killed five Englishmen, an answering fusillade killed five Germans."[7]

From the point of view of the soldiers in the trenches, although not from the point of view of their commanders, the situation between battles was that of a repeated prisoner's dilemma. Despite a near-total lack of explicit communication, a Tit-for-Tat strategy developed, of not initiating attacks but punishing attacks by the "enemy." The strategy enabled both sides to minimize their own casualties.

Choosing Not to Compete

MarketThink sometimes claims that we live in a world of ever-increasing competition among firms, which is to the benefit of the rest of us in our role as consumers. Companies are certainly self-interested and are forbidden by law to collude with each other; thus it seems reasonable that a company wanting to maximize its own self-interest in a free-market environment would have little choice but to compete. The possibility that reciprocity-based co-operation may be the best outcome for self-interested actors suggests a different outcome for industries in which the shadow of the future is large, that is, in industries dominated by a relatively small number of long-lived firms. In such an environment, the competition may well be less than "red in tooth and claw."

Let's return to Whimsley to look at a case in which both co-operation and competition between self-interested firms is possible. There are two daily newspapers in Whimsley: *The Journal* and *The Courier*. The newspapers are sold at the same price and have an equal share of the market, and each owner makes a healthy profit of $3,000 per week. The owners of both dailies are always looking to sell more papers, but to sell more they would have to lower their prices and hence their profits. The *Courier* owners calculate that if they reduce their price by a dollar a week, every newspaper reader in Whimsley would buy their paper. Such an outcome would leave *The Journal* with no profit at all. *The Courier* would not double its profit because of the lower price: it would make a profit of $5,000 rather than $6,000.

But of course the owners of *The Journal* can make the same analysis. They realize that they too can lower their paper's price. And if both newspapers lower their price, they will get only half the market, at a lower price, and so will make a lower profit of $2,000. The decision matrix, shown in Figure 6, is another variant of the familiar prisoner's dilemma.

Courier

		High	Low
	High	*Journal* $3,000 *Courier* $3,000	*Journal* $0 *Courier* $5,000
Journal	**Low**	*Journal* $5,000 *Courier* $0	**Journal $2,000** **Courier $2,000**

FIGURE 6. *The Journal* and *The Courier*. The equilibrium outcome is in bold.

The newspaper owners are apparently trapped. No matter what the other does, each paper's best reply is to lower its price. But if both companies lower their prices, they end up being worse off than if they both keep their prices high. The equilibrium outcome is for both newspapers to drive down their prices until they are making only a minuscule profit, an outcome that leaves newspaper readers happy because they get their news cheaply. Consumer choice drives the price down, and drives companies to compete.

Or does it?

Newspaper companies are not involved in a game with a single move; they are in business for the long haul. In Whimsley there are only two players in the game, and we already know that collective action problems can be overcome more easily in small groups. What's more, each company has an excellent memory for the past behaviour of the other, and can expect to continue to play against each other frequently (daily, in fact) far into the future, so the threat of retaliation is real. The conditions are ideal for reciprocity-based co-operation to take effect.

In their book *Co-opetition*, Adam Brandenburger and Barry Nalebuff describe a similar situation in the summer of 1994 in New York, where Rupert Murdoch's *Daily News* and the rival *Post* dominated part of the market. Murdoch raised the price of the *New York Post* from 40 cents to 50 cents, apparently hoping that the rival *Daily News* would follow suit. But it didn't, and the *Post* started losing sales to the *News*.

The *Post* then took a dramatic step to convince the *News* to raise its prices. In one part of New York (Staten Island), the *Post* went on sale for only 25 cents. Its sales boomed, and it became clear that disastrous consequences would befall the *News* if the *Post* extended its price cut throughout New York City. The *News* got the message and raised its price to 50 cents, at which time the *Post*'s sales on Staten Island stopped. The *Post* had convinced the *News* to co-operate by threatening an extended war, and the *News* had conceded.

The story emphasizes how we must avoid simplistic good/bad associations of behaviour in the face of a prisoner's dilemma. With tales of pollution, overfishing, urban sprawl, and gridlocked streets in our minds we might find it easy to think of all co-operation as good and all free-riding as bad. But from the point of view of the newspaper readers, co-operation among the newspaper owners is a bad thing – so much so that explicit co-operation is labelled as price-fixing, and is illegal.

Another lesson from this story is that we must be careful when we construct the Whimsley tales. It looks like *The Journal* and *The Courier* are doomed to a perpetual price war, and yet the events in New York demonstrate that companies can and do seek to co-operate through tacit forms of negotiation, to their own benefit and to our detriment. There are many industries in which the conditions for reciprocal co-operation are met spectacularly well: they are populated by a small number of large firms playing repeated games, skilled at communication and with the resources to watch their "competitors" carefully.

★

As the success of Tit-for-Tat showed, communicating the possibility of both reward and punishment is key to achieving co-operation among self-interested players. In New York this communication took the form of a largely symbolic price cut on Staten Island, but there are many other ways in which the potential for reward and punishment can be communicated among companies.

One that many of us are familiar with is the tactic of "guaranteed lowest price." When a company announces a "guaranteed lowest price" it looks like a good deal for the consumer. In contracts among businesses, the same tactic is called a "meet the competition" clause: it is a guarantee that the company will match the price of any competitor. But the players in the buying and selling game are not just the vendor and the consumer: the real game is going on among vendors. A guaranteed lowest price offer is a signal to other vendors that it is not worth their while trying to offer lower prices in order to steal business. It is the equivalent of Murdoch's price cut in Staten Island: a signal that defection is not worth it. It prevents price-based competition, and leads to higher prices all round.[8]

Loyalty plans, such as credit cards that give points towards the purchase of a car, are another tactic that makes it difficult for potential customers to switch from one seller to another. When these plans were introduced, they reduced the incentive for auto companies to try to take market share by lowering prices, because customers who had adopted a loyalty plan would be unlikely to switch. The end result is again reduced competition and higher prices.[9] Loyalty plans are another signal to other companies: a mechanism for promoting mutually beneficial co-operation at the expense of the consumer.

An action that is apparently a gesture to consumers turns out to be a signal to other companies. The consumer is simply a resource that companies are trying to get the most out of. One way of doing this is for companies to avoid "overgrazing the commons" and to find ways of co-operating among themselves, restraining their own tendency to aggressively cut prices in search of market share by finding mechanisms of reward and punishment. That many markets are dominated by a few large and long-lived companies gives these mechanisms a chance to take hold. So companies, known for being self-interested, may still be able to co-operate over time without explicit collusion, to the detriment of the rest of us.

Choosing in Groups and Crowds

The key factor in promoting co-operation through reciprocity is what Axelrod calls "the shadow of the future." Carrots and sticks are effective only if there is a good chance that another round of the game will take place: if the future is important enough. If the game may finish before the next round, the threat of punishment and the promise of reward are not so effective, and the opportunity to defect is that much more tempting.

Several factors shape the shadow cast by the future. One is group size: in a small group individuals are more likely to meet each other again, which means they can strike up reciprocal arrangements. A second is longevity: individuals in a stable group are more likely to meet each other again than are individuals in a transitory crowd. A third is the potential for anonymous action: reciprocal co-operation requires that free-riding be detected and punished, and also requires that co-operation be detected and rewarded: anonymity works against detection of both actions.

The possibility of reciprocal action is not the only thing that favours small long-lived groups when it comes to co-operation. The balance of private and public costs also works against large groups. The fruits of co-operation are a public good, shared among all members of the group. In a small group the costs and benefits of a public good are shared among fewer actors, and so each actor has a larger interest in the fruits of co-operation than they would have in a large group. Consider ocean fishing again: if only two countries fish in a particular location, it may make sense for one of the countries to unilaterally limit its own fishing one year, even if the other country continues to overfish, if this unilateral action preserves enough fish to improve its catch the following year. If 10 countries are fishing, the chance that any one country can preserve enough fish to make abstention worthwhile is smaller. If 50 countries are fishing, the chance is minimal. So a small group may, even with some free-riders, still get closer to co-operation than a large group.

Another factor is the relative difficulty of negotiating in large groups. In their divorce case, Jack and Jill have a significant incentive to overcome their antipathy and sort out an agreement out of court. Each of them gains the full benefit of the other's co-operation. Free-rider problems with more participants, such as Jill's coffee-cup littering problem, are more difficult to resolve by negotiation. Jill could negotiate with one person that they will both carry their coffee cup out of the park, but this is not worthwhile, even if the negotiation itself were to cost Jill no effort at all: one less cup is not enough to switch the balance of the incentives in favour of co-operation. Jill would have to negotiate with a group of five others before an agreement is worthwhile.

Finally, any negotiated agreement requires monitoring. In the two-person prisoner's dilemma each player gets the full benefit of the other's co-operation and pays the full price for the other's defection, so that incentives for monitoring are not a problem. Tit-for-Tat exemplifies an effective monitoring of the other player's behaviour: a carrot is given for each and every co-operative move, and a stick is applied for each defection. Sending these signals is a form of communication: those who read each other's signals well can establish mutually beneficial co-operation.[10] In loose crowds, there is less incentive for any individual to monitor the behaviour of others: to track their co-operation or defection, and the consequent weak monitoring makes it more tempting to free-ride. Anonymity is the other side of the monitoring coin: groups in which individuals can act anonymously have a much harder time maintaining co-operation than those in which individuals are easily associated with their actions.

Co-operation is, then, as much about context as it is about the specific individuals involved. Given the right conditions, co-operation can evolve even among actors who care nothing for those they co-operate with, while under unfavourable conditions even well-intentioned actors may fail to act collectively.

Enforcing Co-operation

The "tragedy of the commons" and the prisoner's dilemma have been widely interpreted as moral tales, with the lesson being that co-operation among self-interested people is doomed, and that a central authority is needed to impose co-operative behaviour on a group of people caught in these traps.

The repeated prisoner's dilemma tells us that this lesson is too pessimistic for small, long-lived groups. But we must not take reciprocity too far. Some critics have suggested that Axelrod's work shows that governments' traditional role of providing public goods is not necessary because individuals will, left to themselves, find their way to co-operation.[11] But co-operation cannot be expected to emerge in conditions in which the "shadow of the future" is faint: we should not expect co-operation in crowds. What is more, the tournaments only investigate co-operation among equals. Power inequalities lead to other sources of temptation, such as the option of compelling others to take certain actions.

If collective action is to be sustained, larger groups need to resort to more explicit and formal mechanisms, such as the establishment of an external authority to enforce binding agreements. At the largest scale this becomes the state; and there is an obvious need for compulsion if co-operation is to be established within a group as large as a nation. As Olson points out:

> Patriotism is probably the strongest non-economic motive for organization allegiance in modern times. This age is sometimes called the age of nationalism. . . . But despite the force of patriotism, the appeal of the national ideology, the bond of a common culture, and the indispensability of the system of law and order, no major state in modern history has been able to support itself through voluntary dues or contributions.

Philanthropic contributions are not even a significant source of revenue for most countries. Taxes, *compulsory* payments by definition, are needed. Indeed, as the old saying indicates, their necessity is as certain as death itself.[12]

Elinor Ostrom has investigated and catalogued many cases of the successful maintenance of collective action in small communities in her book *Governing the Commons*. These communities are large enough that a purely informal structure is insufficient, and yet small enough that external compulsion is not necessary. Instead, Ostrom catalogues a rich variety of diverse and intricate mechanisms that govern what she calls "common pool resources."

Members of these communities have found ways of making "a binding contract to commit themselves to a co-operative strategy that they themselves will work out."[13] Ostrom describes communal management of meadows in Switzerland and Japan, and irrigation systems in Spain and the Philippines, and makes reference to the successful management of the commons in England until the Enclosure Acts of the late 18th and early 19th centuries allowed property owners to drive commoners off the land. Ostrom's examples show that the story of the commons need not end in tragedy or in the division of common ground into private plots.

Examples

A few scattered events make a little more sense once we know how co-operation works.

VILLAGES AND CITIES. In most countries it is accepted that co-operation plays a larger role in the life of villages than it does in cities. The reasons for this are clear: villagers meet each other repeatedly and have a chance to develop reciprocal co-operation, while most of the people whom city dwellers meet during their day are inevitably strangers, not to be met again.

It is also not too surprising when that sense of co-operation is not extended to those outside the community, especially if the presence of outsiders poses any threat to the community norms of a village. Community norms are a collective good, and a community that can protect that good against the perils of free-riding can be expected to use the same mechanisms to protect it against external threats.

Co-operation in small communities is notoriously double-edged: it is commonly associated not only with mutual support but also with intolerance, which is the other side of the co-operation coin. Non-conformists, after all, are people who do not co-operate in the maintenance of community norms and standards. If those norms are to be maintained through reciprocity, non-conformists must be punished.

It is not surprising that small communities are seen throughout the world as being not only more co-operative and supportive but also more narrow-minded in their attitudes to new ideas and to changes such as immigration. It is not surprising that non-conformists such as gays and rebellious teens flee small towns in favour of the big city.

PULLING TOGETHER. Social crises are also ideally suited to promote reciprocity-based co-operation, as the benefits of co-operation and the perilous consequences of defection are both enhanced. The "spirit of the Blitz" is still a strong image in the United Kingdom; winter storms bring out the best in Canadians; mining towns, whose residents live in a permanent state of near-crisis, are known for their strong community spirit.

As with co-operation in villages, these crisis situations are two-edged swords, and it is important not to romanticize them. One other aspect common to many of them is, of course, the punishment of the defector: looters of bombed buildings could expect little mercy; the ostracism (or worse) of the blackleg miner is well known. Like it or not, these tendencies are part and parcel of what is needed to bring about co-operation.

GREENHOUSE GASES. Attempts to meet the Kyoto protocol goals of reduced greenhouse gas emissions simply by encouraging individuals to burn less fossil fuel are doomed to failure. Even if all of us agree with the goal, the temptations of free-riding are simply too large for voluntary action to take us to the destination. As a result, while Canada undertook to reduce greenhouse gas emissions by 6 per cent between 1990 and 2012, by 2004 its emission levels had actually grown by almost 20 per cent instead. The failure of individual action to achieve these goals unassisted by other incentives is, however, not evidence that we disagree with the goals of Kyoto or that we would not like to see those targets met.

That most governments have not adopted compulsory measures for greenhouse gas emissions says something about their commitment to the goals of achieving the targets. Of course, we should not expect individual nation states to very easily overcome their own temptation to free-ride on such targets. It is easy to declare support for noble goals, but faced with budget crunches and other demands, and without a mechanism for ensuring co-operation, each government has a temptation to free-ride on the efforts of others.

Along the spectrum from small, tightly knit, and long-lived groups to short-lived, large, and diffuse crowds, the shadow of the future becomes fainter and fainter. At some point, it is faint enough that reciprocity-based co-operation can no longer be maintained and free-riding becomes the optimal individual choice. For shorter-lived and larger groups, individual choice comes into conflict with collective action. In crowds, more formal and coercive means are required if co-operation is to be sustained.

Such coercion may still be voluntary on the part of those who bind themselves to it – Hardin's phrase is "mutual coercion, mutually agreed upon" – but members of a group do give up some of their own freedom when they commit themselves to an enforceable contract. Indeed, in many of the cases that Ostrom explores there is no chance for an individual to opt out of the arrangement. As we move towards the large-group end of the spectrum, structures to maintain co-operation tend to be more formal, and the monitoring agency tends to become separate from the community that it is monitoring. It may have goals and aims of its own, distinct from those of the community it is working for. Co-operation within a group becomes compliance with authority.

There is no clear boundary at which voluntary co-operation and teamwork become compliance with authority. What is important is that in groups of a certain size co-operation and individual choice are at odds with each other, even if all members of the group are in favour of co-operation.

Choosing Temptation

One kind of co-operation is notoriously difficult to achieve: co-operation involving a single person. On the surface, it may seem as if choices involving only one person are almost guaranteed to be effective in giving us what we want: that here, at least, the precepts of MarketThink would be well founded. But externalities exist here as well, not from one person to another, but from one time to another.

The problem is that of temptation: do we do something pleasurable now at the risk of regretting it later? Temptation is like a prisoner's dilemma game in which the moves are sequential instead of simultaneous, and the players are Yourself Today and Yourself Tomorrow. And it is a particularly difficult problem because, as Thomas Schelling points out, Yourself Today cannot make a binding agreement with Yourself Tomorrow.[14] To understand temptation, let's return to Whimsley.

Like many other Whimsley residents, Jack is trying to lose weight, and he is finding this difficult. There is little doubt in Jack's own mind that the enemy is "lifestyle," that is, too many calories and too little exercise.

One evening Jack is halfway through an entertaining novel and knows that there is a big bag of corn chips (one of his particular weaknesses) in the cupboard. He has a choice: indulge himself as part of a relaxing evening, or resist the high-calorie temptation. If he takes the second choice, while the evening might not be as enjoyable, he would feel better about his weight in the morning.

In one way or another, this is a familiar dilemma, and I am sure we could argue the case for either side perfectly well. In his usual manner, Jack writes down his options on paper (see Figure 7). He gives himself two satisfaction points by eating the chips (a more pleasant evening), and three satisfaction points by refraining (feeling better in the morning about his weight). The appropriate choice would seem to be clear: leave the bag in the cupboard. If Jack's satisfaction points were reversed, the choice would seem equally clear: open the bag.

Eat the chips	Don't eat the chips
2	**3**

FIGURE 7. The corn-chip problem: first attempt. The equilibrium is in bold.

But Jack has a little more to write down as he makes his choice. For example, if he chooses to indulge, he gets the good evening right now, but if he refrains he doesn't get to feel better about his weight until tomorrow morning. The payoff time for each choice is different.

It is generally true that benefits received now are preferable to benefits received later. This is the reason why most of us are prepared to pay interest to borrow money: we can then use the money to get something right now instead of waiting to save up. We are prepared to pay the interest on the loan for the additional benefit of getting the payoff now, rather than later. For impatient people, getting the payoff right now is very important, and for patient people it is less so. Just as utilities are each individual's own business, so is our attitude to delayed payoff.

Jack, of course, uses a number to represent his patience (see

Figure 8). When he makes his decision, he is comparing not the relative satisfaction of the options at the time he accrues the benefit, but the value he gives to those options at the time he makes the decision. The "patience factor" is a number between 0 and 1, and multiplies the satisfaction points that Jack gets from choices with delayed payoffs. If Jack has a patience factor of ½, his table would look like this: the value to Jack at decision-time for refraining is 1½ (3 × ½) rather than 3. Jack's impatience means that he chooses to eat the chips rather than leaving them in the cupboard.

Eat the chips   Don't eat the chips

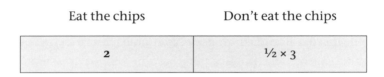

FIGURE 8. The corn-chip problem with impatience. The equilibrium is in bold.

If Jack were a more patient person, his patience factor would be close to 1, and the value at decision time would be only slightly less than 3 points – it would not matter much to him whether he gets the payment now or later. For example, if Jack has a resistance to temptation of ¾, the value at decision time would be ¾ × 3, which is greater than 2, and he would leave the chips in the cupboard. Such a value fits the case in which Jack has a long-term view of things and is quite happy to defer gratification.

At the other extreme, if he had a patience factor of 0, Jack would get no points at all, at the time he makes his decision, for the benefit he is to receive tomorrow morning. This describes Jack as being very impatient: nothing that he would get later is of any importance; all that matters is now. However, he would feel different in the morning when he reflects on how he has just made it more difficult to lose that extra weight.

As a postscript, it could be argued that, just as a number that represents patience is needed to discount benefits received at a future time, so we should introduce a transience factor to describe how quickly the benefit fades. In the morning, the benefits that Jack received from his indulgence are reduced to the condition of having a more relaxed state of mind as a result of his enjoyable evening.

We could then argue that the benefit to Jack after the decision is taken, when he wakes up the next morning, is not 2 points, but is less than 2 points. In this case Jack will end up feeling good the next morning about indulging only if the indulgence payoff is significantly greater than the payoff for refraining. There is a range of patience and transience factors that describe cases in which Jack will choose to indulge, but next morning will wish he hadn't.

These possible outcomes to Jack's decision are just reflections of what we all know about temptation, which is that there are times when it is in our own best interest to refrain, times when indulging is worthwhile, and times when we do indulge but wish we hadn't. Once these possibilities are acknowledged, it is obvious that simply providing as large an array of choices at any time to everyone in a society is not a reliable way of achieving a satisfied populace.

To go back to our trivial example, I for one don't actually want immediate access to corn chips on any particular evening: I would be looking to lose a lot more than Jack's 20 pounds if I did, and would not be more satisfied in any sense.

In their pursuit of freedom of choice, Western industrial societies have provided private industry with a licence to tempt consumers through marketing and easy credit, among other things, whether we want to be tempted or not. As consumers, we still have the absolute right to succumb to temptation or to refrain, but there is an important choice that is increasingly unavailable to us: we do not have the right to place ourselves in a position in which we can avoid temptation. Instead, we are encouraged to seek immediate gratification and to exhibit a low degree of patience.

The considerations described in Jack's choice receive scant attention in most economics texts, but they are far more up front in business books. Alan Murray, the Washington bureau chief for *The Wall Street Journal*, is a strong believer in the consumer as sovereign, but even he accepts that this sovereign entity has advisers who are pretty difficult to ignore. Murray describes the difference that even very mild temptation can make:

> My friend Robert Rosiello, a senior partner at [management consulting firm] McKinsey and Company, likes to say that the most profitable words in the English language are uttered by McDonald's clerks, who ask, "Would you like French fries with that?" Businesses have found that a simple suggestion, made at the right moment, can prompt a sale of a high margin product that otherwise might not have happened. . . . It's no secret that McDonald's sells French fries; if you had really wanted them, you could have ordered them in the first place.[15]

We see this situation all around us. Whether it is deciding to buy a sound system on a credit card or picking up a candy bar while waiting at the checkout, the structure of the problem is the same.

There is no rigorous manner of deducing the values of the payoffs and the temptation factor in any one case. In our particular example, they vary from person to person, from evening to evening. The might depend on the book that Jack is in the middle of, whether the chips are in the cupboard or he has to go to the store to buy them, and a myriad other factors. Again, the numerical phrasing of the problem does not help us much, directly at least, in any particular situation. The strength of the approach is to help identify the kind of factors that will promote one behaviour or another.

There are paradoxes here, but they are not deep ones. There are continual debates over what potentially bad choices society should protect us from, and what choices we should permit ourselves. Society allows and disallows choice inconsistently, and the particular positioning of the line between choice and protective legislation is open to debate, but it would take the most extreme libertarian to suggest that there should be no line at all. What is striking is that, in the current infatuation with the market, opposition to choice in economic situations is seen as almost totalitarian, when in other areas of our life it is a matter of common sense. A glance at how society has dealt with various forms of temptation suggests that MarketThink is barking up the wrong tree when it comes to how much choice we actually want.

ADDICTION. Addictions are a form of strong temptation. Some addictions are strong enough that society deals with them by outlawing them. This is a way for society to say: we know that we cannot be trusted to make a good individual decision about heroin, so we are giving up the right to make that decision. Other addictions, such as those involving tobacco and alcohol, are restricted but not outlawed. Of course, the choice of which addictions to outlaw is partly a political one: the producers of addictive substances tend to promote the right of free enterprise to make a profit, as in the opium wars waged by Britain against China in the 19th century and in the export of cigarettes from Western countries to developing ones. The importing country is often likely to prefer the route of restriction, as Western countries do in the case of cocaine from Colombia or heroin from Pakistan.

Addiction is a choice that, once made, cannot be easily unmade. It is one thing to choose to take heroin for a while, another thing to choose to stop. The Alcoholics Anonymous refrain of "One day at a time" is a recognition of how you cannot look too far ahead if you want to avoid temptation: the patience factor is too daunting over an extended period of time.

SELF-HELP. Whether it is Richard Carlson's "Don't sweat the small stuff" or Stephen Covey's "Start with the end in mind" (one of his *7 Habits of Highly Effective People*), temptation is one of the major subjects of self-help books.[16] "Delayed gratification" has become a ubiquitous catchphrase, the idea being that we are commonly faced with choices between immediate but shallow gratification and a deeper but delayed reward, and that it is usually best to spurn the immediate in favour of the long-term. The problem, however, is that self-help books tend to locate the source of the problem in ourselves, rather than in the environment in which we make our choices.

ART. In his books *Ulysses and the Sirens* and *Ulysses Unbound*, Jon Elster argues that what he calls "self-binding" constraints and their associated restriction of choice – even arbitrary constraints – are a necessary part of good art, whether they take the form of the structure of a symphony, twelve-bar blues, or the restrictions of haiku.

CONTRACTS. Another way of handling temptation is to introduce contracts. By signing a contract, we explicitly give up the right to make certain choices in the future, and open ourselves to the possibility of censure if we break the terms of the contract. By agreeing to marry, we give up our right to have other partners. Whether it is in entering employment, or any other long-term relationship, we give up rights in return for the benefits we expect to get.

In terms of payoffs, a contract introduces an additional factor to be taken account of when considering the indulgence. If we are discovered in our breach of contract, the payoff may be very negative, and even if we are not explicitly punished, our own conscience may impose a cost on us that we may not want to bear.

While contracts can be seen as a way of handling temptation, it is interesting that they rely on exactly the same discount factor as the action they seek to prevent. You can get married now (an immediate benefit) at the cost of giving up the right to affairs later. At the time you make the commitment, an affair is presumably distant and abstract, and rather easy to commit to abstaining from. At some other time the benefits of an affair may be more tempting, but the terms of the marriage contract remain. That the same discounting of future payoffs works in both ways emphasizes how we are not looking here at moral judgments, but at the structure of individual decisions. Employment contracts and commercial contracts are other everyday examples of the voluntary renunciation of choice.

chapter six

DIVIDE AND CONQUER

THE COLLECTIVE ACTION PROBLEM helps us to understand how power is gained and wielded in societies based on individual choice. For example, it helps us to understand the debate over the balance of power between corporations and citizens: whether corporations are powerful or whether the market renders them powerless.

On the one hand we have Naomi Klein arguing: "That corporations have grown so big they have superseded government. That unlike governments, they are accountable only to their shareholders; that we lack the mechanisms to make them accountable to a broader public."[1] On the other hand we have *The Economist* stating that we do have a mechanism to make corporations accountable – the market – and that "customers are in charge" and "companies would run the world for profit if they could. What stops them is not governments, powerful as they may be, but markets."[2]

Does the move to privatize and deregulate mean that we are "handing society over to corporations," or are we turning our societies into a "people's capitalism" based on a guarantee that market forces will respond to our individual choices?

★

One of the most obvious sources of power in a world of choices is the ability to set the agenda, or to change the game. Simply by putting up a shingle, the Whimsley lawyers put Jack and Jill into a position in which their only options were bad ones for themselves and good ones for the lawyers. The lawyers had a position of power, which they achieved by the apparently harmless act of offering Jack and Jill an additional choice. In the prisoner's dilemma, the police put the prisoners in separate cells and refused them the chance to communicate in order to ensure that the outcome of their choices would be beneficial to the police and bad for the prisoners.

If incentives are important in influencing how the players in a game behave, then incentives must also be important in a larger game – that of setting the rules that determine which games we play. In particular, it is not surprising if special interests use their resources to influence the bodies that set rules – which, in a political context, means governing bodies such as the state or multilateral organizations.

Economics textbooks tend to talk about three main actors in an economy: consumers (who make choices), corporations (which respond to market forces), and the state (which sets the rules by which corporations and consumers must play). One of the central questions is "what is the proper role of the state?" – a question that implicitly treats the state as an independent actor standing outside the economy itself. But such a perspective misses the larger picture. Instead of thinking of the state as an external agency, we must think of the state and its ability to set the rules as a resource that is open to a struggle for control. In this larger picture the competition among a variety of interests – including corporations and consumers/citizens – for access to the rule-setting powers of the state becomes a game in itself.

Choosing Not to Vote

The collective action problem influences participation in the political process. Let's start by looking at the simplest act of political participation, voting.

Democracy itself is a public good: people cannot be excluded from the benefits of living in an electoral democracy whether or not they contribute to its functioning. As a result, democracy is subject to free-riding. Individual voters have little incentive to take an active part in preserving a broad-based representative political system.

Intelligent voting requires an investment of time and effort, but the private payoff for such effort is small because in almost all cases any one individual vote makes essentially no difference to the end result of an election. The best choice from an individual point of view is to let everyone else invest the time to vote intelligently, while you go and do something else that benefits your life directly. The logic of the situation is so strong that some political scientists even talk about "the voting paradox": the paradox being that anyone bothers to vote at all given the incentives at work to the contrary.

The rise of MarketThink has not surprisingly coincided with a decrease in voter turnout in countries throughout the industrialized world. We are being told repeatedly that it is okay to follow our own interests, which means that we should not bother to vote. In the past voting has offered intangible but real rewards, such as the feeling of civic pride or of having done your duty, but MarketThink has successfully managed to discredit those rewards.

What is true of voting is true of many other aspects of political participation, and this leaves the process open to capture by special interests. Italian economist Vilfredo Pareto posed this dilemma many years ago:

[If] a certain measure A is the case of the loss of one franc to each of a thousand persons, and of a thousand franc gain to one individual, the latter will expend a great deal of energy, whereas the former will resist weakly: and it is likely that, in the end, the person who is attempting to secure the thousand francs via A will be successful.[3]

The act of opposing "measure A" is subject to free-riding. As soon as the cost in time and effort of opposing measure A exceeds one franc, the best solution for each of the thousand persons involved is to free-ride and let someone else do the work, with the result that no one does. The individual who stands to gain a thousand francs faces no such dilemma. As long as the cost of promoting measure A is no more than 999 francs, that person will still come out on top. Measure A is likely to succeed, and the unhappy thousand will be told that they chose this outcome.

Most of us are affected, in one way or another, by government actions that are subject to free-riding. For instance, even though the supply of clean water is a vital service to each and every one of us, very few people spend any time either thinking about how a clean-water service is maintained or lobbying government to maintain standards. The private costs of doing so are large, and the benefits are inevitably shared widely. But commercial firms tend to have more at stake in certain government actions or policies. A large farming operation, for example, has to bear the costs, directly and privately, of properly disposing of waste. It is in its interests to cut costs as much as possible. Indeed, the legal structure of corporations requires them to act in the financial interests of their owners and to put aside other considerations. In an environment sympathetic to private industry, it is not surprising, then, that the companies lobby for special treatment or for changes to relax legislation and influence procurement actions – and these business interests can easily diverge from the interests of the amorphous "rest of us." Then too, when the party in power believes that people, left to themselves, will get what they want, services such as water treatment and the monitoring of water-system purity can be neglected. The end result is an event such as the 2002 E. coli outbreak in Walkerton, Ontario, when compromised water quality led to seven deaths and some 2,300 illnesses.

Maintaining the electrical transmission infrastructure poses an identical problem, and in the absence of strong control we get the 2003 power blackout in Ontario and the northeastern United States. The result may leave us unhappy, yet no one but ourselves "chose" the outcome.

In some cases the efforts by private companies to influence government actions are so extensive that the boundary between the private sector and the state becomes indistinct. Lockheed, for example, is the largest military contractor in the United States and thus has a considerable and direct interest in U.S. military policy: nearly 80 per cent of its revenue comes from the U.S. government, and much of the remaining 20 per cent comes from military sales to other countries. In 2003 it received $21.9 billion in Pentagon primary contracts. Given that business profile, it would be positively irresponsible of Lockheed if it did not seek access to the corridors of power. And as a major corporation with a major individual stake in the continued growth of U.S. military expenditure, Lockheed faces little in the way of a collective action problem and can act effectively in its own interest by using its resources to influence government.[4]

The results are impressive. A non-profit group that monitors government contracts concluded, "It's impossible to tell where the government ends and Lockheed begins." Stephen Hadley, the national security advisor, is among those who have "worked, lobbied and lawyered for Lockheed." Others include the secretary of the navy, the secretary of transportation, the director of the national nuclear weapons complex, and the director of the national spy satellite agency. According to *The New York Times*, "Lockheed's board includes E.C. Aldridge Jr., who, as the Pentagon's chief weapons buyer, gave the go-ahead to build the F-22." Lockheed gained approval to build "as many F-22s as possible," with a 2004 price of U.S.$258 million each.

Developing military technology on the scale that Lockheed does is a stupendously complex technological challenge: it takes 20 years to develop a major new weapons system. As a result, the last two decades saw "the concentration of expertise, experience, and power in a few hands," with Lockheed "increasingly putting its stamp on the nation's military policies." Lockheed stands at "the intersection of policy and technology," its chief executive, Robert J. Stevens, pointed out, adding that "We are deployed entirely in developing daunting technology," which requires "thinking through the policy dimensions of national security as well as the technological dimensions." Lockheed is not only a supplier to the U.S. military, but is also "framing the questions."

If Lockheed is in favour of measure A, it will most likely get its way.

Companies and Individual Choice

MarketThink is the worldview of the corporate world. The loudest and most consistent voices in favour of individual choice and the market are the spokespeople for private industry and the leaders of major corporations. Yet despite the rhetoric there are many cases in which corporations take a less than enthusiastic attitude to individual choice.

Choice in the Workplace

Corporations recognize the benefits of teamwork. Whether it is Wal-Mart requiring that employees wear identical uniforms and engage in morning singalongs, or high-pressure workplaces demanding that employees demonstrate their commitment by working long hours, companies certainly realize that individual choice and governance by the market have their limits. However keen CEOs are on market forces outside the company walls, they rarely trust the operations of their own organization to market models.

If companies relied on individual choice and the market to organize their internal affairs, they would replace long-term employment contracts with the short-term buying and selling of pieces of work. Companies (if they existed at all) could make it known each time they want to buy a certain piece or kind of work, and pay the sellers according to the rates and terms those sellers offer. But that practice is certainly far from the norm – in fact, it seems totally unrealistic – in most modern economies, which is in itself an indication of the limitations of markets and individual choice.

Indeed, the inapplicability of the market to this key part of any modern economy is an indication of the sharp conflict between the reality of business practice and MarketThink. Inside corporations the collective action problem is addressed organizationally by the establishment of hierarchy and the removal of individual choice, and psychologically by a constant focus on collective effort.

Trade unions have been hit hard by the persistent arguments of MarketThink. The closed shop environment, which requires every employee of a company to be a union member, has been assailed by accusations that it infringes on individual liberty. And so it does, of course – it removes the choice not to join the union. But it does so with good reason. The bargaining power that comes with being in a union is a collective good that companies do not look on favourably, but free-riding provides them with a way out. In a workplace in which union membership is optional, unions are vulnerable. Any gains that union members achieve in working conditions or in salaries are enjoyed by all employees at the workplace, whether they are members or not. These gains are public goods, and individuals cannot be easily excluded from them.

In such a situation, it makes sense to avoid paying your membership dues and to enjoy the fruits of others' commitment. Of course, if everyone feels this way the union loses its membership. The same principle applies to taking part in a strike: it makes absolute sense for individuals to cross the picket lines, because in the end they will still benefit from any gains made as a result of the strike.

It is hardly surprising that many employers are in favour of "freedom of choice" when it comes to union membership and the "right to work": they know the equilibria of these free-rider problems. The rhetoric of choice, put to one side when it comes to company organization, once again comes to the fore when union rights are discussed.

But as in the case of a hockey player choosing not to wear a helmet, it makes sense for individual employees to recognize this problem, and to mandate ahead of time that all employees must join the union and pay their dues – to create a binding agreement that holds them to the better outcome and foils the temptation to defect. The question is whether employees have the right to collectively bind themselves.

Market Discipline

In an attempt to fend off government intervention, corporations commonly argue that market discipline is sufficient to keep them honest. For example, in the case of labour standards in Third World countries, some corporate spokespersons have argued that informed consumers ensure that the corporations behave themselves and treat their workers properly.

Protesters opposing corporate-led globalization have documented how brand-name companies or their contractors mistreat their workers, or how companies such as McDonald's have damaged the environment. Those who believe in MarketThink insist that these companies will inevitably behave better over time because consumers will otherwise turn away from them.

Unfortunately, there is a good reason why individual consumers will not abandon Wal-Mart just because they have heard about the mistreatment of contract workers in Guatemala,[5] or abandon Shell because of its involvement in Nigerian government despotism: such a choice is subject to free-riding.

Part of the consumers' problem is the private cost of obtaining reliable information about the choices available. So they say to themselves: "Yes, I have heard that Wal-Mart could treat its workers and contractors better, but I don't know for sure that such allegations are true, and my individual purchase won't make much difference for them anyway. Also, I personally need a new pair of socks and if the cheapest store I can get them conveniently is a Wal-Mart, well so be it."

The friends of Wal-Mart and Shell insist that this kind of solitary decision is a vote in the ongoing referendum that directs the economy, but we know that individual votes are subject to free-riding, and in this case there is no civic history to countermand that problem, and no peer pressure to help us on our way to the ballot box. "Better for me if I just shop at Wal-Mart and let others take the trouble to go somewhere else."

That the enforcement of good corporate behaviour is subject to free-rider behaviour explains why collective actions such as publicity campaigns and boycotts are needed. If their fate is left to individual actions, corporations will always be given an easy ride. Collective actions help to address the free-rider problem by suggesting that each vote can make a difference (because others are voting too) and by bringing peer pressure to bear on individual decisions (for more on this, see chapter 11).

While private industry sees employment standards legislation, pay-roll taxes, and other government actions as interference to be minimized, it takes a different tack when the subject changes to industrial infrastructure. Even the most pro-market of corporate leaders seems to recognize that private industry alone cannot provide the infrastructure that a modern economy demands.

Infrastructure is a concrete example of a "public good" that is shared among all the companies in an economy. Public money is used to provide the roads, sewage and water systems, and telecommunications systems that industry relies on for its operations.

Less tangible things, such as a well-educated workforce, are also public goods that form part of the industrial infrastructure. Of course, employees work for only one company at a time, and so are "private goods" from the point of view of the company that employs them. But they are also at least partially a public good in that companies cannot easily prevent employees from taking their skills with them to other companies. Each individual company has an incentive to free-ride by taking trained employees from other companies while not investing in training itself.

Left to itself, then, any one company would choose not to invest in the industrial infrastructure. Its best reply to the problem of infrastructure supply is to free-ride on the actions of others. Given that all companies recognize this benefit, a strict free-enterprise system would tend to produce an inadequate infrastructure. But when it comes to the provision of public goods required by industry, corporations drop the talk of competition and discover the virtues of co-operation, collective action, and even government spending. Business lobby groups are formed largely to ensure the provision of these public goods, and the voices of "the business community" – a phrase that makes the shared interests of private corporations explicit – come through loud and clear. This community realizes that individual choice is not enough, and it spares no effort encouraging governments of all levels to provide the infrastructure needed to compete against companies from other locations.

Those who see the world through the lens of MarketThink are reluctant to abandon the virtues of competition in their rhetoric, and yet the provision of public goods is not a story of competition, but of collective action. In the world according to MarketThink, the story of competition is recast with new players: instead of being company against company, it is now region against region or country against country, and we must all pitch in together, overcoming our incentives to free-ride, if our region or country is to prosper.

The double standard is apparent. What's more, the claim that regions and countries are really competing against each other is a half-truth at best. We are not involved in "competition" with trading partners. Trade is in essence a mutually beneficial exchange, not a zero-sum game with a loser for every winner. A prosperous U.S. economy, for example, is not at all a bad thing for Canadian companies.

The Market as a Public Good

All of this twisting of rules to suit the short-term interests of individual corporations raises new questions about the marketplace and how it works in theory and practice. The market certainly has its place, as Amartya Sen reminds us:

> To be generically against markets would be almost as odd as being generically against conversations between people (even though some conversations are clearly foul and cause problems for others – or even for the conversationalists themselves). The freedom to exchange words, or goods, or gifts does not need defensive justification in terms of their favourable but distant effects; they are part of the way human beings in society live and interact with each other (unless stopped by regulation or fiat).[6]

The core of the problem with the market is not the practice of exchange, but the opportunities it gives for manipulation by those with the resources to do so: to turn exchange into exploitation. The only thing that keeps markets healthy in the face of the temptation to exploit others is a strong set of institutions to govern the transactions that take place: "property rights, predictability, safety, nomenclature and so on," according to one list.[7] These institutions are, ironically, features that can only be supplied by collective action. Sen states: "Successful operation of an exchange economy depends on mutual trust and the use of norms – explicit and implicit. When these behavioural modes are plentiful, it is easy to overlook their role. But when they have to be cultivated, that lacuna can be a major barrier to economic success."[8]

It is part of the conceit of MarketThink that "the market" will provide all that is needed for prosperity and freedom. This view carried the day in the restructuring of Eastern bloc countries after the fall of the Berlin Wall in 1989 and the subsequent collapse of the Soviet Union. According to World Bank chief economist and Nobel Prize–winner Joseph Stiglitz, Russia's transition to a market economy would have achieved better results if planners had introduced a market economy based on a strong institutional infrastructure – everything from the solid "legal structures that enforce contracts to regulatory structures that make a financial system work." Instead, the economists who held sway – particularly in the halls of the U.S. Treasury Department and the International Monetary Fund – purposefully neglected the role of institutions, Russian history, and even questions surrounding the distribution of income, and professed a faith in the market that was "unmatched," according to Stiglitz, "by an appreciation of the subtleties of its underpinnings – that is, of the conditions required for it to work effectively." The result was that through the mid-1990s "the Russian economy continued to implode. Output plummeted by half. While only two percent of the population had lived in poverty even at the end of the dismal Soviet period, 'reform' saw poverty rates soar to almost 50 percent."[9]

The single-minded, oversimplified approach of MarketThink works to conceal or distort difficulties, and yet this way of doing things is taken seriously in the most influential centres of global institutions. Taken together, as the post-Cold War collapse of the Russian economy indicates, these aspects make for a dangerous combination.

MarketThink leads as a matter of course to arguments in favour of corporate-led globalization: borders must come down, subsidies and protectionist legislation must be thrown away, free exchange and the market will deliver the goods.[10] But the factors that make some countries succeed while others are mired in poverty are complex, and the "globalization leads to prosperity" story is misleading. One prominent critic of the simplistic formula for success is Harvard economist Dani Rodrik, who argues that when it comes to producing prosperity, "institutions trump free markets." That is, collective action trumps individual choice.[11]

The absence of well-functioning institutions in post-Communist Russia produced widespread corruption, which severely damaged the economy, but then the temptations of corruption are not confined to Russia or other less-well-off countries, nor are they limited to government officials or business-people. The choice everywhere is to follow the norms and expectations of the spirit of the law, or to cheat others and steal, in one form or another. It is a familiar story: the benefits of graft and corruption are private, while the benefits of an economy with a proper system of regulations and norms are shared. If monitoring is insufficient or if, even worse, corruption is an accepted practice, the costs and benefits are those of free-riding. Effective institutions are needed to counteract this temptation, and a stable environment with prospects for the future is needed for the participants in an economy to be able to take the long view and play by the rules of the game: to trade rather than to plunder.

There is no reason to believe that Western economies are somehow invulnerable to the corruption of the market. The incentives are similar for government officials and private businesspeople. In either case, those in positions of power face the temptation to abuse that power. What keeps society whole in the face of this temptation is a framework of institutions that restrain the actions of the powerful, together with strong countervailing organizations. And those institutions, as we have seen, are under continual attack from MarketThink.

chapter seven

THAT OBSCURE OBJECT OF DESIRE

NOW FOR ANOTHER GAME, one that is as simple as the prisoner's dilemma and has as many implications.

Two people are walking directly towards each other along a sidewalk, and they are faced with the problem of avoiding a collision. If both of them, from their own perspectives, step to their left or both step to the right, they avoid the collision and are both happy. If one steps to the left while the other steps to the right, they collide. In this game the best choice for each player depends on the choice that the other player makes, and the best outcome happens when both make the same choice: when their choice is co-ordinated. For this reason, the game is called the co-ordination game.

The co-ordination game is like the prisoner's dilemma in that it involves two people, each of whom has a single choice to make (which way to step) between two alternatives (left or right). In other ways the co-ordination game is the opposite of the prisoner's dilemma:

- In the prisoner's dilemma, each player has an *unconditional prefer-ence*: the player prefers the same choice, irrespective of which choice the other person makes. In the co-ordination game each player has a *conditional preference*: the preferred choice depends on the choice made by the other player.

- In the prisoner's dilemma, each player has an *unconditional preference* regarding the choice made by the other player – each player would like the other to co-operate. The preference is not affected by the choice one makes for oneself. In the co-ordination game each player has a *conditional preference* with respect to the other's choice: it *is* affected by one's own choice.

- In the prisoner's dilemma, the preferences of the two players go in opposite directions: the choice each prefers to make is not the choice that the player wants the other to make. In the co-ordination game the two preferences go in the same direction: the choice that each prefers to make *is* the choice that the player wants the other to make.

- In the prisoner's dilemma, the strengths of the preferences are such that both players are better off if they make their unpreferred choices than if both make their preferred choices: there is a single, predictable, unhappy outcome. In the co-ordination game, there are two equilibria: as a result there are multiple, unpredictable outcomes, which can be more or less happy.

To take a closer look at the co-ordination game, let's return to the town of Whimsley.

Buying Sneakers at Whimsley Mall

Jack's nephew Bill, who lives with his own family in Whimsley, is a style-conscious nineteen-year-old, and when we catch up with him he is off to the mall with his friend Adrian. Both of them are looking to buy a pair of sneakers.

In Whimsley, of course, the simplicity of things extends to footwear, and the stores carry only two brands of sneaker – let's call them "Nike" and "Adidas" – as opposed to the half a dozen or so other brands available in most towns. Still, in the shoe store at the mall Bill and Adrian are confronted with shelf after shelf of footwear. There are liquid-filled shoes with extra bounce, shoes inspired by aerospace engineering ("the technology-packed Nike Shox BB4 is the same hoop shoe worn by Vince Carter"), shoes of all kinds of colours and designs – but there are only the two brands.

Bill and Adrian are faced with a choice of buying Nike or Adidas sneakers. They each have their brand preferences, but these preferences are weak compared to their desire to establish a group identity, and wearing the same brand of sneakers, no matter which it is, is a part of that identity. Adrian would, other things being equal, prefer Nike to Adidas, while Bill would prefer Adidas. Other things, however, are not equal, because if they choose different brands they lose a piece of their group identity.

As genuine residents of Whimsley, Bill and Adrian weigh their choices numerically. If they both buy Nikes, Adrian gets 3 points, while Bill gets only 1. If they both buy Adidas, it is Bill who gets 3 points, while Adrian gets but 1. If they are both stubborn and buy different sneakers, they lose their group identity and so get no points whatsoever. This is the co-ordination game (see Figure 9).

| | | BILL | |
		Nike	Adidas
ADRIAN	Nike	**Adrian 3** **Bill 1**	Adrian 0 Bill 0
	Adidas	Adrian 0 Bill 0	**Adrian 1** **Bill 3**

FIGURE 9. Sneaker preferences at Whimsley Mall. The equilibria are in bold.

- If both buy Nike (top left corner), Adrian gets 3 points, and Bill gets 1 point. If Adrian changes his choice and buys Bill's preference, Adidas, we are in the bottom left corner, in which both get no points, so changing his choice is not a good thing for Adrian. If Bill changes his choice to Adidas while Adrian buys Nike (top right corner), then again both would get no points. Bill may not be doing so well if both buy Nike, but he does even worse if the two of them buy different sneakers. Neither player can improve his outcome by a unilateral action, and so this outcome is an equilibrium for the game.

- If both buy Adidas (bottom right corner), Adrian gets a single point, while Bill gets 3 points. If Adrian changes his choice (top right corner), both get no points. If Bill changes his choice (bottom left corner), then again both get no points. Just as in the case of both buying Nike, neither player can improve his outcome by a unilateral action, and so this outcome is also an equilibrium for the game.

In one case Adrian gets his first choice, while in the other case it is Bill who gets his first choice. But in either case, it would pay neither player to switch, and this is the key to equilibrium. This game has not one, but two equilibria. One equilibrium is for both Adrian and Bill to buy Nike; the other is for both to buy Adidas.

Games with multiple equilibria exhibit *co-ordination problems*. The rules of the game require that the players make their choices independently and simultaneously. There is nothing in the game itself to help Bill and Adrian decide which choice to make. If Bill expects Adrian to insist on the Nikes, he should accommodate himself to that decision and choose Nikes also. If Adrian expects that Bill will insist on the Adidas, he should choose Adidas as well. On the other hand, if Adrian expects that Bill will be accommodating, he should choose Nike.

Let's say that Bill and Adrian both buy Nike shoes, successfully co-ordinating their choices. While Bill is less happy than he wants to be, at least Adrian is happy, so that in one way this story has a better outcome than is possible in the prisoner's dilemma. But in co-ordination problems in general, good choices are no guarantee of happy outcomes. Imagine if both Adrian and Bill preferred Adidas to Nike, but did not know the other's preference (see Figure 10). The surprising thing is that "both buy Nike" is still an equilibrium, even though both of them would prefer to buy Adidas.

| | | BILL | |
		Nike	Adidas
ADRIAN	Nike	**Adrian 1** **Bill 1**	Adrian 0 Bill 0
	Adidas	Adrian 0 Bill 0	**Adrian 3** **Bill 3**

FIGURE 10. More sneaker preferences at Whimsley Mall. The equilibria are in bold.

Without communication, quite possibly they will end up in a bad equilibrium.

Identifying the Real Choice

The role of externalities in the co-ordination game is even more pervasive than it is in the prisoner's dilemma, altering not only how each player feels about the outcome, but also how each player ranks his or her choices. The prisoner's dilemma demonstrates that choice and preference are separate concepts, and that we cannot make inferences about preferences by observing choices; the co-ordination game demonstrates that the nature of choice itself is complicated when choices are tightly coupled.

In situations in which co-ordination is paramount, *the choice being made is not the one it seems to be.* When pedestrians approach each other on the sidewalk, they are not choosing left or right, they are choosing to avoid each other. In the same way, Bill and Adrian are not choosing Nike over Adidas: instead they are choosing to buy the same shoe as the other one is buying. The particular shoe they end up buying is secondary to the problem. While the sales people at the shop may think that Bill and Adrian preferred Nike to Adidas, we know that they did not.

In situations driven by co-ordination problems, it becomes impossible to avoid the context in which the game is played: we are forced to go outside the formal structure of the game to find a mechanism for selecting among the various possible equilibria.

Thomas Schelling identified what he called the *focal point effect*.[1] Anything that focuses the attention of the players on one equilibrium among many may lead the players to expect that others will make choices compatible with this equilibrium, and so successfully co-ordinate their actions. In one example, Schelling, providing no other information, asked a group of students where they would go if they were asked to meet another person in New York on a particular day. A majority of the participants chose a prominent meeting place (the information booth at Grand Central Station) at noon. That is, without communication, they managed to identify a focal point that enabled them to co-ordinate their actions.[2] The goal of game theory is to describe, albeit in a formal and simplified way, real world situations. As game theorist Roger Myerson observes, Schelling appreciated that a "multiplicity of equilibria was not a technical problem to be avoided, but was a fact of life to be appreciated."[3] Myerson argues that Schelling's focal point effect provides a foundation for the social role of concepts such as justice, tradition, and culture, and so constitutes "one of the great fundamental ideas of social philosophy."

At first the focal point effect can seem like a cop-out. Having gone to great lengths to establish a mathematical theory of choice, we now throw up our hands and say "anything may tip the balance": meaningless signals, conventions, traditions, or abstract ideas. And yet in the real world the idea is powerful. For example, social conventions often play the role of focal points: if there is a convention of passing on the left, then a pedestrian will not only choose to pass on the left but also expect others to adopt that convention and do the same: the convention becomes a self-fulfilling prophecy, not because left is better than right, but because any convention is better than none.

If a mutual friend of Adrian and Bill's has just bought Nike sneakers, both may deduce that the other is also more likely to buy Nike than Adidas, and so may choose Nike themselves (regardless of their own preferences) in anticipation that the other will choose Nike.

One of the dangers of using numbers to represent preferences, as the people of Whimsley do, is that they can introduce a perception of authority, objectivity, or precision. Such a perception is entirely unwarranted. I am using numbers here as a convenience so that we can talk about one choice being "better" than another, but that is all. What's more, there is no need for these numbers to be objective, or indeed to have any meaning to anyone apart from the actor making the choice. We are discussing personal decisions, and Adrian's and Bill's ranking of preferences as they shop for sneakers is, as with Jack's ideas about eating corn chips or Jill's opinions on hiring a divorce lawyer, no one else's business. There is no accounting for taste.

The numbers form what is called a *utility scale*. One of the ideas behind rational choice is that people make choices to achieve the best outcome they can, as measured on such a scale, or to "maximize their utility." It is common for this "utility-maximizing" behaviour to be branded as automatically and simplistically selfish. For example, philosopher Mark Kingwell argues that the "notion of rational choice is the basic assumption of most contemporary economic theory."

> The individual person is reduced to the status of a consumer whose "rational" actions are a result of the presumed basic desire to be as happy as possible. That presumption – that every choice made by a person is what he or she thought rational at the time – is in turn the basis of what is known as rational-choice theory. Here, all decisions and actions decline to a base level of perfect rationality where people are always free of manipulation, coercion and necessity.[4]

In game theory, Kingwell argues:

> The world is conceived of as an aggregation of individuals, lacking both class interests and political convictions, who function as utility-maximizing ciphers in a vast web of market relations. For them, "welfare" is defined hedonistically. . . . The individual person is reduced to the status of a consumer whose "rational" actions are a result of the presumed basic desire to be as happy as possible.
>
> I am rational when I act efficiently to realize my goals, irrational when I do otherwise. My happiness or unhappiness, by extension, is just a function of how well or badly I am able to perform this series of choices, moving by stages from means to end. Rational choices are ones that contribute to my personal happiness, allowing me to get what I want and so "maximize my utility functions," as the theorists say.[5]

But Kingwell oversimplifies the idea of "utility functions." It is true that in our prisoner's dilemma examples, the utility functions did not depend on other actors. As Jack and Jill evaluated their options in their divorce case, they did not adjust their points tally to reflect how they felt about the other person getting lots of money or no money. As Jill crossed the park, she did not worry if people would be angry at her: if she had, it might have changed the points she assigned. As *The Journal* and *The Courier* made their pricing decisions, they spared no thought for the fortunes of their competitor. In this sense, the actors involved were selfish.

In Bill and Adrian's story we see something different. As Bill and Adrian assigned points, their assignments reflected a concern about the choice that the other would make. Adrian may be choosing to maximize his "utility function." However, his utility is geared not to the possession of one or another brand of sneaker, but rather to a wish to identify and be identified with his friend Bill. The story expands the idea of a utility function to include a dependence on other people's choices.

If we are to assess problems of status (my utility is increased if people see me as being of higher status than you), of "cool" (my utility is increased by the appreciation of my peers), of altruism (my utility is increased by seeing you happy), and of vengeance (my utility is increased by seeing you unhappy), we must necessarily build this new level of interdependence into our models. As long as we take this step, we can still use a game theory approach to guide our thinking about issues of choice.

Kingwell's argument contains a nugget of truth in that it is indeed difficult to measure utility as seen in this way. Who, after all, can peer inside another's heart? It is far easier to assume that utility corresponds to something easy to measure, like money, which is the route that much use of game theory in economics takes. In fact, as we've seen (chapter 6), corporations are almost required to act as if this is the case, so that when game theory is applied to their actions it makes sense to equate utility and money.

Kingwell is not the only critic who considers the rational choice effort to be misguided. Writer Linda McQuaig also disputes its useful-ness: "The central character in economics is Homo Economicus, the human prototype, who is pretty much just a walking set of insatiable material desires. He uses his rational abilities to ensure the satisfac-tion of his material wants, which are the key to his motivation."[6]

Again, there is a nugget of truth here: much economics discus-sion does tend to identify utility with "material desires." But the con-cept of utility is also not quite that simple, as an increasing number of economists have recognized.

Game Theory: What Is It Good For?

Multiple equilibria are the rule rather than the exception in game the-ory. Even simple games can have an infinite number of equilibria, and this oversupply of solutions is the source of some problems for the theory. In cases in which there is no obvious focal point outside the game that allows co-ordination, game theoretical problems can become intractable; theorists will have difficulty predicting the out-come of a particular situation.

Game theory has a mixed reputation within economics and

political science because of this intractability. While many people in those fields recognize that it contains at its core a more realistic description of many situations than do models built on independent actions, others suggest that such a description is not of much use if it is too complex and intricate to make concrete predictions. The complexities of even as simple a place as Whimsley are such that prescriptions should be made very cautiously, and the real world is more complicated than Whimsley.

Economist and free-market enthusiast David Friedman offers a cautionary view of game theory and its applications:

> Game theory is a fascinating maze. It is also, in my judgment, one that sensible people avoid when possible. There are too many ways to go, too many problems that have either no solution or an infinite number of them. Game theory is a great deal of fun, and it is often useful for thinking through the logic of strategic behavior, but as a way of actually doing economics it is a desperation measure, to be employed only when all easier alternatives fail.[7]

Constructing realistic economic models based on game theory has indeed turned out to be fiendishly difficult. As Friedman suggests, economists often find that in the real world of economic exchange there is not one story and one clear outcome – as they would argue there is in the classical competitive market with its many firms – but many stories and many possible outcomes. Along the same lines, Paul Krugman has made major contributions to the theory of international trade using game-theoretic ideas; and yet he writes that, when an industry is dominated by a few major players:

> These players are bound to realize that they have some price-setting power. They are also likely to realize both that it is in their common interest to agree, at least tacitly, to set prices high, and that it is in their individual interest to cheat on that agreement and undercut their rivals. Is the eventual result a stable cartel, a perpetual price war, or an irregular alternation between the two? Hard to say.[8]

The difficulty of constructing realistic economic models of situations in which choices are tangled is a genuine problem, but it should not divert us (whether we are economists or not) from attempting to interpret the world that we live in, that we see around us every day. As Einstein famously said, theories should be as simple as possible, but no simpler. The absence of a single story as compelling as that of the competitive market should not stop us from recognizing the importance of externalities, and seeing how blinkered the MarketThink worldview is. Presenting the free market as "the way the world works," as MarketThink popularizers do, with its corollaries of consumer power and corporate weakness, is misleading in the extreme when, as Jean Tirole writes in his textbook: "Most markets are served by a small number of firms with non-negligible market power,"[9]

Literary theorist Jonathan Culler talks about ways of making sense of the world:

> Scientific explanation makes sense of things by placing them under laws – whenever a and b obtains, c will occur – but life is generally not like that. It follows not a scientific logic of cause and effect but the logic of story, where to understand is to conceive of how one thing leads to another, how something might have come about: how Maggie ended up selling software in Singapore, how George's father came to give him a car.
>
> We make sense of events through possible stories; philosophers of history . . . have even argued that the historical explanation follows not the logic of scientific explanation but the logic of story: to understand the French Revolution is to grasp a narrative showing how one event led to another.[10]

Game theory is another way of making sense of events in the world around us. For example, Bill and Adrian's visit to the mall indicates that the choice people make might not be so obvious. According to the bottom lines of Nike and Adidas, Bill and Adrian went to the mall and chose to buy Nike, but we have seen that they really went there to express their joint identity through buying sneakers, and that choice depended on other factors and not just on brand. The criteria in their choices were mainly about each other's preferences, and only secondarily about the sneakers themselves. The sneakers are a medium through which they express their identities, and pretty much any sneaker would do the job in a pinch.

What the story of Bill and Adrian suggests is that success can be a matter of simple luck. Bill and Adrian both walked out of Whimsley Mall with Nikes, but that says less about Nike shoes than it does about the almost random chance that led Bill and Adrian to settle on that equilibrium rather than on the Adidas equilibrium.

When the best choice is dictated by co-ordination, trusting individual choice proves to be a mistake. It leads to a winner-take-all world characterized by extreme inequality. While the winners in this world may reap a disproportionate share of the spoils, that overly large amount generally has little foundation in either merit or justice.

chapter eight

JOIN OR GET RUN OVER

IN CO-ORDINATION GAMES INVOLVING MANY PLAYERS, the best choice for an individual player is to do what the others are doing. The end result is a kind of herd behaviour caused not by a mindless following of others but by sensible individual choices. And just as free-riding leads to bad outcomes, so too can herd behaviour.

Calling someone a sheep is not usually a compliment, but sheep act in the way they do for perfectly good reasons. Once a herd is moving, the best choice for any one individual is to join it. Standing in its way or going against the stream is not a sensible choice: it just gets you run over. What's more, each individual who makes the best available choice adds to the momentum of the herd, making it even more unattractive for subsequent individuals to do anything other than join. Herd choices are self-reinforcing.

Herd choices are different from free-rider problems: they have less that is obviously wrong with them, and sometimes they have nothing wrong with them at all. Some herds are happy. But there are times when joining the herd, like free-riding, leads us into a trap from which individual choice cannot help us escape. Many herd choices are part of what have come to be called "winner-take-all" markets,[1] in which individual choice leads to inequality: individual choice is on the side of the powerful. MarketThink would also have us believe that individual choice and the market lead to competition: the option of spending our money somewhere else encourages new entrants into markets and keeps existing ones on their toes. But when the best choice is to join the herd, individual choice leads to monopoly and the eradication of meaningful choice.

Choosing a Nightclub in Whimsley

Let's return to Whimsley, where we again meet Bill and Adrian. After buying their Nikes, Bill and Adrian set out for a Friday evening at a nightclub.

You will not be surprised to hear that Whimsley has only two clubs: we'll call them El Simple and Club One. As they head towards Whimsley's club district (which, of course, takes up no more than a block in the centre of town), they discuss which one to go to. Here is how their reasoning goes:

- They both like the music at El Simple more than the music at Club One. So they give one point to El Simple.
- They both like the drinks at El Simple more than the drinks at Club One. So another point goes to El Simple. It seems that El Simple is the place to be.
- But more than anything, they both want to go to a lively, exciting club filled with other people having a good time. They will give one point to a club for every ten people there, but they won't know how many points that is until they get there.

When they arrive at the club district, a crowd of 50 people has already formed outside Club One, while El Simple is deserted. The choice is clear: tonight Adrian and Bill decide to go to Club One.

What's more, by joining the crowd, Adrian and Bill influence the people who come after them. By choosing Club One they add two more people to the jostling and lively crowd, which makes Club One an even more interesting place to go.

Once a product or destination gets itself established, it becomes the equilibrium choice – "winner takes all." There is no explicit restriction on Bill's or Adrian's actions, but the incentives demand conformity. This is the essence of "increasing returns": the leader in the race gets stronger simply by virtue of being in front, while those behind get weaker because they are lagging.

Once again, we can represent this choice – the choice of nightclub – by a graph (see Figure 11).

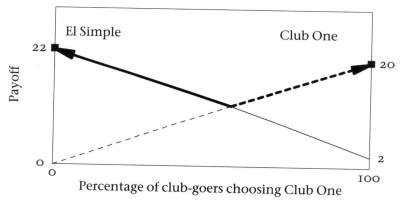

FIGURE 11: Choosing a nightclub. Adrian's choice and outcome depend on how others act. His best choice is the bold line. The two equilibria are marked by squares.

The graph shows the points associated with choosing one club over another, so a high point on the graph is a good thing. The graph shows what happens when 200 people are going to the clubs. To keep things simple, it shows only Adrian's decision. Adrian prefers El Simple to the tune of 2 points to start off with, but assigns himself an additional point for every 10 people at a club.

Imagine Adrian arriving in the club district when all 200 people are at El Simple. In this case the percentage of club-goers choosing Club One is zero, so he is at the left side of the graph. Adrian assigns 20 points to El Simple for the lively atmosphere the crowd makes. Adrian also gives El Simple 2 points for its drinks and music, so it has a total of 22 points. Club One, on the other hand, is abandoned (no points), and Adrian does not like the music or drinks there anyway. So Adrian assigns Club One no points whatsoever. He prefers El Simple by a large margin of 22 points to zero.

On the other hand, if Adrian arrived in the club district to see 200 people at Club One, he would be at the right side of the graph. Despite El Simple's drinks and music, Adrian assigns Club One 20 points and El Simple only 2. Again, the choice is clear: Club One by a large margin.

Finally, if Adrian arrived in the club district to see 110 people at Club One and 90 people at El Simple, he would be in the middle of the graph, where the lines cross. At this point, Adrian has no preference for one place or the other. There are slightly more people at Club One, but only just enough to offset the better drinks and music of El Simple. The point at which the lines meet is sometimes called the *tipping point*.[2] When the clubs are finely balanced, with a similar number at each place, a small group of people choosing one or the other can set a self-reinforcing trend going, as subsequent choices slide up the top line to one edge of the graph or the other. A small action can have a big effect by "tipping" the choice for those who come later.

Imagine people arriving at the club district over the course of the evening. At the beginning, the percentage of people at each of the clubs may be very similar, and so each new person arriving faces a choice that is close to the middle of the graph. But imagine that a few people decide to go to one club rather than the other – say, Club One. Then by their choices they make Club One a more interesting place to be: they push the choice for the next person over to the right side. Now Club One is clearly a bit more lively than El Simple. As soon as the trend starts, it becomes self-reinforcing, with each additional person or group who goes to Club One pushing the choice further over to the right side for subsequent people. The gap between the two clubs gets larger, and the larger it gets the more new people are likely to push it even further over to the right.

A Selection of Herd Choices

Co-ordination Choices

Some herd choices are just co-ordination problems among many people. These are similar to the pedestrians who have to avoid bumping into each other on the sidewalk – the choices are made purely with a view to fitting in with or adapting to what others choose to do. In these situations people commonly look for a focal point – some external indicator that helps them to decide how to co-ordinate choices – to help them make their choice, as in the case of Bill and Adrian buying shoes (chapter 7).

WHICH SIDE OF THE ROAD? An obvious example of a co-ordination choice is the side of the road that we drive on. It matters little whether we drive on the right or left side of the road, as long as we all stick to the same side when we're going in the same direction. Although there is a law that tells us which side of the road to drive on, that law acts primarily as a focal point and requires little enforcement because, once a side is established, we have no incentive to drive on the other side. The problem of choosing which side of the road to drive on has two equilibria: one with everyone driving on the left, and one with everyone driving on the right.

That everyone within a given country makes the same choice doesn't tell us that everyone likes to drive on the right or on the left. All it tells us is that when we are going in the same direction we all like to drive on the same side of the road. This obvious point carries over into worlds such as those of technology and fashion, where we constantly hear that people choose one brand or product over another because that particular item is in some sense better. Change is not impossible (Sweden did change from driving on the left to the right in 1967), but it is difficult, and requires a co-ordinated shift from one equilibrium to another. If we wait for individual choice to move us from driving on one side of the road to the other, we will wait forever.

There's nothing bad here, of course. It is a good thing that we are not tempted to switch to the other side of the road. It's just worth remembering that the choice we are really making is not the one we seem to be making.

GETTING INTO A RUT. A second traffic-related example comes from China just before 200 BC, under the rule of Emperor Qin. This emperor is perhaps now best known in the West for the terracotta army that accompanied his burial, a tribute that reflected his influence in making China a single country. As one part of that consolidation he built a network of new roads. Carts travelled even more slowly along the rough roads than they had to, because they all had different axle lengths so that each cart had to make a new and different rut in the road. Emperor Qin dictated that carts should be made with a standard axle length, so that each cart could run in the tracks made by its predecessors. The result of this decision was a smoother and quicker journey for each individual cart. And while some of Qin's laws may have needed strict enforcement, it is unlikely that this one did, because any one cart-maker had little incentive to deviate from the norm.

Again, the key point here is not the particular axle length that Qin chose – within reason, any would do – but that he made a choice of a particular length. In the face of co-ordination problems, any decision is better than none: the emperor was simply the person in a position to make it. And again, the decision to standardize was a good thing, because it provided a focal point that allowed individuals to co-ordinate their actions.

THIS YEAR'S COLOURS. Now it is time to look at a co-ordination problem that does have a downside. That the phrase "this year's colours" means anything at all reflects how industries from fashion to the auto industry to home furnishing have managed to co-ordinate their decisions about the colours they use in their products. As part of this effort, twice a year the members of an organization called The Color Marketing Group (CMG) meet to make forecasts of colour palettes for the coming years, not only for clothes, but also for home furnishings, cars, and recreation.[3]

The CMG is an association of "Color and Design Professionals." It produces a set of colour directions for consumer markets and for "contract industries" that include hospitality, retail, and office furnishings. The consumer market is further subdivided, and specific colours are chosen for each branch. For example, the consumer directions forecast for 2006 included a section for transportation, which included colours such as Georgian Bay (which "balances the blue and green of both Technology and Organics for a fresh clean color sparked by silver fleck") and Obi ("Transportation brings this rich saturated brown to differentiate the Über Luxury world from growing mass extravagance").

The CMG describes its palettes as "forecasts," and its website reminds us that "CMG's Forecast Palettes are color 'Directions,' not directives"; but this is just being cute because in practice these forecasts are self-fulfilling. Although the organization has no authority – there is no compulsion for manufacturers to adopt the predicted colours – in practice each manufacturer is faced with a choice between having its products complement those of others or of clashing, and in most cases clashing is a bad idea. The CMG forecast provides a focal point that helps its members co-ordinate their actions to achieve a better outcome for each of them.

So the manufacturers are generally happy with the outcome, and at first blush consumers would seem to benefit too, at least where clothes are concerned, in that they get to mix and match colours from several manufacturers without being tied to any one company. But there is an aspect of this co-ordination in which the interests of manufacturers and consumers clash.

Manufacturers have a common interest in encouraging people to buy not just one item, but many items, each year. If next year's colours are chosen so that they don't match this year's, then that one new shirt really needs a pair of pants to go with it. As one example, in her "Making Light" weblog, Teresa Nielsen Hayden remembers the "Big Khaki Push":

> Remember that one? Ads everywhere saying "Hemingway wore khaki"? We'd all been wearing black for several years. We had black levis, black skirts, black leather or denim jackets, little black dresses – a great installed base of basic black clothing, plus the colored stuff we wore with it. I hadn't heard anyone sighing for the return of khaki, and if I had, I'd have pointed them to one of the WASP mail-order catalogues. What's the big deal with khaki? It gets dirty too easily, and for a lot of people it's an unbecoming color. But there's only so much new black clothing you can sell a happy consumer who already has a closet full of black-and-co-ordinates; so the clothing industry pushed khaki remorse-lessly.[4]

The idea that "the clothing industry pushed khaki" sounds conspira-torial, but there is no explicit conspiracy here. Achieving collective action among the members of the clothing and interior design indus-tries is not difficult, after all. There is little of the free-rider problem here (save for the cost of sending someone to the biannual CMG con-ference) and a lot of the herd. The CMG is a way in which companies can co-ordinate their actions in the pursuit of their own individual interests in promoting new purchases, which can be helped by mak-ing last year's colours look dated and stuffy as quickly as possible. While the clothing industry may have pushed khaki in the 1990s, it can now deride anyone who would choose that colour.

Aimee Desrosiers, a colour expert with Boston-based California Paints, asks, "How many shades of khaki do you have in your closet?" She suggested that red would be a big colour in 2005 because it says "I'm going to do what I want and don't care what people think."[5]

For instance, the whole idea that a colour such as Lapis ("Crowds will cheer for this favourite Fashion blue enhanced by Techno-effects for surprise and luminosity") would be "popular" in 2006 is disingenuous. In reality consumers would buy Lapis-coloured items in 2006 whether they wanted to or not because Lapis-coloured things (or things that go with Lapis) would be everywhere. As the new equilibrium takes hold, our existing clothes will not match, and will start to look outdated. And, theoretically, we will all go out and buy a matching shade of red to show how independent we are.

This is not to say that people are being tricked, or making stupid decisions. There is such a thing as colour co-ordination after all, and for many people clothes, to pick one example, can be an important factor in determining how they prosper in their workplace or social circles.

Evolving Choices

While focal point equilibria form quickly once an external focal point is recognized, other herd choices are made by a few people (or other actors) at a time, so that the equilibrium is the result of a gradual evolutionary process, in which different strategies may be tried until one strategy comes to dominate others. Again, some of these choices have nothing wrong with them at all, while others end up leaving us in unhappy places.

GEOMETRY OF THE SELFISH HERD. Game theory can be used to analyze the results of Darwinian evolution as well as the results of social choices. As one example, the biologist W.D. Hamilton provided an explanation for the formation of herds based on the behaviour of individual animals.[6] Imagine thousands of wildebeest spread out over a large plain, and imagine that the main threat to these animals is attack by lions, which can appear randomly, essentially "out of the blue," anywhere on the plain and kill the nearest wildebeest. What behaviour on the part of an individual animal will provide it with a good chance of surviving?

To answer this, we can draw an idealized, geometrical picture of a herd, with the wildebeest spaced evenly on a square grid, each of them 10 metres from its neighbours. Each animal is surrounded by a "danger zone" with an area of 100 square metres. If the lion appears in that area, no other wildebeest is closer, and that particular wildebeest is in danger of becoming dinner for Leo.

If a particular animal chooses to move away from its grid point and takes up a spot in the middle of a square of four others, a little geometry shows that its "danger zone" shrinks to only 50 square metres. It therefore has a better chance of not being attacked by a lion. Wildebeest that have a tendency to surround themselves by others therefore have a greater chance of survival, and over the generations the proportion of wildebeest with a tendency to cluster in a herd grows. On any given day, the herd may form at any point on the plain. However, once a grouping starts to form, the herd instinct will lead the remaining scattered wildebeest to move towards it. The equilibrium is self-reinforcing.

This simple arrangement is, of course, not all that can be said about the herding of wildebeest, or all the animals would pile into one huddled mass. Considerations such as the need to find food and drink will tend to make the animals spread out even at the risk of being eaten. Like the other stories in this book, this one describes only a piece of reality, not the whole picture. The stories are still useful, however – up to a point, the herding tendency is a helpful trait for individual wildebeest to have. Just as the focal point of the CMG's forecasts can help the individual members of the clothing industry co-ordinate their choices until those members seem to be monolithic, so a herd, which provides safety in numbers and looks like collective action, can form as the result of individually selfish decisions on the part of its members.

ZEBRA STRIPES. The selfish herd is just one example of how thinking of biological variations and genetic mutations as if they were a "choice" can clarify the natural world. Animals do not really choose their genes, of course, but John Maynard Smith and others realized that game theory could tell us not only about rational choices but also about the factors driving biological evolution and the outcomes they produce.[7]

In biological evolution, the payoff for players with successful strategies is an increased chance of survival and reproduction compared to others, other things being equal. Consequently, genes for successful strategies are propagated to the next generation in greater numbers and in time genes for successful strategies proliferate while genes for unsuccessful strategies disappear. From time to time, genes mutate and new strategies appear: under the pressure of evolutionary selection, successful ones will spread and unsuccessful ones will fizzle out.

After many generations of change, the population settles into a stable state, at which point successive generations look the same as each other. The surviving strategy (or mix of strategies) is the equilibrium strategy, in this context commonly called an evolutionarily stable strategy or ESS. Such strategies turn out to be equilibria for a game between "rational" players; for example, in the case of the prisoner's dilemma, the ESS is to free-ride. Just as we know that when a game is at equilibrium no player can improve the outcome by choosing an alternative strategy, so we can say in the language of evolutionary game theory that an ESS cannot be invaded by a "mutant" strategy. Another way of saying the same thing is that an ESS does better against itself than any available alternative. With each generation, there may be small numbers of mutants who try out different behaviours, but if none does better than the prevailing strategy, natural selection ensures that those alternatives die out.

Co-ordination games have many equilibria – and the diversity of natural life is surely the best testament possible to how many different solutions exist to the problem of survival – and the ones that succeed depend crucially on the details of the environment. As just one simple example, consider the problem of camouflage for herding animals. The vivid black and white stripes of a zebra make no sense if each animal is isolated against a brown or green background. It does make sense for an individual animal seen against a background of black and white stripes. The predator has a hard time picking out one individual animal against the confusing background. A brown animal in such a herd would stand out and be an easily isolated target. On the other hand, while having black and white stripes is one solution to the problem of camouflage, it is an unusual one: a herd of plain brown animals also works, and is the more common solution.

WALKING TO SCHOOL. Moving from the animal world to the human, we can consider an evolutionary equilibrium that is not a good one. Instead of taking place over evolutionary time scales, social co-ordination problems are worked out over shorter times, but they may still involve a continuous stream of decisions made by successive generations of choosers. In these circumstances, as a guide we can go back to the graph (Figure 11) representing Adrian's choice of a night-club: we slowly slide up one branch or the other of a choice, to the equilibrium at one edge or another of the graph.

Many children face a choice each morning of walking to school or being driven. Fewer children walk to school now than used to be the case. As a result, the sidewalks are emptier than in times past; they are perhaps more dangerous, and certainly less inviting for those children who do still walk. Next week or next year, some of those children who now walk may complain a little harder to their parents about the long and boring journey, or some of the parents may worry a little more about the empty and exposed sidewalks that their children are navigating, and as a result perhaps a few more children who are now walking will get driven to school. This is another twist in the spiral, as their decision to stop walking makes the sidewalks still more empty, and perhaps drives off a few more students. And so it goes: a relatively small drop in children walking to school can start a spiral of emptying sidewalks that can end with a major change in habits for many people.

Faced with the observation that few children walk to school anymore, we commonly hear that this tendency represents our preferences: that "people won't walk" anymore. But this is oversimplified. What we are seeing is one equilibrium among many, and perhaps not the best one. There is an equilibrium in which no one wants their children to walk along empty streets, and so no children walk, but there is another equilibrium in which many children enjoy walking with groups of other children, and parents feel safe about their children because there is safety in numbers on the busy sidewalks.

Too many cities have concluded that empty sidewalks are a result of our preferences rather than the other way around, of our preferences being the result of empty sidewalks: they think that because no one walks anymore this means that no one *wants* to walk anymore, whereas the truth may be that no one walks simply because no one else is walking. But once a city takes it as a given that most children will be driven to school, there is no need for the city to even build sidewalks in new subdivisions, and there is more temptation to build fewer, bigger schools rather than more, smaller, easily accessible schools. With these decisions, the empty-sidewalks equilibrium becomes even more entrenched: we are trapped in an outcome that was the result of individual choices, but that may not represent our true preferences.

Individual choices left to themselves cannot change cities with empty sidewalks into cities with busy sidewalks. To switch from one equilibrium to another requires a kick in the opposite direction. In some cities groups of parents and others have joined together to try to provide this kick and move the trend in the opposite direction, hoping that a small increase in the number of children walking to school may prompt a bigger increase; that the more children walk, the busier the sidewalks, the better chance of finding someone to talk to on the way, the safer and more enjoyable it is.

THE PLACE TO BE. Hay-on-Wye is a small town on England's border with Wales. It has 2,500 inhabitants and 40 bookshops. Why are there so many booksellers in such a small town, where they provide maximum competition for each other, where customers can compare prices and deals among the various shops? If these bookshop owners behaved according to the oversimplified model of the competitive market, they would try to set up stores in towns without bookshops rather than operating in a small town already saturated with them.

But these store owners know their business and have a perfectly good reason for setting up shop in Hay-on-Wye. The town has become a well-known destination for book shoppers, who often travel great distances to spend the day browsing the shelves there. The benefits of being a part of this shopping scene outweigh the dangers of competition. And, of course, the more bookshops there are, the more of a destination the town becomes. Bookstore owners know the benefits of being in a herd.

Increasing returns from geographical concentration apply to many industries other than bookshops. At one time northern California's Silicon Valley was just one place among several where new-technology companies were forming, but at some stage it became "the place to be." Once it reached this tipping point its future was secure, and Silicon Valley became synonymous with the new-technology boom. The more new companies set up in Silicon Valley, the more it became a place for talented programmers to live. The more talented people moved there, the more companies found it an attractive place to be. The more Silicon Valley firms were successful, the easier other Silicon Valley firms found it to get venture capital.

Around all these self-reinforcing spirals of growth were other benefits: the area developed a whole set of services and expertise that new-technology firms can use, from prestigious conferences to trade magazines to service companies. Ironically, for technologies that are supposed to make distance irrelevant, being on the spot turned out to be crucial.

Even more than Silicon Valley, Hollywood is a prime example of how concentration leads to more concentration. According to Peter Grant and Chris Wood:

> No production capital of any contemporary cultural genre comes close to rivalling the dominance that Los Angeles exerts over moviemaking. . . . Seventy per cent of the filming happens in Los Angeles, ten times the amount done in the next-largest U.S. centre of New York City and six times the combined production of the next four English-language countries with film industries – Canada, the United Kingdom, Australia and New Zealand.[8]

The stories of herd choices tell us that success may have little to do with intrinsic merit. The herd may form at the south end of the valley or the east side of the valley – it is not that important which one gets chosen as long as there is a herd to join. It is not so much the people there, but rather the cycle of increasing returns that leads to success. Even in the highly individualistic cultures of Hollywood and

Silicon Valley,[9] the truth is that success has much to do with the accidents of history.

THE MATTHEW EFFECT AND INCREASING RETURNS. The parable of the talents says, "For unto every one that hath shall be given, and he shall have abundance: but from him that hath not shall be taken away even that which he hath" (Matthew XXV:29). Herd choices exhibit this "Matthew effect," in which those who already have the most stand to gain even more as the game continues.

Another name for the Matthew effect is "increasing returns to scale" or just "increasing returns." When a big company has an advantage because of its size, and so gets bigger still, its "returns" increase as its scale increases. Cities can exhibit the same kind of dynamics. The growth of Hollywood and other centres that dominate an industry is a result of cities becoming more attractive destinations for firms in a particular industry the larger they get.[10]

There are many different sources of increasing returns in addition to the geographical ones. One source that is common in knowledge-based industries is "learning by doing," whereby a firm with an early lead in experience uses that experience to increase its lead: each new piece of knowledge or skill it gains makes subsequent developments easier.

INCREASING RETURNS BY DECREASING COMPETITION. Another source of increasing returns is the knowledge and resources to use the existing intellectual property system to your own advantage, or even to shape that system. The more a firm or cartel has the ability to change the rules of its industry to suit itself and to restrict competition, the more it can get ahead. As an example, large pharmaceutical companies have unparalleled experience with the patent system, and can use this knowledge and resources to make the most of that system to their own benefit.

One of the effects of corporate-led globalization has been to extend the value and scope of patents through the World Trade Organization's Agreement on Trade-Related Aspects of Intellectual Property Rights (TRIPS). Historically many of the world's richest countries, including the United States and Japan, got their economies growing by relying on copycat industries. The United States copied the inventions that had boosted the United Kingdom's cotton industry in order to build its own industry in that sector, and Japan copied techniques from other countries to build its own steel industry. But these routes are now being closed off for today's underdeveloped countries as the reach of the patent system has become global. The race is on to establish private ownership of valuable knowledge.

Some of the ways in which pharmaceutical companies take advantage of the patent system amount to what Indian physicist Vandana Shiva calls "biopiracy": the capture of biological knowledge that already exists but has not been patented, by companies that know the importance of those patents.

A prominent example is the patenting of products based on the Indian neem tree. Neem has been used for centuries as a biopesticide and medicine. Neem datun (toothbrushes) are in common use throughout India. Shiva describes the privatization of the knowledge that has developed throughout India regarding the neem tree and its properties:

> For centuries, the Western world ignored the neem tree and its properties: the practices of Indian peasants and doctors were not deemed worthy of attention by the majority of British, French, and Portuguese colonists. In the last few years, however, growing opposition to chemical products in the West, in particular pesticides, has led to a sudden enthusiasm for the pharmaceutical properties of neem. Since 1985, over a dozen US patents have been taken out by US and Japanese firms on formulas for stable neem-based solutions and emulsions – and even for neem-based toothpaste.[11]

W.R. Grace, the owner of four such patents, has established a base in India, setting up the "world's first neem tree-based biopesticide facility." Shiva points out that Indian organizations have been producing and selling neem products, including pesticides and toothpastes, for years. Such local industries have not attempted to patent the processes they use because the methods are based on common

knowledge. Shiva describes the patent activities of the pharmaceutical companies as the "privatisation of biodiversity and the intellectual commons."[12] It is a new form of enclosure being practised on
the powerless by the powerful.

Just how much the patent system is a game played only by the
West can be seen in Africa, where in 1997, according to one report,
"26,000 patent applications were filed to the African intellectual
property organisation. Only 31 came from resident Africans."[13] When
the key piece of expertise is the ability to work the system, we'll see a
few big winners taking the lion's share of the pie. That these companies continue to grow is not so much testament to their inventiveness
as to their ability to plunder the unprotected inventiveness of others.

Choosing Our Schools

What makes a good school is a complicated question, and what
makes a good school system is even more complex, but we can still
learn something from simple stories. During a time when calls for
"school choice" are commonplace, it is worth understanding a little
about how choices work when it comes to schools. We shall see that
many flavours of school choice may turn out to be on the side of the
already fortunate and work to leave the unfortunate worse off than
they are now.

MarketThink would have us believe that opening schools up to
individual choice, allowing parents to move their children from one
school to another and allowing schools to choose which students
they admit, will force schools to compete for students, and that as a
result the quality of schools will improve.

In Canada the Fraser Institute is an influential promoter of these
ideas. Its 2001 report *Can the Market Save Our Schools?* collected papers
that argued in favour of school choice. The report clearly stated its
position:

> Developing an educational market, where schools are allowed to com-
> pete more freely for students, will produce better educational results for

more students. . . . The public's goals for its education system would be more attainable if we encouraged schools to respond to the demands of parents rather than those of the bureaucracy.[14]

In the United States the Walton family – heirs to the Wal-Mart fortune and numbers 10 to 14 in *Forbes* magazine's 2005 list of the wealthiest people in the world – have been supporting increased school choice by putting their money behind groups that favour bringing choice and the market into the school system.

The scope for choice is much broader in the post-secondary educational system than it is in most school districts, and we can learn something about school choice by looking at the forces at work in university choices. Economist Robert Frank observes the difference between choosing to attend an elite U.S. university and making other exclusive purchases, such as a Porsche sports car:

> The salient difference between a university and the producer of a sports car is that although the attractiveness of a sports car does not depend on the average skill level of its buyers, the attractiveness of a university depends strongly on the average intellectual ability of its students. Applicants want to be at a school whose students are accomplished, partly because they can learn more by interacting with such students, but also because that's where the best employers concentrate their recruiting.[15]

The same argument holds for high schools and elementary schools. David Jesson of York University tracked the progress of 28,000 successful elementary school children in England and found that, while it made little difference whether they went to state schools or independent schools, their performance did depend on whether they were surrounded by other smart children. When 20 bright students were in the same year group at a school, they scored much higher than students of similar ability who were not surrounded by strong peers.[16] When looking for a school for their children, many parents naturally want to surround their children with smart children, and they want their children to be in schools that have good links to prestigious universities (that is, schools that have an established history of successful students).

When it comes to choosing a school, the best you can do is to join the herd. The best educational choice for most parents is to try to get their child into schools that other parents want their children to attend: to choose a school that is already popular. We know already what to expect from such a structure: a few schools will become recognized as elite, and many children in other schools will be left behind.

School choice can be expressed in several ways. Even in a system in which all schools are state schools and everyone must send their children to the nearest school, there is "choice by mortgage." Prestigious catchment areas attract more people; school vouchers or credits enable parents to move their children outside the public system; and charter schools provide alternative schools within a public school system. And then there are parallel public and private systems. Beyond this, there are issues regarding the universality or targeted nature of a school choice system (vouchers for everyone or just for a few?), whether vouchers can be "topped up" by parents, and whether and how schools get to select from among the students who apply. All of these variants can make a real difference to the outcome.

In Whimsley some years ago, when Jack and Jill's children were going to school, parental choice of high schools was introduced to improve school quality. The Whimsley model was simple: students could choose to apply to any school in the area, and schools could then choose their students from among those who applied.

There are, of course, only two schools in Whimsley: Eastern High School and Western Collegiate. Their exam results are published in *The Journal* and *The Courier* each year. Some years ago, Jack and Jill (they were still married at the time) were looking at which school their child Jean should apply to. They looked in the paper to see that although the two schools were not far apart, Eastern got somewhat better scores than Western. Jack and Jill reckoned that Jean would get a better education surrounded by the higher-achieving students at Eastern. They filled out the application form putting Eastern in first place, and Western in second.

Of course, everybody else looked at the same exam results, drew the same conclusions, and also put Eastern as their first choice. When it came time for the schools to pick their students, Eastern got to pick the cream of the crop. The result was that all the students high on the achievement list gravitated to Eastern, while Western was left with the lower half. Next time the results were published, Eastern was not just a little ahead of Western, it was well ahead. And once Eastern was well ahead of Western, it became more important for parents to get their children into Eastern.

Those who get into Eastern are happy – they are surrounded by high-achieving students, and when they apply to universities the admissions officers will believe that they went to a good school. Those who are left in Western are not so pleased: even the brightest students in the school don't work that hard because they are surrounded by lower-achieving classmates.

There are still the same number of students and still the same number of schools. It is still the case that half the students go to Western and half go to Eastern. Introducing this model of choice in Whimsley did not improve the average marks of Whimsley students, but it did polarize the system so that the top students did better and the lower students did worse. Even under the most favourable circumstances, when everyone makes the best choice they can, and even when factors such as incomes make no difference at all, as in this case, individual choice leads to stratification.

★

The achievements of the other students are not the only thing that makes a school attractive. School resources also have an effect. Other things being equal, everyone would want their kids to go to a school with abundant resources rather than to one with limited resources.

A few years later Whimsley changed its approach to school choice. The town returned to a model in which school funds were held locally, and each school took the children in its catchment area. If they wanted to choose a different school, Whimsley parents had to move.

A little later, as the results continued to show Eastern ahead of Western, house prices on the eastern side of town started to go up, because more and more parents were looking for houses in the area. The wealthier parents had a greater chance of making the move, and Eastern was soon inhabited by a very affluent student body, while Western had a much less affluent population. Polarization ensued, with Eastern getting better equipment from its expanded tax base and Western being unable to keep up with its more meagre resources. Visitors to Eastern would have been struck by the modern equipment, the interesting classrooms, and the well-tended grounds. Visitors to Western would have come away with the impression of an ill-cared-for, badly maintained, and poorly equipped environment. And just as this atmosphere influenced visitors, so too did it influence students: the Eastern students were more likely to respect their surroundings and themselves than were the Western students, some of whom would take their frustration and resentment out on the school buildings.

In one way the end result was much the same as before: Eastern continued to beat Western in the rankings, and the gap between the two widened. In another way it was different: Eastern was not inhabited so much by all the higher-achieving students, as by all the wealthy students. While it could be said that wealthier families have the resources to provide a rich home curriculum, or that the parents of wealthier families are more likely to value the educational system (probably having spent more time in it) and are more likely to know their way around the system, the end result is still polarization, not an overall improvement in the system.

These models of school choice are one-dimensional. In reality the schools that get the best rankings must have both a population of good students and the resources to teach them well.

Whimsley changed its approach to school subscriptions one more time, allowing a limited number of vouchers to families from the Western catchment areas. Eastern could select a limited number of students from among those applicants. The parents of these students might not contribute as much to the school funding as those who lived in the catchment area, but they would be the high-achieving students and likely to contribute to the reputation of the school.

Of course, everyone still wanted to get into Eastern High School. Parents had a choice of moving into the catchment area or of applying for one of the additional spaces. The result was a combination of the previous two policies.

Eastern chose all the high-achieving kids with rich parents. The remainder of its school population was made up of some of the rich kids who were not so high-achieving, together with some of the higher-achieving kids who were not so rich. The kids who were neither high-achieving nor rich were of no interest to Eastern whatsoever, and were doomed to study at Western.

Note that some high-achieving and poor students have now had the opportunity to move out of Western, and could act as poster kids for the new egalitarianism, but in practice the Eastern student body was still overwhelmingly rich (see Figure 12). Schooling is, as Robert Frank and Philip Cook point out, embedded in a "winner-take-all" market.[17]

	Low Achievers	High Achievers
Poor	Western	Mixed
Rich	Mixed	Eastern

FIGURE 12. School selection in Whimsley. Eastern gets most of the high-achieving kids and the rich kids, while Western gets the remainder.

The best schools attract applications from the best students, who make the school better by being there. The schools with the best resources attract the wealthy parents, who add further to the resource base of the school, either by private donation or property tax depending on the system in use. The leftover schools end up with the leftover students, and have neither the talent nor the resources to raise themselves out of their lowly placing. And if there is any correlation between ability at school and income, perhaps from a "home curriculum" that benefits from better educated parents (on average) and more resources, the polarization is enhanced further.

Universities are subject to many of the same pressures as schools. The fad for ranking schools by publishing tables of test results has spread across many countries in the last few years. At the same time magazines (such as *Maclean's* in Canada) publish rankings of universities. We are told that these report cards not only give us choice but also create incentives for schools and universities to improve. What's more likely is that they will lead to increased inequality, with the top schools getting ever more exclusive and the poor schools being worse than ever. While we will have choice in theory, in practice parental and student choice will be as restricted as ever, as wealthy parents with the resources to build their children's resumés from toddlerhood push to get their children into the best schools.

It is best for students to attend a university that is high in the national rankings, even when they believe that the particular university is not necessarily the best suited to them. The key consideration is that others – including future employers or graduate programs – will interpret their university of choice as a reflection of their ability. As a result a lot of good students apply to the top universities, who get to pick the cream of the crop and keep the cycle going. Frank reports how, in U.S. universities:

> When Cornell's Johnson Graduate School of Management jumped from 18 to 8 in the Business Week rankings in 1998 . . . applications for the following year's class rose more than 50 percent. To an extent rivaled perhaps only by the market for trendy nightclubs, higher education is an industry in which success breeds success and failure breeds failure.[18]

Trusting that individual choice and the market will improve school performance is a mistake. It benefits those fortunate enough to be relatively high achievers in school and those who have wealthy parents, at the cost of others less fortunate. The end result is a plundering of available resources by a few, and not the promised rising tide that lifts all boats.

In the 2001 Massey Lectures, Janice Gross Stein gave a perceptive and open-minded discussion of how the culture of choice affects our public institutions. She considers school voucher credit programs in the United States, Chile, and Ontario – places in which a voucher enables students the choice of leaving the public school system and signing up at a private school. Her conclusions are that even in the program she most favours (that in Milwaukee), when it comes to the overall quality of education ("efficiency") there is not much to be said for vouchers: "On both dimensions of efficiency – cost and effectiveness – there is little hard evidence that voucher students did significantly better than those who stayed in the public schools."[19]

She does say that the voucher program had some positive effects on equity: that some students from low-income families used the vouchers to attain a better education than they otherwise would have had. When we look closer, we can see why Stein can make this assertion.

In Milwaukee, the sole place where this more equitable outcome was found, the voucher program had three characteristics that made it different from Whimsley (or, in fact, from most voucher programs suggested in other locations). First, it was restricted to a limited and relatively small number of students. This restriction prevented the large-scale polarization that we saw in Whimsley. Second, it was targeted at a specific group of students at the lower end of the income scale. When voucher programs are made universal, as in Cleveland and Chile, they had the opposite effect of reinforcing inequality because "current private-school users consumed most of the vouchers." Instead of promoting mobility, the program simply subsidized those who already had the money to leave the state system. In Chile and Cleveland, vouchers became a subsidy of better-off families and private schools. Such a subsidy is even more likely to create polarization when parents are permitted to "top up" vouchers, because only those with the funds to provide this topping up will use them. The third restriction on the Milwaukee program was that schools were not permitted to cherry-pick the best students from among those who applied; instead the applicants were selected by lottery. The program was, Stein points out, in some ways more similar to an affirmative action program than to a market solution.

Even in the best case, of Milwaukee, there are doubts over the success of the school choice program.

> Students who remain in the poorest schools lose their most articulate champions for change and improvement. . . . [Vouchers] are a form of

means-testing that historically has created social stereotyping. . . . Targeted programs are also likely to engender resentment among those who are not eligible: parents who are dissatisfied with their local schools but do not qualify for a voucher because their income is just above the line. . . . It is precisely this political dynamic that pushes the creation of universal, rather than targeted, voucher programs, with pernicious consequences for equity.[20]

Thus even where school choice programs have good outcomes, those outcomes vanish if the program is expanded. And to the extent they are successful, their success comes from restrictions on the ability of schools to choose their students. Harry Brighouse makes some interesting suggestions of ways in which schemes could be designed to promote equity rather than promote stratification:

Require oversubscribed schools to select their intake from applicants by a lottery, and create financial incentives for a school to achieve, or approximate, a prescribed mix of class backgrounds and ability levels among its pupils. Lotteries evoke suspicion perhaps because they are associated with gambling. But they are impartial selection mechanisms, which generally achieve a mix of pupils roughly mirroring the mix of applicants. They are not novel: the Milwaukee Public Choice Program [the same program described by Stein] in the USA, which uses state funded vouchers to send children from low-income families to private schools, requires oversubscribed schools to select by lottery, the fairest method.

Lotteries would have at least one bad effect: increasing the incentive for targeted marketing to increase the proportion of "desired" pupils in the applicant pool. So financial incentives to encourage schools to attract an appropriate mix of children are necessary.[21]

Whether such schemes would work well is open to debate. What is clear is that any scheme of school selection based on individual choice is prone to the logic of the herd, and so to outcomes characterized by inequality and stratification. If such outcomes are to be avoided, programs must be wrapped around with restrictions and random elements such as lotteries to prevent those who know how to work the system from doing so. And if these restrictions and concerns are not front and centre of any school choice scheme, then whatever the phrasing used by their promoters, the end result will be a plundering of public resources by those with the ability to do so. When the Fraser Institute asserts that "market education will offer poor families greater educational equity, invigorate the state system, encourage parental involvement in their children's education, and foster social harmony,"[22] its researchers must either be ignorant of the true dynamics of individual choice or using the appeal of individual choice and the apparent empowerment it provides as a front for an agenda of stratification and inequality.

Choosing Our Technologies

A network is a system of interconnected objects. There are social networks, computer networks, phone networks, and so on. Choices that involve networks inevitably, because of the interconnected nature of networks, involve externalities, and commonly produce herd choices.

These so-called "network externalities" have become the focus of much attention in the worlds of computing and new technology. The externalities arise because the value of a network service increases as the size of the network expands. Having a telephone is useful only if others have a telephone too. A fax machine is useless if no one has a fax machine to receive the documents you send. When you choose instant messaging software, there is no point in searching out the best messaging software from a technical point of view – the only sensible thing is to choose what your friends are using.

Network externalities apply to more than physical networks. Personal computers are made from complementary components including hardware, operating system software, and application software. Compatibility among computers is an important attribute for ease of sharing of information, ease of maintenance, and ease of learning. Compatibility is a source of network externalities and so of herd behaviour in the computer industry. To understand how network externalities work, we look at one particular piece of the computer: the keyboard.

Choosing QWERTY

In 1985 economist Paul David wrote an influential essay, "Clio and the Economics of QWERTY." The acronym in his title comes, of course, from the typewriter and now computer keyboard layout, which is another example of increasing returns at work. The QWERTY layout is not necessarily efficient, but was established as the early standard in an area in which standards are important. The amount of irritation and frustration that would be caused if keyboard layout changed from typewriter to typewriter and computer to computer is easy to imagine. No one would seriously claim that I have chosen to type this book on a computer with a QWERTY keyboard because the layout reflects my preferences, partly because the omnipresence of this system makes it scarcely noticeable.

Just as Adrian and Bill went to Club One because it was lively (and thus ended up making it more lively), and just as we all use the QWERTY keyboard because it is standard (and so help to make it more standard), so other cases in which it makes sense to join the herd lead to a single well-entrenched but not necessarily predictable – and not necessarily optimal – outcome. Markets do not lead us inexorably to the best solution; instead, the particular equilibrium that markets select may depend on the quirks and accidents of history.

There were many possible solutions to the problem of establishing a keyboard layout, and QWERTY is not necessarily the best, but the benefit of consistency meant that QWERTY, once it got a lead, was able to hold off all comers. It is not the case that if there were a better keyboard layout, we would switch to it (which would happen if the market for computer keyboards was an ideal competitive market). The importance of consistency has so far outweighed any benefits of better layout design.

Other Network Effects in Technology

An archetypal story in network economics was the triumph of the VHS videocassette format over its competitor, the Beta, which was regarded by many as technically superior. The VHS triumphed because it got a head start in the number of movies available in the format. The more movies that were released on VHS, the more sense it made to release the next movie on VHS too, regardless of which was the better technology. The triumph of VHS was driven by herd dynamics, not by the laws of the ideal competitive market.

If you want to buy word-processing software, there are many incentives to buy Microsoft Word that have nothing to do with the quality of the product itself, but everything to do with its widespread adoption. You can send a Microsoft Word manuscript to a publisher, and you can exchange Microsoft Word documents with colleagues and acquaintances. You can ask other people how to use the program because so many people use it. Other software, including programs developed by companies other than Microsoft, is designed to be compatible with it. The merits or deficiencies of the software itself fade into insignificance.

The role of network externalities is even stronger when it comes to Microsoft Windows itself. Although other operating systems, including Macintosh and Linux, are available for personal computers, these are essentially confined to niche markets, primarily because the network externalities of buying Microsoft Windows are so strong.

Network externalities are one of the major reasons for the runaway success of a series of companies in the technology world. The pace of technological change does mean that new areas of technology open up in succession, but within each of those areas any winner is likely to be a very big winner. The first supplier of a network product to get established has a built-in advantage that almost inevitably leads to its further growth.

The point here is that choices in network-dominated environments are bound to consume themselves. The result is an effective, if perhaps short-term, monopoly – and a holder of a monopoly is powerful, while a consumer faced with a monopoly has few practical alternative choices.

The Internet is the jewel in the crown of the "new economy." Many MarketThink proponents see it as exemplifying the two key characteristics of free-enterprise capitalism: consumer sovereignty and innovation. Here is a typical claim heard on behalf of the Internet and the new economy:

> The economics-textbook notion of perfect competition, with countless buyers facing countless sellers, all armed with the same information, all aggressively pursuing their own interests, is closer to reality today than it has ever been before. The world, in short, has become a more perfect bazaar.
>
> [The new economy] puts power in the hands of consumers by (1) vastly expanding their choices; (2) vastly increasing the abundance, quality, and usefulness of the information they have at their disposal; and (3) forcing businesses to compete to please them.[23]

The idea is that we have more intense competition among companies than before because the global reach of the Internet means that a company in Scotland can compete with a company in Nova Scotia, and a company in York, England, can compete with a company in New York. In addition, we can all use the Internet to make better-informed choices among these various suppliers.

This picture of the continually expanding computer industry is incomplete. There is another side to the story, and it is all about network externalities and herd behaviour. After all, the new economy has certainly not done away with geography when it comes to company location. Silicon Valley has, through a mixture of different kinds of increasing returns, maintained its role as the hub of new-technology companies. There are other reasons why the Internet is subject to increasing returns.

For example, Yahoo! established itself early on as a search engine and went on to become the prime "portal" site for those wanting a home page on the Web. Here you can list your favourite headlines, stock quotes, weather reports, and cartoons on one convenient page, as well as take advantage of free e-mail and discussion groups.

Yahoo!'s success came at the cost of many failures. Excite and other competitors went by the board. Yahoo! lives by advertising, and advertising-driven sites are prone to increasing returns. Why would anyone advertise on a rarely visited site? So the market for Internet portals is not at all like a bazaar, with a whole lot of stallholders consistently driving each other's prices down: it is more like a one-time-only tournament, where the winner gets to live in a relatively uncompetitive world. Indeed, Yahoo!'s only competition looks likely to come from even bigger companies, such as Microsoft and AOL, which want to use the portal as a loss leader.

Amazon, the principal successful bookseller on the Internet, also shows how increasing returns pay off. Amazon chief Jeff Bezos made it as *Time* magazine's 1999 person of the year at the height of dot-com fever. His 35-year-old smiling face on the cover of the magazine was emblematic of the "new-era entrepreneur." Amazon's online bookstore was the first significant venture into online selling, and seemed to set the stage for a whole new generation of retailers. Many of those other retailers have failed, however. It has become clear that transferring Amazon's success with books to other goods is a difficult endeavour.

It has also become clear that, although in principle the consumer may be sovereign on the Internet, able to switch vendor at the click of a button, that's not quite how things work. Issues such as trust and reputation mean that few people will go to an unknown site to save a few pennies when they can go to a widely recognized site instead. Do you feel comfortable giving your credit card number to this company? How do you know they will deliver what you order, on time and in good shape? And if it turns out to be not what you hoped for, will they take it back? Increasing returns and networks are at work again: the more people use a site, the more it is trusted. And if trust is an important factor when shopping for something as cut and dried as a book (which, let's face it, is supposed to be the same product wherever you buy it), it will be vital for other items such as clothes and home furnishings.

The difficulty of establishing trust in the face of uncertainty has been one of the biggest challenges facing those who would sell on the Internet. Unglamorous issues such as delivery charges and return policies have crippled many an online seller. We are drawn to those sites that others have already visited. We trust our credit-card numbers only to vendors that have already established themselves. The cycles of increasing returns are at work, and they tend to lead, as always, to a single big winner.

With technology, as with nightclubs and schools, it is often a mistake to say that we choose one particular technology over another because we prefer it, or that we end up using one technology rather than another because we like it better. Usually we are not choosing a product based on its merits, but we are wisely choosing to use what others use.

It is also a mistake to claim that winners in the technology stakes have added value in proportion to the profits that their companies make. Club One made lots of money and El Simple made none, but that was purely the result of a random fluctuation that started the ball rolling in its favour. Had the ball run some other way, El Simple would have been the big winner. Had Microsoft Windows not won the operating system battle, some other operating system would have done so and that system would, over time, have gained many of the capabilities of Windows. It might have been a bit better, it might have been a bit worse, but as consumers our situation would not be much different: we would still have little in the way of real choice.

In addition, many of the profits of the big-winner technology companies are derived from their monopoly status, however fleeting it is. Microsoft can charge a lot for Windows because in today's world for many people it is the only choice that they have.

Fooled by Randomness

MarketThink has adopted the language of evolution and the "survival of the fittest," and has made of it a myth that fits what its proponents want to see. In this myth, competing companies produce products or adopt strategies and fight it out among themselves. Survival of the fittest guarantees that "the best" wins out as consumers select it above all the others. The market provides a forum for both continual mutation in the form of innovation, and continual selection in the form of success or failure in the marketplace. Those who survive, and deserve to survive, are those who, through talent and hard work, develop the best products.

MarketThink mythology is propagated by shelf upon shelf of hagiographic business books that relate the special qualities of this or that heroic entrepreneur that took them to the heights of success. Not surprisingly, luck does not come high up on the list. For instance, the blurb on the back cover of Michael Lewis's *The New New Thing*, the story of Silicon Valley entrepreneur Jim Clark, proclaims that Clark is not "a businessman," but "a conceptual artist."

> Clark tries to fill out an investment profile for a Swiss bank, where he intends to deposit less than .05 percent of his financial assets. When asked to assess his attitude toward financial risk, Clark searches in vain for the category of "people who sought to turn ten million dollars into one billion in a few months" and finally tells the banker, "I think this is for a different . . . person."[24]

Or here is *Time* magazine on Jeff Bezos of Amazon.

> Every time a seismic shift takes place in our economy, there are people who feel the vibrations long before the rest of us do, vibrations so

strong they demand action – action that can seem rash, even stupid. Ferry owner Cornelius Vanderbilt jumped ship when he saw the railroads coming. Thomas Watson Jr., overwhelmed by his sense that computers would be everywhere even when they were nowhere, bet his father's office-machine company on it: IBM.

Jeffrey Preston Bezos had that same experience when he first peered into the maze of connected computers called the World Wide Web and realized that the future of retailing was glowing back at him.[25]

The worship of the entrepreneur that is part and parcel of Market-Think conveniently ignores the role of luck. If Clark and Bezos are wealthy, it's because they are smarter, more energetic, more imaginative, more courageous – damn it, just more heroic – than their vanquished competitors.

In his engaging book *Fooled by Randomness*, currency trader Nassim Taleb spelled out the role of luck in modern success stories. Currency trading, like setting up a high-tech company, is characterized by a large degree of randomness and uncertainty. Taleb provides us with a good reason to ignore books like Michael Lewis's and other business success stories. To make his point clear, Taleb looks at some cases in which luck is the only factor at work, rather than being just one factor. He shows why it is dangerous to rely on past performance as an indicator of merit or future success.

> If one puts an infinite number of monkeys in front of (strongly built) typewriters, and lets them clap away, there is a certainty that one of them would come out with an exact version of the Iliad. . . . Now that we have found that hero among monkeys, would any reader invest his life's savings on a bet that the monkey would write the Odyssey next?[26]

Taleb uses the concept of "alternative histories" to introduce the idea of what happens when history is told only by the winners.

> Imagine an eccentric (and bored) tycoon offering you $10 million to play Russian roulette, i.e. to put a revolver containing one bullet in the six

available chambers to your head and pull the trigger. Each realization would count as one history, for a total of six possible histories of equal probabilities. Five out of these six histories would lead to enrichment, one would lead to a statistic, that is, an obituary with an embarrassing (but certainly original) cause of death. The problem is that only one of the histories is observed in reality; and the winner of $10 million would elicit the admiration and praise of some fatuous journalist (the very same ones who unconditionally admire the Forbes 500 billionaires).[27]

Taleb also tells about reading a book called *The Millionaire Next Door*: "An extremely misleading (but almost enjoyable) book by two 'experts', in which the authors try to infer some attributes that are common to rich people." The authors examined a collection of successful, wealthy people, and only wealthy people, which made their study, according to Taleb, subject to a condition that he calls "survivor bias," which springs "from the fact that the rich people selected for their sample are among the lucky monkeys on typewriters. The authors made no attempt to correct their statistics with the fact that they saw only the winners." This mistake is chronic among "professionals," he says: "Because we are trained to take advantage of the information that is lying in front of our eyes, ignoring the information that we do not see. . . . In a nutshell, the survivorship bias implies that the highest performing realization will be the most visible. Why? Because the losers do not show up."[28]

What we don't ordinarily see are books written about smart, driven, and adventurous entrepreneurs who, through bad luck or no fault of their own, never make their fortunes. There are no TV documentaries about the gymnast who, after years of early morning practice and high achievement, breaks her ankle and ends her career. To prove that being bold and talented leads to success, it is not enough to show us bold, talented, and successful people; we also need to take into account those bold and talented people who, for whatever reason, don't make it.

One of the biggest single changes to society over the last 25 years – the period of time when MarketThink came to dominate our cultural scene – is a massive growth in inequality. The claims that the extravagant rewards seen by the captains of private industry would trickle down have proved false.

Why have societies endured this return to massive inequality? Part of the reason has to be the widespread acceptance of Market-Think. In a culture of choice, we have accepted, first, that in a market society rewards are proportional to the difference a person makes, and, second, that such market-driven outcomes are fair. Successful companies are by definition worthy of their success: they have identified and filled a niche that others failed to identify, or they have produced a product that is more appreciated by consumers than is the product of their competitors. Any wealth accumulated by the CEOs of these successful companies is, ipso facto, deserved and justified: it is simply a reflection of their market value. The rewards, however extravagant, are both fair and just.

Jeff Rubin, chief economist for the Canadian Imperial Bank of Commerce, suggests, "Society has adopted the goals of economics as its own," and "Governments of all political stripes have bought into the importance of deregulating markets, privatizing public services and reining in public spending. Individuals have accepted responsibility for their own welfare."[29] In other words, if those at the top have collected almost all the gains of the last quarter-century, then good for them. If the rest of us have failed to do so, well that's our own lookout. If we grumble sometimes, that's just sour grapes.

Once we have a more realistic view of the dynamics of individual choices, and of herd choices in particular, the lessons to be learned from such unequal rewards look different. The perspective of herd choices suggests that many of the very rich got that way, not because of their contribution to the betterment of society, but because they were lucky enough to be in the right place at the right time. They have more in common with lottery winners than heroes.

chapter nine

THE DEVIL YOU KNOW

IN THE STORIES TOLD SO FAR in this book, the participants have all had "perfect information." Everyone involved knows what is going on. In the real world, as Nassim Taleb's book explains, we must often act in the face of uncertainty.

Herd behaviour can often arise in such situations, but the effects of imperfect information go even further than that. For example, given imperfect information two people who have the opportunity to make an exchange – something that would possibly benefit both of them – might still prefer to walk away from the transaction. The reasons for this outcome are tied to what is called "asymmetric information," and the situation is known as "the market for lemons." It happens when one side of the exchange knows more about the item being traded than the other. In such a situation, someone selling an item of good quality will find it difficult to sell that item unless its quality can be proven ahead of time.

The market for lemons situation explains why outsider groups such as immigrants find it difficult to obtain suitable jobs even when employers are not discriminatory, why fast-food franchises can prosper even if no one likes their products very much, and why start-up businesses find it difficult to raise money. It also adds to the explanation of why movie studios are tempted to make predictable movies, TV channels carry predictable programs, and independent producers have a difficult time getting funding. It shows why predictability trumps quality.

The market for lemons scenario is akin to many other cases in which the promise of individual choice turns sour (sorry about that) and in which choice, in the hands of people who control resources, becomes a tool to extend inequality.

Jack Goes to the Movies

One Friday night Jack sets out to see a movie at Whimsley Theatre.[1] Being small and simple like everything else in Whimsley, the theatre shows only two movies – it happens to be *Spider-Man* and *Star Wars* – both of them opening that day. In the papers that morning *The Journal* gave *Spider-Man* a good review and *Star Wars* a bad review, while *The Courier* did the reverse.

All the moviegoers come to the theatre for the first showing with opinions based on the particular newspaper they read. They all know that their opinions, being based purely on a single newspaper reviewer, are far from definitive but better than nothing. Let's say they all know that the reviewers are right two-thirds of the time.

Jack reads *The Journal*, and so he is inclined to see *Spider-Man*. Still, he tries to approach the theatre with an open mind. He is the third person to arrive at the theatre, and sees a man and then a woman lined up for the auditorium showing *Star Wars*. What should Jack, good Whimsley resident that he is, do? He knows that the man who arrived first must want to see *Star Wars* because he thinks it is the best movie. After all, he was the first one to arrive and line up and thus could not have been influenced by other people. Now, seeing this man lining up for *Star Wars*, Jack has two pieces of information – his own private information from the review he read, and the revealed knowledge that something prompted the man ahead of him to choose *Star Wars* rather than *Spider-Man*.

Next, Jack considers the woman who has also lined up for *Star Wars*. Like Jack, she saw the man in front of her head for *Star Wars* and would have realized that he thinks *Star Wars* is likely to be the best movie. If her own private opinion is also that *Star Wars* is likely to be the best movie, she would certainly have joined the line for that movie. If she thought *Spider-Man* likely to be the best movie she would have been aware of one opinion in favour of each movie. She would have to flip a coin or use some other way of breaking the tie, and there was a 50 per cent chance of her choosing either film.

Seeing both the man and the woman lined up for the *Star Wars* theatre, and having thought about the implications of their choices, Jack now knows that the man believed that *Star Wars* was probably the better movie and that the woman had at least an even chance of also believing *Star Wars* to be better. Their actions give Jack more than one signal in favour of *Star Wars*. Even though his private information is one opinion in favour of *Spider-Man*, his sense of logic tells him to join the lineup for *Star Wars*.

Then too, all the people following Jack find themselves in the same boat. No matter which review they have read, they find the opinion of the reviewer outweighed by the knowledge that a number of people before them decided on *Star Wars*, even though all of those people probably hadn't yet seen the movie, and even if (according to which review they read) *Spider-Man* might well be the better movie. This phenomenon is sometimes called an "information cascade," because a little public (shared) information has a big effect.

Jack's choice of which movie to see is not governed by the logic of increasing returns: Jack will not necessarily enjoy the movie more because other people are also happening to be watching it. Instead, the governing factor is uncertainty, or lack of information. Faced with uncertainty, Jack is in a position in which his best move is to trust the judgment of others rather than his own shaky knowledge, even though he knows that their judgment is, like his own, based on shaky knowledge. In an arena governed by uncertainty, even a little shared information – and even if it is less than perfectly trustworthy – can produce large changes in the outcome.

Just as with free-riding and network effects, a bad outcome can occur even if everyone involved makes the most of the information they have. Jack and the others who file into *Star Wars* are not being stupid, and they are not being unduly led by the opinions of others – they realize that the information others have is just as dubious as their own. They are making perfectly good choices, but sometimes these choices lead to bad results. *Star Wars* wins big in Whimsley, not because it is the better movie, but simply because the trendsetter happened to read *The Courier* rather than *The Journal*. Others used the information they had available to make sensible and apparently independent choices, but they ended up simply following the trend.

Choosing Our Fashions

One feature of the trends set in motion by information cascades is that they are fragile. Everyone going to the movie knows that they are basing their choices on limited and uncertain information. If a few people buck the trend and start a lineup for *Spider-Man*, those who follow them may also head in to see the web-slinger. Information cascades tend to lead to trends that are boom or bust in nature, being short-lived and dramatic. We see them around us in fashion trends, stock-market bubbles, and other transient happenings.

The idea that financial markets are driven by herd-like behaviour is nothing new, although the bursting of the dot-com stock bubble and the 1997 Asian financial crisis gave new impetus to the idea. Over 60 years ago John Maynard Keynes portrayed the stock exchange as being like

> those newspaper competitions in which the competitors have to pick out the six prettiest faces from a hundred photographs, the prize being awarded to the competitor whose choice most nearly corresponds to the average preferences of the competitors as a whole; so that each competitor has to pick, not the faces which he himself finds prettiest, but those which he thinks likeliest to catch the fancy of the other competitors, all of whom are looking at the problem from the same point of

view. It is not a case of choosing those which, to the best of one's judgement, are really the prettiest, nor even those which average opinion genuinely thinks the prettiest. We have reached the third degree where we devote our intelligences to anticipating what average opinion expects average opinion to be.[2]

The image may be outdated, but the logic remains pertinent, and it is perhaps worth mentioning that in addition to being a brilliant economist Keynes made a lot of money on the stock market.

Once we see that small things can make a big difference, we get tied into ever more involved circles of decisions. If it is in my interest to choose what you have chosen, then it is not surprising that companies will spend a lot of money creating the appearance of inevitable success. If an advertising campaign can convince Adrian that Bill is going to choose Nike rather than Adidas when he goes to the mall, then Adrian is more likely to buy Nike himself. We end up being driven not by established trends, but by potential trends, not by what is cool but by what we think is likely to be cool tomorrow. Success can be a self-fulfilling prophecy.

If MarketThink is correct, Nike and Adidas would both be wasting the massive amounts of money they spend on their lifestyle and image-based advertising campaigns. They would also be wasting the millions they pay sports stars to endorse their brands. But Nike and Adidas are not foolish companies, and they spend their money for good reason: they know that identity and image have a lot to do with why people choose brands. Their advertising creates a connection between their brands and an image that is attractive to the target of the advertising, whether that target is rebellious skateboarders, sports-minded women, or some other target of the day. Such a connection is a none too subtle nudge that gets the herd forming and then moving in the direction of the brand being advertised.

That the image used to drive herd choices is often one of independence and unorthodoxy is ironic, but not unusual. Another example of such a seemingly contradictory message is the long-running advertising campaign for Sprite driven by the slogan "Image is nothing." Here, Sprite is both pointing out that choosing a soft drink based on image is not the way to get a good soft drink, and at the same time the company is trying to establish itself as the drink to choose if you want to be seen as independent-minded.

Self-confessed ex-mall-rat Naomi Klein highlights both the uncertain, interdependent, and co-ordinated nature of the supposedly individual choices made in the search for coolness and the huge profits to be made from them:

> The quest for cool is by nature riddled with self-doubt ("Is this cool?" one can hear the legions of teen shoppers nervously quizzing each other. "Do you think this is lame?") Except now the harrowing doubts of adolescence are the billion-dollar questions of our age. The insecurities go round and round the boardroom table, turning ad writers, art directors and CEOs into turbo-powered teenagers, circling in front of their bedroom mirrors trying to look blasé. Do the kids think we're cool? they want to know. Are we trying too hard to be cool, or are we really cool? Do we have attitude? The *right* attitude?[3]

But which picture of the modern fashion marketplace is more accurate: the MarketThink idea of independent pursuit of the best price/quality ratio, or the fragile, recursively interdependent, herd-driven picture suggested by Klein? Both Malcolm Gladwell and Klein document the phenomenon of "cool-hunters," a phenomenon that shows just how uncertain and unpredictable the world of trends is. According to Klein, "The idea was simple: they would search out pockets of cutting-edge lifestyle, capture them on videotape and return to clients like Reebok, Absolut Vodka and Levi's with such bold pronouncements as 'Monks are cool.' "[4] She continues:

> Of course all this has to be taken with a grain of salt. Cool hunters and their corporate clients are locked in a slightly S/M, symbiotic dance: the clients are desperate to believe in a just beyond- their-reach well of untapped cool, and the hunters, in order to make their advice more valuable, exaggerate the crisis of credibility the brands face.[5]

Given this frantic activity to find the particular mix of stimulus and response that will let a company ride the herd of consumer choice to success, it is ironic that Gladwell started *The Tipping Point* with a story of totally random success: the revival of Hush Puppies. In late 1994, he points out, sales of the classic shoes had fallen to a dismal "30,000 pairs a year, mostly to backwoods outlets and small-town family stores." Wolverine, the company that made Hush Puppies, was thinking of phasing them out. Then word got out that the shoe "had suddenly become hip in the clubs and bars of downtown Manhattan." Sales exploded – to 430,000 pairs in 1995, then four times that number the following year, and even more the next – until "Hush Puppies were once again a staple of the young American male." According to Gladwell, when the shoe won a prize for "best accessory" at the Council of Fashion Designers awards dinner in 1996, the president of the firm gratefully "accepted an award for an achievement that – as he would be the first to admit – his company had almost nothing to do with."[6]

Choosing Our Culture

The story of fashions is like that of other cultural industries. In their exhaustive look into the world of TV and movie economics, Peter S. Grant and Chris Wood explain that it's a tossup when it comes to predicting the success or failure of individual projects:

> The risk factor in launching new works of popular culture is impossible to overestimate. Simply put, the great majority of cultural products do not succeed: few people buy the CD or watch the movie, and the investment in the creation of the intellectual property is not recouped. Adding to the risk is the blunt fact that research and pre-testing are notoriously ineffective in the realm of popular culture. Until audiences actually experience a creative product, it simply cannot be evaluated. In advance of the actual release of the title, *nobody knows*.[7]

The economics of moviemaking have led the industry to be

dominated by a small number of large companies. The work of making a single film carries huge "fixed costs" (the amount of money that has to be spent before the product even sees the light of day), including both production costs and promotional campaigns, while subsequent copies of the movie can be made essentially for free. This means that a successful movie can generate far more money than do successful products of other kinds, because after the fixed costs are covered each subsequent "sell" is essentially all profit. Then again, only those corporations with fingers in many pies can make the most of the rare successes by cashing in not only on the movie, but also on the TV rights, the cross-promotions with fast-food companies, the video game, action figures, and so on, making the playing field even more uphill for independent producers. Because few movies (or CDs, or books) are commercial successes, and *nobody knows* which those few will be, then, as industry analyst Larry Gerbrant puts it, "If you have to live and die one film at a time, you're probably going to die."[8]

There are also reasons, from the perspective of choice, as to why it is difficult for independent producers to make a dent in the movie world. It is not impossible, of course, as hits such as *My Big Fat Greek Wedding*, Michael Moore's *Bowling for Columbine*, and others attest, but these are rarities.

Consider two movies, which we will call *Blockbuster* and *Indie*. *Blockbuster* is made by Hollywood, has a production cost of $150 million, a cast led by two A-list stars, many spectacular special effects, and the tie-ins of a Burger King toy and video game. *Indie* is made in Canada, has a production cost of $2 million, a cast of largely unknown actors, and no special effects. To recoup the expenses of *Blockbuster*, its owners plan to open it simultaneously in nearly 10,000 screens in all the major theatre chains of several countries.

They will promote it with talk-show appearances from the stars and extensive advertising, and to coincide with the movie's premiere they will release a song from the soundtrack (complete with a video that includes bits from the movie). Meanwhile, *Indie* has no budget for promotion, and hopes for a release in a limited number of theatres in Toronto, Vancouver, and a few other major Canadian cities.

In this scenario several factors favour *Blockbuster* over *Indie*, even in those cities in which *Indie* is playing. The first factor is the herd-forming effect of a little public information. Even in Toronto and Vancouver, the number of people who are aware of *Indie*'s impending release is small, while mass audiences have seen the commercials for *Blockbuster* (featuring some extravagant explosions), watched or read an interview with the star, and seen the music video. Seeking out information costs time and effort: it is as if you need to go grocery shopping and can either go to the store just down the street or drive all the way across town to a store that may or may not have what you are looking for. Chances are you are going to try the closest store, even if it is no more likely to stock what you want than the distant one is. It is just easier. In the absence of any information about *Indie*, why would you take the risk?

Second, with *Blockbuster* playing on several thousand screens worldwide, there is no doubt that it is going to be seen by a lot of people. So the next week the newspapers report the box office figures, with *Blockbuster* at or close to the top and *Indie* nowhere to be seen. Advertisements can trumpet *Blockbuster* as the "number one movie in [insert country here]." Again, this is not reliable information, but it is marginally better than nothing, and that is all that is needed for yet more people to choose *Blockbuster*.

With openings for big movies happening on a wider and wider scale, and with new blockbusters coming out every week, the showing time for even the biggest movies is limited. There is little room for word of mouth to help a movie grow, although it still does happen. Critical reviews, even if they pan a movie, do little to sway the viewing figures for most movies. To the extent that reviews do play a role, *Blockbuster* wins again, because it receives more review attention than *Indie* does.

Finally, there is an "increasing returns" aspect to movie-watching. Many of us enjoy talking about movies with friends, reading the reviews of movies we have watched, or seeing the stars on television.

We like the feeling of being part of a big event. We can only partake of these pleasures if we watch a movie that lots of other people are watching, or others have seen.

So, whether *Blockbuster* is better or worse than *Indie* (and, after all, there are many good movies put out by big studios and bad movies put out by independents), it is almost guaranteed to be seen by many more people.

In the face of the endless shouting from the Hollywood industry, the whisper of an independent movie industry is drowned out.

It is not obvious at first that there is a problem here. If people go to what is less than the best movie, well surely that's okay as long as they enjoy it? But there is a problem, and it has to do with diversity. We have seen how what Grant and Wood call the "curious economics" of cultural industries – meaning increasing returns, partial information, and other factors driving herd behaviour – give advantages to the biggest players in the game, helping them get bigger and encouraging them to use their leverage more and more. What's more, they need to tell stories that will play across the world, and the success of the Hollywood machine means that everyone from Finland to Fiji knows Manhattan and Los Angeles, Brad Pitt and Julia Roberts, the X-Men and Spider-Man. In short, U.S. cultural references have, by virtue of herd choices, become global cultural references.

The difficulties faced by moviemakers outside the Hollywood sphere have nothing to do with freely made consumer choices, and everything to do with the logic of the herd. Jack Valenti (head of the Motion Picture Association of America) speaks for Hollywood when he declaims:

> There should be no artificial governmental barricades which bar or limit entry. Competition should flourish. It is citizens in each country who decide what movies they want to see, what TV programs they want

to watch. This kind of competition stirs creative juices. It lifts the level of quality in the creative community.[9]

He is, however, wrong. Competition in such a market does little but put money in the pockets of those who are already wealthy, regardless of the quality of their productions. The program of the free-traders and deregulators, summed up by politician Preston Manning during the 1997 Canadian election campaign, is based in an unreal world: "The cultural industries are going to have to learn to work in the same sort of free trade environment that other industries operate in. . . . We aim to provide a level playing field."

It sounds reasonable, and yet the playing field that Manning, a founder of the conservative Reform Party, would have provided is anything but level. Those of us bombarded daily by the tenets of MarketThink faith find it difficult to get our heads around the idea that a barrier-free world exhibits less competition – genuine competition – than one in which countries develop and employ cultural protection legislation. It seems counterintuitive, but it is true. The U.S. movie industry is the QWERTY of culture; the one we are familiar with, the one that looks and works the same everywhere. But diversity in culture is, unlike diversity in computer keyboards, a desirable thing, and alternatives to QWERTY – even high-quality alternatives that many of us would choose were we ever to get the opportunity – need protection if they are to survive.

Jill Buys a Lemon

Jack's visit to the movies shows how certain choices can lead to poor outcomes, but there is more to uncertainty than was apparent in that story. The question is: how do moviemakers respond to such behaviour on the part of their audiences? To see this side of the story we look at a case in which uncertainty is inescapably high: the buying and selling of used cars or, as it has become better known, the market for lemons. In a famous paper, George Akerlof investigated why it is that the price for second-hand cars – even those that have been out of the showroom a short time – is so low compared to new cars.[10] He showed that the reason has to do with information: specifically, that the seller of a second-hand car knows more about the quality of the car than the buyer does, and that the buyer, knowing this, fears being cheated. As Akerlof notes, his paper was addressing the consequences of the very natural question, "If he wants to sell that horse, do I really want to buy it?"[11] In such a situation it makes sense for car buyers to instead choose the more predictable purchase of a new car.

Jill is looking for a replacement for her car and decides that a second-hand car is the way to go. She picks up a copy of the local auto trader magazine and a guide to used car prices, and starts looking for a deal.

Jill considers trying to get a four-year-old Toyota Corolla. The price guide suggests that an average car of that type and age is worth $12,000. The catch is the difficulty of telling whether a particular car is in good shape or whether its braking system or something else is just about to go.

In Whimsley, of course, instead of a scattering of all qualities of used cars, there are only two qualities. Half of the four-year-old Corollas in town are in bad condition (lemons) and the other half are in good condition (plums); but the buyers won't know which is which until after they have made the purchase and driven the car for some time.

The owners of plums want to sell their cars for $13,000 or more, while the owners of lemons want at least $9,000. Jill wants a good-quality car and is prepared to pay $14,000 for it. As a fallback position, she would be content with a lemon as long as she can get it for no more than $10,000. There are plenty of sellers who would like to unload a suitable car at these prices, and it looks as though Jill will find a seller with no problem.

Just before she picks up the phone to call one of the sellers, Jill pauses and tries to imagine how the negotiations might go. Even though she would be happy to pay $14,000 for a plum or $10,000 for a lemon, she knows that she can't tell just by looking whether a car is a lemon or a plum. As a result, she cannot trust that a high price indicates a car of good quality: a car offered for sale at $14,000 may be a plum, but then again there is nothing to stop a lemon owner from putting the car on the market at $14,000. If she offers $14,000 she is as likely to get a lemon as a plum, and she is not prepared to pay $14,000 for a car that might well be a lemon. She is prepared, however, to take a reasonable chance and offer the average price, as recommended by the used car guide, of $12,000. That way, she will have at least an even chance of getting a decent deal. Having sorted that out, she reaches for the phone.

But then she stops again. Wait a minute, she thinks. If I offer $12,000 and the seller accepts it, doesn't that mean that the car is worth less than $12,000 to the owner? Jill knows that plums are worth $13,000 to their owners. There is no way the owner of a good-quality car would sell it for $12,000. So if her offer is accepted, that means she's getting a lemon, and she doesn't want to pay $12,000 for a $10,000 car.

She pauses with her hand on the phone. Is there a way out of this predicament? She has just proved to herself that she can't buy a plum at the price she is prepared to pay, but perhaps she can at least buy a lemon. She would be prepared to pay $10,000 for a lemon, and she knows that the owner of such a car would accept that offer because lemons are worth only $9,000 to their owners. Is there a catch? She thinks a while. No, there isn't. So she picks up the phone and gets ready to buy a lemon.

This story shows how, in contrast to MarketThink claims, some exchanges cannot be consummated, even if both parties would benefit from them. If Jill could identify a good-quality car, she would be prepared to pay $14,000 for it. If the owner of a plum got an offer of

$14,000, that person would be happy to accept the money. But despite this promising alignment, plum owners cannot sell their cars, and Jill has to settle for a cheap, low-quality car instead. There are particular problems in buying and selling high-quality goods, especially if it costs money to produce higher quality and if the seller cannot prove that her or his item is of higher quality than others.

This is where "asymmetric information" comes in, which is what stops the exchange from happening. The sellers know more about the quality of the goods they are selling than the buyers do. The buyers will therefore be inclined to "play the averages" when evaluating the prices they are prepared to pay: that is, sensible buyers will not offer top prices because they know there is a realistic chance that they will not be getting top-quality goods; instead they make an offer based on the distribution of good- and bad-quality goods. Such an offer is not what the sellers of high-quality goods need in order to make a profit, and it drives them out of the market.

In Whimsley there are only two qualities of car, but the argument also holds true in more realistic cases in which there is a spectrum of qualities. As the top-quality items are pulled from the market, the average price that buyers are prepared to offer is lowered, and the second-rank sellers drop out. The market unravels until only the cheap and poor-quality items can be sold.

Another consequence of the market for lemons situation is that *predictability trumps quality*. Economists break goods into distinct classes, based on what consumers can and cannot know. A used car is an *experience good,* which has to be experienced before a buyer can know the quality. This is in contrast to a *search good*, for which a buyer can know the quality before purchase. There are also *credence goods* – buyers may never be able to tell from their own experience whether or not the product delivers what it promises. Examples are fluoride toothpaste, goods where you pay extra because of how they are produced (free-range eggs, hormone-free beef), or the purchase of services from experts such as auto mechanics or lawyers. In the cases of both experience goods and credence goods there are incentives for the seller to cheat, so that if customers can find search goods that are a reasonable alternative to experience goods or credence goods, they will tend to flock to those more predictable markets.

In the case of used cars, one such alternative is to buy a new car, because manufacturer guarantees and consumer reports make a purchase less risky. In the real world (as opposed to Whimsley), some good-quality used cars do get sold, but the number is fewer than would be expected.

In an attempt to overcome the problems of asymmetric information, buyers and sellers of experience goods and credence goods can engage in efforts to supply trustworthy information or obtain reliable information. Jill might take the car to an independent garage for an inspection. Actions on the part of the seller are called "signalling," and actions on the part of the buyer are called "screening." However, these are typically costly actions, and it is rarely in the interests of either party to spend what would be required to entirely resolve the uncertainties. At some intermediate level, the additional cost of gaining or revealing more information becomes more than the information is worth.

When choices go wrong, externalities are often the source of the problem, and the market for lemons is no different, although the externality at work is more subtle than in some other cases. The sellers of lemons exert an externality on the sellers of plums, with the buyer acting as a conduit for that externality. By offering their lemons for sale, they lower the average price that buyers are prepared to pay, thus making life worse for the sellers of plums.

A Basket of Lemons

Let's take a look at a few cases that exemplify the market for lemons.

INSURANCE. In the insurance industry the lemons problem goes by the name of "adverse selection."[12]

Despite their best efforts to gain the necessary information, insurance companies typically know less than their customers do about the specific risks they are taking on in the contract for insurance. For example, while an insurance company may find out some things about a person applying for life insurance (whether the applicant smokes, or whether health problems run in the family), there are other things that the company doesn't know, but the applicant does. The result is that when setting their rates, insurance companies have to play the averages, just like Jill did when buying her car. Insurance companies spend a lot of time and money finding out as much as they can about their applicants, and they prepare their actuarial tables carefully. Within these limits they play the game very well, but there is still an inherent lack of knowledge on their side of things.

The adverse selection comes about because insurance companies know that if they set their rates based on the average requirements of the population, a good number of the more healthy customers would probably walk away from the offered rate, concluding that the rates are too high for the small risk they are running. But customers who are bad risks would be only too happy to take the offered rate, because they know it is a good deal for them. Any offered rate, then, is likely to attract only those clients whom the insurance company would rather not deal with. The result would be insurance available only at high rates, even for low-risk people.

One way out of this problem is to remove the element of individual choice on the better-informed end of the exchange. Insurance companies typically offer group plans (to employees of a given company, for example) in which participation is compulsory. By removing the element of individual choice and requiring everyone to take part, it turns out that almost everyone benefits. The healthy members of the group get insurance at a rate that, while not ideal, is better than the high rate it would have cost if they were having to go it alone. The unhealthy members get insurance at a good rate given their situations. The insurance company gets a customer base that it can plan for, because the averages are applicable. Once again, the idea that restricting choice can lead to an improved outcome for everyone is, to quote one economics textbook, "quite surprising to most economists."[13]

DISCRIMINATION IN THE JOB MARKET. When employers hire employees, asymmetric information again comes into play. Employers find it difficult if not impossible to know ahead of time whether any one particular applicant for a position will turn out to be a productive employee. As a result the employer's first inclination is to play the averages when deciding on how much, or how little, compensation to offer potential applicants. But employers do know that prospective employees already holding a job will, if they have been successful or productive, have been rewarded by their current employers, and are not likely to be tempted away from those jobs by lower offers. Thus, they reason, if they make a lower offer most of the applicants will be of lower quality; hence employers have an incentive to lower the offered salary even further. The employment market can unravel, making it difficult for employees to change jobs.

Given that in the presence of asymmetric information predictability trumps quality, in the case of employment this means that if there is a class of people about whom the employer has reliable information, that class will be favoured when it comes to getting a job. Here is the root of the old-boy network, the importance of the college tie, and the value of contacts. If the applicant has been through the same university courses as the employer, or knows some of the same people, it makes absolute sense for the employer to choose that applicant from the pool. Applicants get divided into two groups: predictable insiders and outsiders of uncertain quality. The insiders have a built-in advantage, not for reasons of merit but for reasons of information.

This is a kind of discrimination, but it does not come from what Nobel Prize-winning economist Gary Becker calls "a taste for discrimination," in which an employer has an explicit preference for hiring a particular kind of worker. Instead, it is simple common sense on the part of the employer. But it also represents a concrete barrier to outsider groups, such as immigrants or women or people of colour or, in fact, any group not well represented among those doing the hiring. Contrary to MarketThink claims, competitive markets do not ensure that employers hire the best applicant for the job.[14] Being the best is not good enough: an unfamiliar applicant also has to *prove* that she or he is the best. These people are in a Catch 22 situation: they cannot get the job until they can prove their ability, and they cannot prove their ability until they get a job that lets them excel.

The same logic works when it comes to admittance to elite universities. If the admissions officer knows an applicant's school, that officer has a sense of what the applicant's grades mean and, in general, has knowledge of the milieu that the applicant has come out of. From workplaces to universities to other influential social networks such as exclusive clubs, a series of barriers of unfamiliarity exist that keep outsider groups outside.

THE MAKING OF A STAR. It isn't just the employment market for "regular" jobs that has a lemon-like sourness to it: the same goes for other areas in which the value of an applicant is not demonstrably obvious and there is a one-off, tournament nature to success. How do you get a first film role? A position at a highly paid trading house? A recording contract? All, to some degree, are gambles by those who give out the contracts.

No one really knows who will have that on-screen charisma, that split-second judgment, that combination of voice, looks, and presence that make a star in the worlds of movies and TV, trading, or singing. As a result, social networks play a big role in the discovery and making of stars.

For example, the June 7, 2005, edition of *USA Today* ran an inquiry into the value of a Harvard degree. The focus was on the Harvard "brand," but part of the article consisted of interviews with a series of successful Harvard graduates from years gone by. One woman noted that Harvard had the ability to pick, from among all the smart applicants, those who would become stars in whichever area they chose to enter. A man (a senior partner at a high-profile law firm) recalled that he got his break solely on the basis of his Harvard degree – even though his courses had not prepared him for the job he applied for, the Harvard name was enough to give him the job over other applicants. Seen in this light, the observation about Harvard picking stars is clearly putting things backward. If Harvard does somehow pick "those who will be stars" from among the applicants, this is only because the very fact that they are chosen – and that they go to Harvard – puts them in line for stardom.

Some kinds of stardom do not depend on the hard-to-define *je ne sais quoi*, and these kinds of stardom are less dominated by the well connected. It is small surprise, then, that the world of sports is the most highly travelled route to stardom among the poorer sections of society. It is relatively straightforward to tell whether athletic applicants have what it takes to be a contender in the 100-metre sprint: just put them on the track and watch them go.

INVOLUNTARY UNEMPLOYMENT. MarketThink has a quick answer for the problem of unemployment. Those who are out of a job are asking for too much money, and they should be prepared to work for less: they are unemployed by choice. In fact, the argument usually goes, they are just plain lazy. But the unemployed are faced with other problems, including one of asymmetric information: offering to work for low wages is not a signal to employers that you really want to work; it is a signal that you are not a productive worker – that you are a lemon – and employers do not want to hire lemons. While the idea of asymmetric information certainly does not provide the only answer to the MarketThink assertion, it does explain why offering to work for less than the going rate does not guarantee a person a job. After all, the market for jobs of all sorts and at all levels of salaries and wages tends to be "thin": there are always fewer jobs available than there are people looking for jobs.

RENTING APARTMENTS. Proponents of MarketThink argue against the existence of mandated minimum standards (such as provision of hot water) for rental accommodation, just as they argue against minimum wages and other government interference in the economy. Such standards, the argument goes, limit the range of choices available to prospective tenants and make them, as well as prospective landlords, worse off.

The renting of apartments is another case of asymmetric information. Prospective tenants cannot tell by inspection, for example, whether an apartment's heating system is on the verge of breaking down, whether its cooking facilities work adequately, whether the walls are crumbling under that fresh coat of paint, or whether insects will creep out in the middle of the night. As a result, the market for rental accommodation is "thin," with a noticeable shortage of demonstrably good apartments. Minimum-quality standards are a way of meliorating the problem by removing the worst lemons from the basket and thus preventing the complete unravelling of the market.

FUNDING NEW IDEAS. The competition for funding or gaining credit among those trying to set up a new company is not at all fair. Investment banks and other potential funders of inherently risky new ideas cannot readily distinguish the good prospects from the ones that will fail: the next big thing from the dud. Of course, there are good proposals and bad proposals, and the choices made by banks are not random, but they *are* uncertain.

As a result, banks are reluctant to offer the financial backing that a good idea may deserve. Credit and start-up funds are hard to come by, even for good ideas and sound plans. In the jargon of the financial sector, "credit rationing" – a dearth of credit for new enterprises – is common.

As they are in getting a job, in breaking through the information barrier personal contacts are one of the best ways of moving from being an outsider to an insider. A personal recommendation from someone who knows both applicant and potential funder cuts through the fog of uncertainty. So it is the unconnected, those without private financing, who are most vulnerable to credit-rationing and the failure of the markets. The ranks of successful entrepreneurs are overpopulated by the well connected and those with access to private funds. The rich are indeed different from you and me: they have access to money.

Still, as with all of our other examples, credit-rationing is not absolute. Counter-examples exist, and by their nature they are compelling tales of hard-won success in the face of adversity. These heartwarming and inspirational dramas just go to show, we hear in portraits of successful business leaders, how talented and hardworking these entrepreneurial heroes are. But this is "survivor bias" (see chapter 8), and it does not demonstrate anything of the kind. A few swallows do not a summer make.

Choosing Where to Eat

One of the defining features of the North American urban landscape is the fast-food franchise or chain operation. McDonald's is the proto-type for many other such businesses, from the ubiquitous (Starbucks, Wendy's and Tim Hortons, Pizza Hut, Taco Bell, Dairy Queen, and so on, the list depending to some degree on where you live) to the smaller ones trying to break into the market (Saint Cinnamon, vari-ous pita places, New York Fries, and others).

The growth of the franchise-operation model has come about for two main reasons. One is purely economic: chain and franchise operations have economies of scale. By centralizing marketing and purchasing operations, McDonald's and others can carry out large-scale advertising campaigns. They can cross-market with Disney by selling toys to complement new movies, and cut down on purchasing costs by using their bargaining clout with their suppliers. But a sec-ond reason is that the franchise model is built on predictability. If there is a virtue to McDonald's, it is that it provides a reproducible experience: "At least you know what you're going to get." This is in contrast to the independent restaurant market, where reputation is difficult to establish, and maintain, and new customers don't know quite what to expect.

Perhaps this is why even some of those who deride the homoge-nization wrought by globalization and the spread of American culture can sometimes be found eating at McDonald's or Wendy's. When you are out of town, visiting an unfamiliar place, or perhaps just stop-ping for lunch on a long drive, do you head for the local greasy spoon or a fast-food franchise? Often the latter, because at least you know what you'll get. A Big Mac is a search good; an independent restau-rant meal is an experience good.

On the part of the customer this does not represent a "bad choice." The market for lemons explains why the failure rate for new restaurants is high in many cities. The problem is not one that pits high-quality expensive restaurants against cheap diners; it is one of restaurants (of whatever budget) providing good value for money or not. Delivering good value in a meal requires money, effort, and skill. Restaurant owners may choose not to spend the money that it takes to produce good value. Customers looking for a meal know they face an uncertain choice and may not be prepared to gamble on getting good value for money when they know that there is a strong possibility that the restaurant will provide poor value. When customers hedge their bets, good-value restaurants are driven out of business, leaving only the "lemons": the restaurants serving lower-quality food but at least offering known value for money. And these lower-quality restaurants will have a difficult time competing against the large-scale franchise operations, which may have equally low-quality food.

When homogeneous chains drive out independent restaurants, customers are not "getting what they prefer." Instead they are doing the best they can in an environment in which a lack of information puts potentially good choices out of reach. It is not simply a matter of preferring the predictable to the unpredictable, or the safe choice to the risky: the problem is that when customers do not know in advance the quality of what they are going to buy, the quality that is available in a certain price range becomes predictably low.

Some restaurants do achieve good reputations and do survive and prosper, just as good-quality used cars do get bought and sold. But this happens against the odds. The competition does not take place on a level playing field; independent restaurants are playing uphill against the predictability and economies of scale of the franchise operations.

What does this mean? Simply that companies such as McDonald's may be successful even if people don't like their food all that much. We commonly see success as an indication of popularity, but the market for lemons shows that the kind of popularity needed is of a very narrow and conditional kind, and that a food environment based on predictable franchise operations may win out over an environment based on independent businesses, even if those independent businesses might be able to provide better value on average. In another environment, in which clear information about the quality of independent restaurants is available, we may well choose differently.

Squeezing the Lemons

There are ways of at least partially addressing the lemons problem, and some of these are being practised. They require either driving the lemons out of the market or providing ways in which the information gap can be bridged.

One approach is for independent producers to collaborate and promote a system for recognizing and establishing quality. The Michelin ratings system for hotels and restaurants provides a way in which these businesses can pay money to establish a guarantee of quality. The Appellation Controlée system among French vineyards is another system for establishing quality. Competitions are another way of establishing quality: foodstuffs and books and movies proudly display their prize-winner labels from industry competitions. Such efforts are co-ordinated, collective actions and rely on a critical mass of interested people to get started. All of these initiatives help consumers to avoid having to play the averages, the activity that we know drives the high-quality providers out of the market.

Government minimum-standards regulation represent a second approach.[15] Health and Safety regulations ensure that hotels and restaurants meet at least a baseline standard. Other regulations, such as truth in advertising or the regulations that require foodstuffs to meet content requirements before they can use certain names (a product calling itself cheese must contain dairy products, for instance), also help to keep the more egregious lemons out of the market. Such efforts are limited, and big business mounts a relentless opposition to regulation. While that opposition is often expressed in terms of freedom of action and freedom of choice (regulation removes consumer choice), the effect of deregulation is often to allow lemons to enter a market, and in turn the presence of lemons shifts the averages and can drive out the high-quality providers, leaving the field free for the predictable franchises. The end result of deregulation is often less choice for consumers, because the market for lemons tilts the balance in favour of big, predictable players.

Other efforts to overcome the information gap come from the

consumer side, and provide opportunities for consumers themselves to gain the information needed to make informed choices. The highly successful effort of the Campaign for Real Ale (CAMRA) in the United Kingdom to promote the benefits of independent beer producers and to provide information about the quality of independent beers is an example of how this can work. CAMRA set out to challenge the idea that the British public had somehow "chosen" the poor-quality mass-produced beer it was being served. It is not always clear whether the existence of consumer groups such as CAMRA is simply a healthy part of a market economy or a protest against what the market economy is providing, but one of the founders of the campaign was Trotskyist Roger Protz, who clearly saw his efforts as a challenge to the big companies that were producing most of the beer. The organization's beer festivals, *Good Beer Guide,* and other efforts have had a major impact on the British brewing industry. The CAMRA website asserts: "No new breweries were set up in the UK for the fifty years before we were founded. There are now around 300 new brewers producing real ale, part of a massive real ale revival." In his introduction to the *Good Beer Guide,* Protz states, "In spite of the best efforts of the global brewers who dominate British brewing, there is greater choice today than at any time since the Good Beer Guide was first published in the early 1970s."[16]

It is often seen as elitist to decry the spread of predictable and homogenized culture in any form, but CAMRA's success suggests otherwise – and it poses a dilemma for MarketThink. Was it the case that British beer drinkers in the 1970s preferred the product of global breweries to the efforts of local breweries? The MarketThinkers would claim so, because the big breweries were successful and local breweries were few and far between. If customers wanted small-brewery beer, the market would have provided it. In the post-CAMRA world, is it the case that beer drinkers' tastes have changed? That they now prefer the products of smaller breweries? It becomes clear that there is no such thing as "the market." Instead, there are different kinds of markets, some with wide choices, some with narrow choices. Which one we get may depend on many things, including collective action on the part of consumers. CAMRA's success is all the more surprising because the taste of beer is relatively easy to assess – a single glass is relatively cheap – and thus the pressure of asymmetric information is not as strong as it is with many other products. One of the easiest things that governments can do to promote real choice, as opposed to promoting the choice of ignorance, is to help squeeze the lemons by subsidizing consumer advocacy groups of this type.

The standard MarketThink response to asymmetric information is that even a small number of well-informed consumers – those who read the consumer magazines, check the movie and restaurant reviews, try out an unknown product or establishment and spread the word – act as information arbiters, helping lazier consumers become well informed. Gladwell's *The Tipping Point* is full of examples of such "connectors, mavens, and salesmen." As a result, MarketThink argues that government or anyone else has no need to worry: the market will provide all the necessary choices, with no collective action required. Information will be provided by word of mouth.

But the success of CAMRA demonstrates that there does need to be a critical mass of such people to carry word-of-mouth information, and that this is why the market for experience goods is vulnerable to invasion by high-volume and predictable goods. The cost of information to the uninformed consumer is higher if experts are few and far between, and it is lower if experts are thick on the ground.

For example, let's see how individual choices can work when two kinds of products are available: products that depend on word of mouth for their reputation; and intensively marketed "brand-name" products (see Figure 13). This situation could describe the British beer market (independent breweries and big breweries) and many other markets as well, including fast-food restaurants (small-scale operations and the big chains), movies, and clothing.

The makers of "word-of-mouth" products cannot afford large-scale marketing efforts, which is why they rely instead on word of mouth to spread the news about their offerings. In Figure 13 the sloping line represents the payoff to a consumer for choosing one of these word-of-mouth products. High on the right-hand side of the graph, at

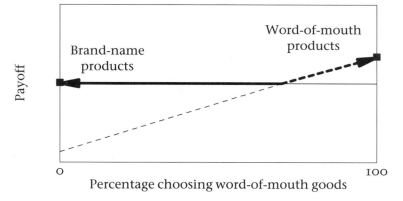

FIGURE 13. Brand-name vs. word-of-mouth products. When these products compete against each other there can be two equilibria. The graph shows a low-information equilibrium on the left and a high-information equilibrium on the right.

the end of the sloping line, is the payoff that comes from choosing a word-of-mouth product when everyone else is also choosing word-of-mouth products. In this case, information is easy to find, and all consumers can reliably get a high-value product based on word-of-mouth information. The payoff is therefore high.

At the lower left side of the graph is the payoff that comes from choosing a word-of-mouth product when hardly anyone else is doing so. In this case, information about quality and value is difficult to come by, because word-of-mouth information is scarce or non-existent. Consumers who nevertheless decide to select a word-of-mouth product have two possible options. One option is to make the effort to obtain reliable information. In that case the cost of the effort has to be subtracted from the payoff obtained by choosing the product, leading to a low total payoff. A second option is to choose without investing the effort, in which case the market for lemons scenario comes into play: consumers could end up with a poor-quality product, with a low payoff once again. Either way, then, the word-of-mouth product line slopes downwards to the left side of the graph.

The horizontal line in the middle of the graph represents the payoff that comes from choosing a brand-name product. There is no problem of finding information about these products: intensive promotion means that most people know, whether they want to or not, more or less what to expect from these products. The payoff does not depend on word of mouth, which has nothing to add to this case, and thus it is the same on both sides of the graph.

There is an interesting similarity here to the choice of which nightclub to go to (Figure 11). As in the choice of nightclub, this one also has two equilibria. One is a "high-information" equilibrium, at the right side of the graph, representing the case in which active word of mouth keeps quality high among independent producers. The second is the "low-information" equilibrium, at the left side of the graph, representing the case in which almost all consumers are choosing a brand-name product and a paucity of word of mouth – or none at all – makes asymmetric information an issue for consumers.

The point at which the lines cross is a tipping point. To the right of this point, the best option is to choose a word-of-mouth product. By making this choice you become informed yourself, and the choice adds to the informal systems of local expertise that sustain and ensure good quality among the producers of these goods. Successive choices by a group of consumers "slide up the line" to the high-information equilibrium at the right of the graph. To the left of the tipping point, the best option is to choose a brand-name product. By making this choice, you opt out of the word-of-mouth market and thereby make information about word-of-mouth products a little harder to find. Successive choices by consumers "slide along the line" to the low-information equilibrium at the left side of the graph, driving independent producers out of the market and leaving us with a choice between lemons and a predictable product.

Once again, if brand-name companies invest in a heavy marketing push or (in the case of a large-scale franchise operation) an intensive construction effort, they may be able to move consumers to the left side of the tipping point. If they can do this we end up living in a low-information world in which choosing brand-name products is the best choice. In this low-information world brand-name products,

with their promise of predictability, make us collectively more ignorant and leave us with the worse of the two equilibria. In such a
world, the only way of moving to the high-information equilibrium
is to make a collective effort to improve word of mouth (as CAMRA
did for British beer) or to find other ways of making the cost of information low.

In any one case, of course, there will be more to the story than
shown in this graph. In the case of cultural products, for example,
watching the same movie as your friends are watching brings increasing returns. In the case of fast-food chains, economies of scale come
into play. And not all consumers face the same sloping line when it
comes to word of mouth: those surrounded by wine enthusiasts, for
instance, will find it easier to distinguish good wine from bad, as long
as there are enough enthusiasts to keep the good wineries in business.
In the real world, as opposed to the simplified world shown on the
graph, a brand-name product will also reach part of its market
through word of mouth, and word-of-mouth and brand-name products will co-exist. Still, given these variances, the basic mechanism
illustrated here is shaping our outcomes and confounding today's
widespread faith in markets.

The market for lemons shines a light on the commonly heard
disparagement of anti-globalization protesters as elitists who would
deny others the right to choose. In a widely quoted piece on the subject, Paul Krugman tells readers that "Nobody forces you to eat at
McDonald's." He says that although the activists opposed to globalization in general and the World Trade Organization in particular

> talk of freedom and democracy, their key demand is that individuals be
> prevented from getting what they want – that governments be free, nay
> encouraged, to deny individuals the right to drive cars, work in offices,
> eat cheeseburgers, and watch satellite TV. Why? Presumably because
> people will really be happier if they retain their traditional "language,
> dress, and values." Thus, Spaniards would be happier if they still
> dressed in black and let narrow-minded priests run their lives, and resi-
> dents of the American South would be happier if planters still sipped

mint juleps, wore white suits, and accepted traditional deference from sharecroppers ... instead of living in this "dreary" modern world in which Madrid is just like Paris and Atlanta is just like New York.

Well, somehow I suspect that the residents of Madrid and Atlanta, while they may regret some loss of tradition, prefer modernity. And you know what? I think the rest of the world has the right to make the same choice.[17]

Krugman argues that multinational companies have broadened our choices and are giving us what we want. But, as Figure 13 shows, when global franchises use their monetary power to replace networks of informed consumers with media-based advertising, they make us collectively more ignorant. The market does not respond to our preferences, it responds to our choices, and these are two different things. In this case as in so many others, the logic of individual choice does not give us what we want.

chapter ten

FREE TO CHOOSE, BUT EXPLOITED

ONE PARTICULAR KIND OF CHOICE is the decision to exchange or trade one thing for another, such as money for goods. Exchange seems like a straightforward thing, but many of our notions of exchange are based on what happens between relatively equal participants. When the participants are of very different status, exchange becomes a little more complicated.

By definition exchange is a voluntary transaction, and so it would seem that power has little to do with it. Even when consumers buy something from a monopoly, they always have the choice of not buying: there is no compulsion in the act of exchange. But then again, power can be effectively exercised without the need for coercion, and when participants are of very different status the line between what is voluntary and what is involuntary gets blurred, and power enters the equation even when there is no explicit compulsion at work. Indeed, voluntary exchange and exploitation can exist hand in hand.

Power, Relationships, and Context

The word "power" can be used in different ways and different contexts. Here I am concentrating on the idea of power imbalance, or one person's power over another. In this use of the word, a person cannot be powerful without someone or something being in a corresponding position of powerlessness. In a sexist society, a man who is a bottom-rung employee during the day may still be "head of the household" at night. Is he powerful or powerless? In and of himself, he is neither. In relation to his employer, he is powerless; in relation to his wife, he is powerful. We often speak of giant corporations as "powerful," but if we are to understand the mechanisms of power we must be more precise. The power of a company with respect to its employees is one thing; that with respect to its suppliers another; that with respect to its competitors another still; and that with respect to its customers yet one more. Power emerges from the interactions between people.

But power is not just a relationship; it is a relationship in a specific *context*, and in some cases the context can determine what happens as much as the relationship itself, and can lead to surprising outcomes. Just as the prisoner's dilemma is a situation that muddles the idea of preference by preventing perfectly good individual choices from being turned into happy outcomes, so too do other situations muddle the idea of power by preventing the apparently powerful from exploiting the apparently powerless. We have seen that game theory provides a way of approaching questions in which the structure of the situation is important, and we have seen that the equilibrium of these games is not always what we might expect. We can apply the same kind of thinking to questions of power as we do to questions of preference.

In *The Selfish Gene* Richard Dawkins describes a particularly dramatic illustration of how context can change power relations.[1] He describes an experiment in which two domestic pigs were placed in a large sty where they could get food by pressing a lever with their snout. In this experiment, when the lever was pressed at one end of the sty, a trough at the other end dispensed a serving of food. The pig had to press the lever and then race to the other end of the sty to eat. The experimenters chose their pigs such that one of the pair was "dominant" over the other. The surprising result was that the subordinate pig ended up getting more food than the dominant pig: the power relationships were turned upside down.

To see why this is so, we need to think of the problem from each pig's point of view. If the subordinate pig pushes the lever and runs to the trough, the dominant pig will already be there and will prevent the weaker pig from eating. As a result, the subordinate pig soon gives up pressing the lever, and neither pig gets any food.

If the dominant pig pushes the lever, the subordinate pig gets to eat until its bigger sty-mate arrives to push it out of the way. The subordinate pig has an incentive to wait by the trough, because it gets at least some food. The dominant pig has an incentive to push the lever, because it also gets at least some food. This arrangement is an equilibrium. The arrangement that the subordinate pig pushes the lever is not an equilibrium, because the pig can improve its outcome unilaterally by not wasting its time pushing the lever.

This surprising equilibrium holds even when the sty is long enough that the subordinate pig gets almost all of the food, as long as there is some left for the dominant pig to eat when it arrives at the trough. So the subordinate pig ends up "reclining idly by the trough" and eating heartily, while the dominant pig does the work of pushing the lever, running back and forth across the sty, and collecting the leftover food. Hardly a picture of dominance.

Choosing Stability

Power is usually associated with the ability to coerce, but just as the dominant pig may end up eating less than the subordinate pig, so too are there circumstances in which the powerful end up helping those they can coerce, even when the powerful are governed by purely selfish motives.

Until now we have been concerned only with situations in which people or other actors have choices to make. We have not investigated the possibilities of one party forcing the other to take one action rather than another, and yet such coercion is commonplace in the real world. It is time to look at interactions that are coercive.[2]

Consider a band of bandits roaming from town to town, taking whatever they want. Each time the bandits plunder a town there are two effects: the bandits become richer, and the citizens of the plundered town are made poorer.

Roving bandits have only a short-term relationship, if that is the word, with any town through which they pass. There is no incentive for the bandits to hold back in the extent to which they plunder, because they have no interest in the health or otherwise of the town.

Successful bandits can effectively conquer a territory, graduating from bandits to warlords. Instead of stealing from a town once only, they become entrenched in some geographic area and extort money from it on a regular basis, as a tax or perhaps as a protection fee. At this stage there is a change in the dynamic of the relationship between the warlords and the citizens of the area. An impoverished and starving citizenry can provide little in the way of taxes, so the warlords now have an interest in the continuing prosperity of the area they rule. Even purely self-interested warlords may cut back on the rate at which they extort the citizens of their territory so as to maximize their long-term income. Just as in the repeated prisoner's dilemma, there is a tension between the short term (take as much as possible right now) and the long term (restrain the takings in order to get more later). The shadow of the future plays a role here as well, and it forces a more co-operative relationship than if things were seen only in the short term.

Feng Yu-hsiang was a roving bandit in 1920s China who made the move to stationary warlord. As Mancur Olson describes him, he "was noted for the exceptional extent to which he used his army for suppressing thievery and for his defeat of a notorious roving bandit called White Wolf. Apparently, most people in Feng's domain wanted him to stay as warlord and greatly preferred him to the roving bandits."[3]

Here again it is the structure of the situation that gives rise to the outcome, rather than the nature of the warlord or of the citizenry.

Once the shadow of the future comes into play, the outcome improves for both warlord and population. As Olson says, warlords have an incentive to "use their power, at least to some degree, in accord with the social interest, even when serving the public good was not part of the intention." Olson calls this unintended consequence the "second invisible hand," complementing Adam Smith's "invisible hand" of the market.

Individual thieves have no influence over the area in which they ply their profession, while organized crime, aspiring to a monopoly on crime in an area, would prefer a prosperous neighbourhood with more money available for the taking. As a result individual thieves engage in burglary, while organized crime relies on protection rackets. Individual thieves will add to the level of lawlessness in an area, by definition, while organized crime will exert efforts to crack down on crime other than their own in order to provide fertile grounds for their own activities.

Olson's recognition of the "second invisible hand" blurs the line between coercive and voluntary acts. We have seen that, properly framed, supposedly free individual choices can lead to inequality (that is, to one set of people gaining considerable wealth while others gain nothing) and that the free-rider problem can mean that many people are saddled with unfavourable laws even under democracy. Here we see that even when the members of one party have the ability to take whatever they want from others, circumstances exist in which that ability will not be exercised and autocrats will, purely out of self-interest, provide public goods. The stability that ruthless autocrats rely on to maximize their own wealth is something that may be valued by their subjects.

To point out that autocracies can provide public goods for their people is not to claim that autocracies are fine societies to live in; just that we must not be too surprised if people appreciate the benefits of stability. Mussolini may have been a dictator, but he famously made the trains run on time. Saddam Hussein ruled brutally, but the rate of violent death has increased during the lawless years following his overthrow.

Choosing to Be Exploited

Choices have costs, which are commonly called *transaction costs*. If a pig farm sets up at the end of your street, you have the right to move house, but making that choice comes with a cost: moving house is an expensive proposition. If your employer treats you unfairly you can always move to another job, but a job search is often a lengthy and uncertain process.

The popular renditions of MarketThink usually gloss over the issue of transaction costs. If you are unhappy in your job, you should get a new one. If you are unhappy with a purchase, you should return it and buy somewhere else. If you are unhappy with your apartment, you should just move. Still, the nugget of truth at the heart of Market-Think is that the ability of consumers to walk away is a valuable one. In a competitive market in which transaction costs are close to zero, consumers do have a source of real power.

But as transaction costs increase, so too does the power associated with the ability to walk away decrease. If companies can find a way of imposing a cost on the decision of a consumer to switch to another product or service, the balance of power in that relationship also switches. Even small transaction costs can lead to a significant power imbalance.

To take this further, it could be argued that there is a continuum of choices, from free exchange to compulsion, that carry different transaction costs. If you are imprisoned it is because you have chosen not to pay the cost of escaping (bribing the guard, perhaps). If you live in a cruel dictatorship it is because you have chosen to remain rather than to pay the cost of fleeing into exile: after all, refugees who do flee dictatorships are plentiful, so the choice does exist even if it is risky. Regional barons or warlords who persecute their populace more than they do their neighbours will face an exodus to surrounding domains. At the other end of the spectrum, if you choose to go and buy something at a neighbouring store, it still costs you time and effort to go there.

The MarketThink worldview divides society into two components: the market and the state. In this view, the market is the world of choices and voluntary exchange, while the state has a monopoly in force. The existence of transaction costs shows that such a black-and-white picture is oversimplified. There is a continuum of transaction costs from freedom to dictatorship, from free choice to coerced acquiescence. Even powerful states have limits on their ability to compel – as illustrated by the existence of pervasive black markets in the Eastern bloc countries during the time of the Soviet government – while we are all subject to some forms of compulsion by private industry, from workplace rules to security guards at the shopping mall. We can, then, speak of power in modern industrial societies, despite the apparent lack of coercion, in just the same way we can speak of power in autocracies.

Free Exchange as Exploitation

MarketThink claims that in the absence of coercion, interactions in our society are mutually beneficial exchanges that need no external enforcing mechanisms or regulations. If these exchanges were not mutually beneficial, the argument goes, then one or the other of the parties would walk away and the exchange would not happen; therefore the exchanges that do happen must be mutually beneficial.

The prototype exchange is that of the consumer purchase, but the idea of a free exchange goes beyond consumer transactions. According to MarketThink, the employer and employee are equal participants in an exchange. Landlord and tenant, insurer and insured, contractor and contractee, bank and loan applicant: all, according to the theory, are relationships based on an exchange that is of more or less equal benefit to both parties. Internationally, arrangements between nations, companies and governments, and the IMF and debtor nations are all relations of exchange. What keeps the otherwise powerful in check is not good intentions, but the market – the ability of either party to walk away.

Many cases exist in which economies of scale or other factors such as network economics or fashion-driven purchases guarantee that an industry will be dominated by one player or a few major players. In such a situation the option to buy somewhere else is limited: think of buying cable-TV, airline tickets, or word-processing software; or think of working in a mining town or an oil town in which a single employer dominates the labour market. These examples involve choices that as consumers we are most likely to make with a feeling of resentment: we grumble as we accept the cable-TV bundle, we grumble about the price of gasoline, but we pay up anyway. And Market-Think argues that even exchanges with monopolists (with the exception of the government) are still mutually beneficial: that while we may not have the option of buying elsewhere, we do still have the option of not buying at all. Gary S. Becker and Guity Nashat Becker describe exchange as "the bedrock of the market system – that shopkeepers and consumers, workers and management, or suppliers and customers do not voluntarily make a deal unless both sides expect to benefit."[4]

Increasing returns may make it difficult for us to find alternatives to Microsoft Windows, but it is still true that no one makes you buy a computer. By entering into the exchange we have demonstrated that we gain by it, and so there is clearly no coercion happening, and therefore we have nothing to complain about. Yet others would argue that to buy Microsoft Windows is to come under the sway of Microsoft's evil empire. So which is it? When we enter into deals with oligopolies and monopolies, are we exploited or are we partners in a mutually beneficial exchange?

The answer is, both and neither. It is a false dichotomy. We have seen how limitations to choice are not on/off switches, but are a gradual restriction as a function of increasing transaction costs. In a similar fashion, as the partners in an exchange move along an axis from equality to inequality, the exchange itself moves from equal bargaining to exploitation, even when no explicit coercion takes place.

This is a bit abstract, so let's get concrete. Let's look at a dramatic example of individual choice in the face of a monopoly.

One of the characters in Stephen Frears's film *Dirty Pretty Things* trades fake passports and immigration papers to illegal immigrants in exchange for one of their organs – a kidney, perhaps. He then sells the organ so that it can be used in transplant operations. When accused of exploiting immigrants, the character defends his actions:

> You give me your kidney, I give you a new identity. I sell the kidney for ten grand, so I'm happy. The person who needs the kidney gets cured. So, he's happy. The person who sold his kidney gets to stay in this beautiful country, so he's happy. My whole business is based on happiness.[5]

From the organ-trader's point of view, there is no coercion here, simply free exchange that makes each participant better off. Granted, in his presentation the organ-trader glosses over the danger of the operation, but he also has power even in the absence of compulsion. The source of his power is that he has a monopoly on something that the illegal immigrants desperately want.

This kind of story prompts us to ask about the boundary between choice and coercion, and about the boundary between legitimate bargaining and illegitimate exploitation. Most of us would agree that there is something wrong in the exchange of bodily organs for immigration papers, and that there would still be something wrong even if the organ-trader speaks the truth when he says that the operation is as safe as a visit to the dentist: and yet the argument of the organ-trader is hard to dismiss. It is true that the immigrant could simply opt not to make the trade. The exchange is what economists call "Pareto efficient": both players are made better off by it, and the exchange could not be improved without making at least one of them worse off.

Dirty Pretty Things is a fictional film, but decisions such as these are not merely fictional. Poor people make desperate decisions every day, and some of these become subjects for debate. Is prostitution a free exchange? What about surrogate motherhood? Child labour in Third World countries? Immigrant workers leaving their families to find jobs? Addicts buying drugs on the street? Taking a high-interest loan to tide you over to your next paycheque? Poor countries accepting toxic waste from rich countries? All, we could argue, are free exchanges. All, we could argue, are exploitative. The answer is that they are both.

Most of us feel uneasy about such exchanges, even when faced with the argument that the alternative (no exchange) would be worse for both participants. The root cause of our uneasiness is that the exchanges are made between manifestly unequal participants, and in such exchanges the distribution of the benefits conforms to the so-called Matthew effect: those that are already rich get most (see chapter 8). In game theory this result is called the Nash bargaining solution – referring to the John Nash who developed the concept of equilibrium that is the basis of modern game theory and whose life is described in Sylvia Nasar's *A Beautiful Mind* (later made into a movie).[6] Nash showed that the outcome of bargaining between two people (or, of course, other players such as corporations) depends on their "disagreement point," or the ease with which they can walk away from the situation: that is, on exactly that ability to walk away that consumers are supposed to have in a competitive market. The player who can walk away more easily is in the stronger bargaining position, and gets most of the benefit: the weaker player gets the scraps.

The Nash bargaining solution suggests that when a wealthy company hires a poor labourer, the position of both may be improved, but the already wealthy company will gain almost all of the benefit of this trade, while the poor labourer will find his or her own situation improved by just a small amount.

In the case of *Dirty Pretty Things*, the organ-trader likes his £10,000, but he doesn't need the money nearly as badly as the illegal immigrants need their papers, so he is in a position to turn his back on them if they refuse his offer. In the case of buying addictive drugs, the cost to the consumer of choosing not to buy is high, and it is widely accepted that the exchange is not free. In the case of customers buying Microsoft Windows or a cable-TV contract, the deal similarly carries a cost of walking away that leaves the customer open to exploitation.

★

The reason that we are dismayed by the outcomes of so-called "free exchanges" between unequal actors is that at some point we come to believe that the situation is no longer one that calls for bargaining. It is instead a situation that calls for altruistic action. And here the MarketThink picture of free exchange falls down: whether we acknowledge it or not, almost all of us at some point turn away from the idea and reject it.

Imagine, for example, that Jill sets out from Whimsley for a long walk one day, and at dusk she is out on the hills far from anywhere. Then she stumbles, not just down a hill but down an abandoned mineshaft. Fortunately she is not harmed, but she cannot get out by herself. She calls out, but no one hears her. Her predicament is dire. Night falls, and the next day dawns. Still no one hears her.

But the next day Jack also sets out for a walk, and takes a route that Jill showed him when they lived together; the same route Jill took the day before. Jack passes by the mineshaft. He hears the calls from within the mine, and stops. He could help Jill out, but he doesn't have to do it for free. He offers to help her out for a price of $10,000 and sends down a contract to that effect. Jill signs, reckoning that she would rather pay $10,000 than be left to die. Jack helps her out and ultimately collects the money.

What is wrong here, most of us would agree, is that Jill's predicament becomes a matter for bargaining. Given a situation of desperate straits, we tend to believe that the appropriate response is to help, not to bargain. Free exchange with someone as vulnerable as Jill is in this case is tantamount to robbery, a way of thinking that has been recognized for centuries – indeed, built into laws that protect people in positions of vulnerability from high-interest money lenders, for instance – but that is now becoming questionable again in the atmosphere of free-market logic.

Why we hold this belief is complicated and bound up in ethics, and this is not a book on ethics. Part of it, however, is surely that we believe a society in which vulnerable people are treated the way Jack treats Jill is not a society we want to live in. We can all imagine being in Jill's place, and we know that we would like to be helped rather than having to become indebted because of an accident. Also, we recognize that a society that treats its weakest members in the way that Jack treated Jill is likely to end up in a bad way, with a large class of irrevocably poor and desperate people who have no prospect of any but the slightest improvement in their state. Morality in this situation becomes a cultural norm that helps to maintain a healthy society.

So there is a transition here, somewhere along the spectrum, in which free exchange becomes exploitation. Although MarketThink purists could argue that Jack has not taken anything from Jill, and that the organ-trader has not taken anything from the immigrants, most of us would agree that what has happened is a form of theft.

The dynamics of bargaining, or of exchange among unequals, shows how exploitation can take place even within a framework of what is apparently free choice. Then again, we know too about the possibility of collective action among the more cohesive groups in society – which are also the groups with the most resources and the most access to the corridors of power – and how this possibility lets them fix the rules of the game itself. It is only to be expected that they will use this ability to move choices into the realm of "free exchange," knowing that they will benefit most. What looks like free exchange, individual choice, and the market is instead plunder. And that is what the trends in inequality suggest: almost all the gains in wealth during the last two decades have gone to those at the top.

Free exchange is entirely compatible with exploitation and plunder. Meanwhile, autocracy is compatible with stability and even the provision of public goods. How, then, to distinguish one from the other? This is not just a question of tricky wording, it is a question of what kind of society we actually live in. It suggests that the formal structure of democracy and free markets is not enough to rule out exploitation and plunder – characteristics usually associated with repressive regimes.

chapter eleven

BEYOND WHIMSLEY

IN AN IMPORTANT SERIES OF PAPERS, Rachel Kranton and George Akerlof (the latter of "market for lemons" fame) made one of the more successful efforts to apply game theory ideas to complex social questions – in particular setting out to broaden the "utility" that the players of their games maximize by incorporating into it the idea of "identity."[1] Taking the idea of identity from the disciplines of psychology and sociology, Akerlof and Kranton postulated that each of us carries around a *self-image*, in the form of an internalized set of prescriptions of how "a person like us" should behave under certain circumstances, and that our choices are ways of expressing who we are.

There is no need to posit a single source for this self-image: social conventions and expectations, internal psychological factors, genetic makeup – any and all of these produce our self-image. Whatever its source, if we violate the set of prescriptions that govern our identity, we experience an anxiety that game theory expresses as a cost: it reduces the utility that we would otherwise gain from the choice that produces this anxiety. Gender roles are an obvious example of how self-image can influence the choices that people make. A man who chooses an < option that society regards as feminine can experience a sense of anxiety, because it damages his image of his own "manliness." Similarly a woman might experience anxiety if she acts in a way that society says "a good mother" should not act.

Such considerations start to take us away from the formulaic, one-dimensional characters of Whimsley and, more importantly, of standard economics textbooks. They bring us closer to the real world. What's more, these ideas shine a new light on a whole set of real-world behaviours that have commonly been seen as "self-sabotaging choices" (property destruction in ghetto riots, for instance) or as genetic predisposition (women who abandon prestigious career paths), and show that these may be perfectly rational responses to social exclusion. But these responses do not lead to good outcomes.

The Ultimatum Game

The "ultimatum game" is one of those things that game theorists like to explore. So seemingly trivial it can hardly be called a game, it is even simpler than the prisoner's dilemma. According to Martin Nowak, Karen Page, and Karl Sigmund, it goes like this: "Two players have to agree on how to split a sum of money. The proposer makes an offer. If the responder accepts, the deal goes ahead. If the responder rejects, neither player gets anything. In both cases, the game is over."[2]

Many economists argue that the only rational action of the responder is to accept any offer given. Let's say the players are asked to split $10, with offers allowed in increments of $1. As Sigmund, Ernst Fehr, and Nowak explain it:

> The only rational option for a selfish responder is to accept any offer. Even $1 is better than nothing. A selfish proposer who is sure that the responder is also selfish will therefore make the smallest possible offer and keep the rest. This game-theory analysis, which assumes that people are selfish and rational, tells you that the proposer should offer the

smallest possible share [$1] and the responder should accept it. But this is not how most people play the game.[3]

In real life – and the game has been tried out in many cultures in many places around the world – about half of the responders reject offers below 30 per cent, so that neither party gets any money at all. What is more, proposers often recognize this likelihood and make surprisingly generous offers, with the majority of them offering 40 to 50 per cent.

So what is happening here? Are humans being irrational in making such high offers and in refusing low offers? Or is our idea of rationality mixed up?

The answer lies in the utility function that most of us maximize. The assertion that "even $1 is better than nothing" insists that the monetary payoff in the game is the only outcome that individuals care about. But such an action is only "rational" (that is, utility-maximizing) if utility is the same as money. Once we accept that a player's utility may include some aspect of self-image, we can see why rejecting a low offer can make personal sense. As Jon Elster points out, "People have material interests, but they also have a need to see themselves as not motivated exclusively by material interest."[4] Accepting a low offer would impose a cost on our self-image (am I the type of person who can be bought that cheaply?) that is just as real as the money being offered, and that at some point outweighs that offer.

One way of thinking about this problem is to imagine the construction of a game in two stages. The first stage is to construct what we might call a "bare" game, which is a game in which utility and money are the same thing and there is no account taken of identity or other interpersonal utilities. The second stage is to add the effects of identity to the mix to "dress" the outcomes and so produce the real-world version of the game being played.

We can see how this works in the case of the ultimatum game, which I further simplify here in order represent it more clearly. In this version, the players are given $10 to share, but the proposer has only two possibilities: offer an even split or offer the responder a token amount of only $1. The game is a little different to the other two-player games that we have seen so far in that it is sequential: instead of both players making their moves simultaneously, the proposer moves first, followed by the responder. We can still represent the game as a two-by-two matrix, but we must remember that the moves have to take place in order.

| | | PROPOSER | |
		Even Split	Token Offer
	Accept	P $5, R $5	**P $9, R $1**
RESPONDER			
	Reject	P $0, R $0	P $0, R $0

FIGURE 14. The bare ultimatum game, with only two proposals allowed. The proposer's outcome is marked as P, the responder's as R. The equilibrium outcome is marked in bold.

Figure 14 shows the possible outcomes for this case. If money and utility are the same, the responder would accept even the token proposal, and so the equilibrium is for the proposer to offer a single dollar to the responder. The proposer cannot improve this outcome by her or his own actions, and the responder cannot improve it either.

The second stage is to construct a "dressed" game, in which the responder sees the token offer as an affront (see Figure 15). To accept the token offer would damage the self-image of the responder, to the tune of, say, 2 units. Knowing that a token offer would be rejected so that neither player gets anything, the best option for the proposer is to offer an equitable split so that each gets $5 rather than nothing.

PROPOSER

		Even Split	Token Offer
	Accept	**P 5, R 5**	P 9, R -1
RESPONDER			
	Reject	P 0, R 0	P 0, R 0

FIGURE 15. The dressed ultimatum game, with only two proposals allowed. The proposer's outcome is marked as P, the responder's as R. The equilibrium outcome is marked in bold.

All real-world games are "dressed." The underlying private evaluations of costs and benefits are inevitably and unavoidably covered up by our own moral codes, the expectations of society, and personal likes and dislikes, among other things. The choices in this game are not irrational; they just have a richer utility function. The results are not unique to this game, of course, but apply across the board: research into how people really play these simplified games and why goes back to Anatol Rapoport, who carried out extensive studies of how people play the prisoner's dilemma.[5]

Jill Hits the Ceiling

Now let's look at a slightly more elaborate case in which identity again plays a crucial role.

Jill is looking to move from her job in the backrooms of Whimsley Bank, an investment concern, onto the testosterone-charged floor of the trading room. She evaluates the costs and benefits of the move, and meanwhile her boss is also thinking about the possibility of moving Jill. We'll see what both are thinking.

In listing the factors that Jill and her boss take into account when making their decisions, we will follow Kranton and Akerlof and go further in incorporating the effects of identity. They suggest that one player's actions may influence not only that person's own self-image but also the self-images of others around them. As a result there is a possibility that those other players may respond by rejecting the first player in order to restore their own identities.

For example, a woman undertaking something traditionally seen as a "man's job" may challenge the self-images of the men holding that job: they may feel that the masculine qualities of their job, something that they feel proud of being able to do, are compromised if a woman can do the job just as well. They may respond by rejecting the woman in order to preserve their own self-identities. Someone from a lower social class who embarks on a prestigious career may influence the self-images of those left behind, who may in response accuse that person of having "ideas above their station."

First, let's listen to Jill as she considers her options.

- *Money*. I know there is more money to be made on the trading floor than there is here in my backroom job. That's worth 2 points to me.
- *Challenge*. If I get a transfer, I expect the new job to be more challenging. That is worth something too: I'll assign the new job an extra 2 points.
- *Self-image*. I do feel uncomfortable at the prospect of being immersed in the masculine world of the trading floor. I may have to act more "like a man," and I may have to "squeeze the female part of [me] into a box, put on the lid, and tuck it away."[6] In short, there will be a cost to my feminine identity. I assign the new job a value of minus 3 for this damage to my self-image.
- *Welcome*. I am a bit worried about the welcome I'll receive. Will I be seen as challenging the masculinity of the floor? If I act masculine, will I be seen by my new co-workers as pushy? And will they reject me in response?[7] I assess this risk as worth a cost of minus 2.

If she takes the job, Jill will gain 4 points from the challenge and salary, but will lose 5 from the combination of her loss of self-image and her concern at the reception she will receive. So her best move is to stay put. She decides not to take the job.

Let's look a little closer at Jill's motives in avoiding the trading floor. First, she likes the idea of the job in a strict sense – she believes that she has what it takes to do it and that she would like doing it. But a job is not simply a collection of tasks. The conventional business world says that this job requires certain characteristics: aggression, competitiveness, decisiveness, risk-taking, even courage. In short, according to that world, it takes balls. There is a whole culture here that Jill is going to become a part of, and it is not a culture she is accustomed to. This is where the question of identity comes in. Everyone has a certain self-image, and along with that self-image comes a set of expected behaviours. If she were to move into this masculine world, Jill would run counter to those behaviours, and the idea of this makes her uncomfortable. She would risk losing her identity. The same may be true for a man taking a job as a nurse or kindergarten teacher, or for a woman becoming a firefighter. A lot of this is purely cultural, and not part of the job – it used to be that bank tellers and psychology professors were male, and things can change – but the costs associated with self-image are just as much a part of Jill's decision as the salary is.

The second reason is a fear of rejection. This is Jill's assessment of the likely reaction to her. By moving into this world and demonstrating that it can be done by a woman she would be challenging and threatening the self-image of the male traders. She realizes that they would feel a little less sure of the masculinity that their profession supposedly requires. There is a cost to the traders associated with Jill's entry into their world. There is a chance that the cost to the existing traders of driving her out would be less than the cost to them of tolerating her and possibly feeling less manly.

Jill's choice has consequences that go beyond her own career and has an impact on the prospects of other women. As a result of Jill's choice the trading floor remains a predominantly masculine environment, a place that continues to be unappealing to other women who consider a move there. The arrangement with "all men on the trading floor" is an equilibrium from which we cannot escape through individual choice alone.

★

Now let's look at the decision from the point of view of the bank. It is, after all, a commonplace MarketThink assertion that the market will force firms to eradicate hiring practices based on anything other than merit. Is there an incentive for the bank to put Jill on the trading floor? Jill's male boss looks at things this way:

- *Performance.* I'm sure Jill could do the job well. That is, she could carry out the tasks associated with the job: she has the motivation, the skills, and the experience to do the job. I'll assign her anticipated good performance a value of 3 points compared to her nearest competitor (who is male).
- *Team Performance.* As a responsible manager, I am worried about the atmosphere on the team if Jill joins. I'm concerned that her presence would disrupt the good-natured, if sometimes coarse, camaraderie that does so much to encourage hard work on the part of the team members. If Jill's presence does disrupt the atmosphere, it may make a difference of minus 1 point per team member, and there are currently ten people on the team.
- *Rejection.* The team may recover their spirit by rejecting Jill. The cost of such actions would be 5 points, spread across the team. In addition, if the team does take such action, they will detract from Jill's performance, to the tune of 4 points.

Looking at these possibilities, the manager decides that whether or not the team acts against her, adding Jill to the trading floor will not improve the performance of the team. And if they do act against her, things will be worse still. Purely in the interests of the bank, he decides to hire her nearest competitor instead. Given the environment, even if the best candidate is female any bank that moves women onto the trading floor will suffer in comparison to its competitors.

So whether Jill makes the decision or her boss makes the decision, the equilibrium outcome at Whimsley Bank is for the trading floor to be all-male. Being the equilibrium does not mean it is a good outcome, though. It may be that it is one of several possible equilibria, some of which could have better outcomes. For example, an all-women trading floor could be another equilibrium: if the trading floor were full of women, Jill would suffer neither the loss of identity nor the fear of rejection, and she would decide to move. Meanwhile, men may fear that it would be unmanly to take a trading-floor job if all the traders there are women. And if the tipping point for acceptability is less than 50 per cent of the population, then there will be equilibria, as there are in many professions, consisting of a mix of both genders: in which there are sufficient from both sexes to make the profession welcoming for both male and female newcomers. But, of course, moving from one equilibrium to another requires a change sufficient to reach the tipping point of a self-sustaining population of women: it requires a co-ordinated and collective action. The existing equilibrium is a fine outcome for the existing male traders, at the cost of the self-excluding female potential traders.

The role of sexism here is subtle. All the external world sees is that Jill does not apply for the job and there are, after all, several possible reasons for this decision. Perhaps she knows she "doesn't have what it takes." Perhaps she isn't qualified. Perhaps she values her home life too much. But we have the privilege of knowing her thought processes and as a result we know that, even though she could do the job, even though she knows she could do the job, even though she wants the pay and status that would come with the job, she is excluding herself from it and remaining in her relative ghetto. There is no need for the bank to discriminate and no need for the men of the trading floor to do anything other than demonstrate their masculine solidarity in order to frighten off intruders. Jill's self-exclusion is not a bad choice: we have seen that it is the best choice available to her in the circumstances, and that she makes it for good reasons. But the end result of the good individual choices of the women at her bank is a bad set of outcomes for each and every one of them: the persistence of segregation and exclusion.

Choosing to Reject

Identity, in one form or another, is a strong motivational factor in many decisions. Taking account of identity helps us to move beyond the simplistic association of utility and money. It is, for example, simply not true that money is the only, or even perhaps the major, motivator of workplace performance. One strong motivator is that some people identify themselves as skilled professionals. They work hard and carefully because producing a good product bolsters their self-image. As we have seen, identity can also hold people back in their progress at work.

Identity plays a role in other contexts also. One that Akerlof and Kranton explore is that of apparently self-destructive behaviour such as vandalism in poor and socially excluded communities.[8] Members of such a community can take one of two attitudes to the dominant culture: they can adopt it (despite not being a part of it) or oppose it.

Those who adopt the dominant culture face the same dilemmas that Jill faced: dominant groups often identify themselves by exclusionary criteria, and the pursuit of a career that is traditionally associated with the dominant group comes at a cost of compromising or losing one's original identity. What's more, the dominant group may respond by excluding those from outside who attempt to adopt their culture, and those in the excluded community who oppose the dominant culture may make life difficult for those who adopt it.

Those who oppose the dominant culture are also faced with a dilemma. The prescriptions for the oppositional identity may involve antisocial or criminal activity that maintains their oppositional identity only at an economic cost to themselves and those around them.

Such a picture leads to several possible equilibria. One is for all members of the excluded community to adopt the dominant culture. Another is for all members of the community to oppose the dominant culture. A third is a mixed equilibrium that includes some of each identity.

The "all adopt" equilibrium may appear to be the "best"

outcome, but it is viable only when the dominant group does not reject the excluded group. If the cost of adopting the dominant culture brings with it a loss of identity and a continued exclusion from that culture, the individually "best choice" may be to instead oppose the culture. The option to adopt the dominant culture is most likely to be pursued when there are significant career opportunities for large numbers of people from the excluded group.

If adopting the identity of the dominant culture and choosing its associated prescriptions yield few such opportunities for advancement, the equilibrium outcome is one in which some or all of the excluded community reject the dominant culture and adopt an identity that has different sources of validation.

For example, Akerlof and Kranton describe disruption by Mexican-American male students in a West Texas high school, quoting the only such student whose family had made it into the middle class: "We were really angry about the way the teachers treated us. They looked down on us and never really tried to help us. A lot of us were real smart kids, but we never figured that the school was going to do anything for us."[9]

In that kind of environment an individual Mexican-American student has two choices: to adopt the school-promoted identity and follow its prescriptions – working hard, being obedient, and so on – or to reject it. If individual students figure that the school is not going to do anything for them, then adopting the prescribed identity gains them nothing and they risk being seen as a traitor by others who reject the school. But adopting the oppositional culture and following its prescriptions – provoking fights with students of other schools at away football games, breaking rules regarding alcohol, illegal drugs, and smoking – can provide them with a sense of integrity, and at the same time they avoid the cost of rejection by peers.

The choice is not, though, simply a matter of peer pressure. While the reaction of other Mexican-American students is part of the picture, it is only one part. Other factors in the choice are the reaction of the school authorities and the internal sense of self, dictated in part by the existing school dynamic. Choosing what seems to the outside world to be self-destructive behaviour becomes a rational response to a high degree of exclusion.

A Backward Glance

This book is based on the idea that a good or "rational" choice is one that provides the most of something that is called "utility," but throughout it has specified that "utility" in different ways. This is deliberate, because utility means different things to different people. For some, the thrill of a fast roller-coaster ride is a significant source of utility, for others it is simply a source of nausea. For some, thrash metal music is electrifying, for others it is as much fun to listen to as fingernails on a blackboard at high volume. There is nothing right or wrong about these preferences; they are simply a matter of different tastes. The idea of "rational choice" has nothing to say about the formation of preferences. It just says that we choose what gives us the most utility.

The utility-maximizing Homo Economicus has been widely criticized as a simplistic picture of human motivations. In response, game theorists justify their apparently cynical assumptions about the selfishness of so-called "rational" behaviour by arguing that the utility may include sympathy for other players (so the utility of player A may be increased by a high score for player B) or spite (the utility of player A is increased by a low score for player B), as long as these utilities are all worked into the scores for the game ahead of time. The difficulty of measuring these internal motivations is too often used as a rationale for ignoring them, so that in too many MarketThink stories the idea of utility is identified with purely private costs and benefits, or more simply still with money. But as the idea of utility becomes based on more realistic scenarios, and as our choices are recognized to be more complex than choosing between apple juice or orange juice, so too do externalities become more and more important, and the dynamics of our individual choices become more tangled.

The notion of utility, then, becomes increasingly complex as we move through the examples in this book. In the story of their divorce, Jack's and Jill's concerns were limited to monetary outcomes. When Jill was deciding whether to drop her paper cup or not she did worry about non-monetary gains and costs, but her utility function was a purely private one: the actions of others affected her only through the number of coffee cups she had to see as she walked through the park. When Jack was deciding whether or not to buy a new car, his concern was broader, and included not only the qualities of the car he was to buy, but also his social status – with the way in which he was viewed by others in his neighbourhood.

The co-ordination game is built on a utility function that is sensitive to other people's actions. Many of our consumer choices were seen to be governed by notions of what is fashionable or cool, notions that depend on how people view each other and how we respond to the gaze of others. The inclusion of complex psychological and sociological ideas such as identity into the "rational choice" model leads to even more complicated and intricately tangled dynamics, in which "individual choice" is an unreliable and treacherous guide in our pursuit of prosperity and happiness.

We can draw a few simple lessons from all of this messy real-life complexity.

INDIVIDUAL CHOICE DOES NOT GIVE US WHAT WE WANT. Some critics argue that the market in its purest form leads to bad results, and so people must be making bad choices. Others maintain that people with free choice will make good choices, and thus individual choice will make us happy. But there is a third option: people make good choices, but end up badly off anyway.

A lot of people shop at Wal-Mart, but – whatever MarketThink would have us believe – these shopping trips are not votes in favour of a Wal-Mart-shaped city. They do not demonstrate that we are happy in a Wal-Mart-driven world, and it is quite possible that we would prefer to have a city with smaller and more central stores. We need the chance to pursue those visions too.

MarketThink asserts that regulations for national media content or urban planning demonstrate a lack of trust in the public to make its own choices: that people left to themselves are incompetent. It maintains that individual choice is all we need to get us where we want to go. Critics of MarketThink too often accept this assertion, and point out the obstacles that prevent people from making good decisions, notably the flood of advertising in which we are all immersed. But most people do make reasonable choices most of the time. It's just that good choices are not enough.

FREEDOM OF CHOICE PROMOTES THE PRIVATE, DEGRADES THE PUBLIC. There are predictable ways in which individual choice fails to give us what we want. The temptation to free-ride means that anything public or shared, such as an unpolluted environment or a compact city, is vulnerable in a world of individual choice, even if everyone values these things highly.

FREEDOM OF CHOICE PRODUCES INEQUALITY BASED NOT ON MERIT BUT ON LUCK. When the choice is between joining the herd and being trampled by it, we end up in a winner-take-all society, with most of us losers. The winners have much in common with lottery winners, and their rewards are out of proportion to the benefits they have brought to society.

FREEDOM OF CHOICE DOES NOT PRECLUDE THE EXERCISE OF POWER. When value-cloaked ideas such as the "right to work" are used to provide a cover for attacks on trade unions, political power is being exercised. People opposed to those attacks need to be able to assert that collective action and collective choice are legitimate values too. When homogeneous and predictable products from global companies drive out local vendors, economic power is being exercised. Consumers need to recognize that we are not getting what we want, and that instead we are ending up with less choice as asymmetric information takes hold and local networks of expertise unravel. We need the right to act together.

FREEDOM OF CHOICE DOES NOT PRECLUDE EXPLOITATION. The idea of free exchange is at the root of MarketThink ethics – who enters a free exchange if it does not make them better off? – but free exchange in itself is far from problem-free. Can there be, for instance, such a thing as free exchange between unequal parties? In that kind of an exchange the stronger party can afford to walk away from the transaction if they decide it is not to their benefit. The end result is that the lion's share of the gains go to those who can afford to walk away.

PREDICTABILITY DRIVES OUT QUALITY. Good-quality offerings at the right price will not always find buyers. When one side lacks certainty about the quality of the goods being offered, exchange becomes fraught with uncertainty and many potentially beneficial exchanges fail to take place.

In an advertising-driven world, the franchise model drives out the independent vendor, regardless of quality. In a socially segregated world, the alternative to affirmative action is not hiring by merit, because the market for lemons tells us that insiders will always have a built-in advantage over outsiders, regardless of quality.

SOCIAL EXCLUSION IS SELF-SUSTAINING. The preservation of identity is a powerful force shaping the choices that we make. Our identities and self-images come with a set of prescribed actions that support and maintain exclusions and disadvantages. Members of excluded groups face a no-win choice: abandon the pursuit of the benefits that are enjoyed by the dominant group, or continue that pursuit at the cost not only of losing their identities but also of being rejected by both their own communities and the dominant group.

The ideas of MarketThink clearly work within a limited domain. They do provide insight into some areas of our lives in which only private costs and benefits matter and there are no side effects to our choices, in which we are impervious to the choices made by others. They are limited to choosing between similar commodities in a world in which quality can be appraised at sight (no lemons here), and increasing returns and network effects are negligible.

To sell this picture of choice as "the way the whole world works," as MarketThink does, is overreaching on an epic scale. To appreciate the richness of the world around us is to appreciate that externalities and the tangles they produce are pervasive: that (to go back to chapter 2), society is more like a liquid than a gas.

It is time to place collective action back on the table. Of course collective action does have its difficulties, but the ideals of collective action have no more been destroyed by, for instance, the failure of communism, than the ideals of individual choice were destroyed by the Great Depression of the 1930s.

Most of all, it is time to embrace complexity. This book is about a worldview; it does not pretend (as MarketThink does) that a single solution exists to solve all our problems. Jane Jacobs got it right 45 years ago when she wrote of the problems of cities:

> City processes in real life are too complex to be routine, too particular-ized for application as abstractions. They are always made up of interactions among unique combinations of particulars, and there is no substi-tute for knowing the particulars. . . .
>
> Being human is itself difficult, and therefore all kind of settle-ments (except dream cities) have problems. Big cities have difficulties in abundance, because they have people in abundance. But vital cities are not helpless to combat even the most difficult of problems.[10]

Societies, like cities, have difficulties in abundance. It is a prereq-uisite for successfully overcoming these difficulties that we recognize the complexity of the world we live in. Doing so demands that we reject the worldview and prescriptions of MarketThink and recognize that the "right to individual choice" is a fool's gold. A reliance on individual choice will lead us not to broadly based prosperity, but instead to ever-increasing inequality and the loss of those things that we hold in common.

NOTES

One A World of Choice

1   Piketty and Saez, "Income Inequality in the United States, 1913–1998." The relevant data are in Table A4, and are updated to 2002 in a supplement on Emmanuel Saez's website.

2   Piketty and Saez, "Evolution of Top Incomes." All figures were adjusted for inflation.

3   Piketty and Saez, "Income Inequality in the United States."

4   Stein, *Cult of Efficiency*, p.199.

5   "The Case for Brands," Editorial, *The Economist*, 360, 8238 (September 2001), p.3. For the corporate consultant's quote, see "Who's Wearing the Trousers?" *The Economist*, Sept. 6, 2001, online edition <http://www.economist.com/displaystory.cfm?story_id=770992>.

6   Clive Crook, "Globalisation and Its Critics," *The Economist*, 360, 8241 (Sept. 27, 2001), online edition <http://www.economist.com/surveys/PrinterFriendly.cfm?Story_ID=795995>.

7   Friedman, *Lexus and the Olive Tree*, p.10.

8   Tony Blair, campaign speech, London, June 23, 2004 <http://www.labour.org.uk/news/tbpublicservices0604>.

9   See Stein, *Cult of Efficiency*, pp.199, 200, 202.

10 "Transcript: Bush, Kerry debate domestic policies," CNN, <http://www.cnn.com/2004/ALLPOLITICS/10/13/debate.transcript2/index.html>.

11 The White House, "Specifics on the President's Plan to Strengthen

Retirement Security," Feb. 28, 2002 <http://www.whitehouse.gov/news/releases/2004/08/20040809-9.html>. A 401(k) is a type of retirement plan in which employees save and invest for their own retirement. The name comes for the section of the Internal Revenue Code that established these plans.

12 There are psychological aspects to choice, outside the scope of this book, that also explain why unlimited individual choice does not necessarily give us what we want, and show how a proliferation of choices can add stress, dissatisfaction, and bad outcomes to our lives. These psychological aspects are discussed in an engaging manner in Schwartz, *Paradox of Choice*. Some of the important work in the area has been carried out by Daniel Kahnemann and the late Amos Tversky, whose work uncovered subtle dependencies regarding how choices are framed and emphasized the importance of our adaptation over time to new situations.

Two Good Choices and Bad Outcomes

1 Sen, *Choice, Welfare and Measurement*.

Three Private Choices and Public Failures

1 The list is based on Schelling, *Micromotives and Macrobehaviour*, p.216. The definition of the multi-player prisoner's dilemma is based on Schelling's list, p.218.

2 Sen, *Development as Freedom*, p.128.

3 The example is cited in many economics textbooks. See, for example, Lipsey, Ragan, and Courant, *Microeconomics*.

4 Schelling, *Micromotives and Macrobehaviour*, p.213.

5 Friedman, *Hidden Order*, pp.7–9.

6 Krugman, *Accidental Theorist*, p.76.

7 Dushoff, "License to Pollute."

8 Krugman, *Accidental Theorist*, p.172.

9 *The Washington Post*, March 15, 2005, p.A01.

10 Monsanto Biotechnology Production Information website <http://lscgw1.monsanto.com/biotech/bbasics.nsf/product_information>.

11 Tenner, *Why Things Bite Back*, p.138.

12 Benbrook, "Troubled Times Amid Commercial Success," pp.2–3.

13 Ibid.

14 Environmental News Service, "Herbicide Resistant Weeds Spring up in Bioengineered Soy Fields," May 4, 2001 <http://www.ens-newswire.com/ens/>.

15 Royal Society of Canada, *Elements of Precaution*, p.123.

16 Gordon, "Plan Obsolescence."

17 The London congestion issue is discussed in Surowiecki, *Wisdom of Crowds*, ch.7.

18 Quoted in Susan Pigg, "Belle of the Big-Box Bookstores," *The Toronto Star* (Business Section), Feb. 3, 2001.

19 See Jacobs, *Death and Life of Great American Cities*, pp.436, 433.

20 Ibid., p.29.

21 Ibid., p.433.

Four Arms Races and Red Queens

1 Oswald, "Happiness and Economic Performance," p.1830.

2 Marx, "Wage Labour and Capital," p.83.

3 Letter to the editor, *The New York Times*, Jan. 17, 2001.

4 See Schelling, *Micromotives and Macrobehaviour*.

5 Heath and Potter, *Rebel Sell*, p. 191. In the United States the title is *Rebel Nation*.

6 Ibid., p.129.

7 Ibid., p.322.

8 Ibid., p.114.

Five Co-operation and Its Limits

1 See Olson, *Logic of Collective Action*, p.1.

2 Ian McEwan, *Enduring Love* (London: Jonathan Cape, 1997), pp.14–15.

3 For the arguments here to hold, the number of times the game is repeated must be indeterminate. In the real world, where the distinction between one "move" and the next is rarely obvious, the restriction is not usually important.

4 See Axelrod, *Evolution of Cooperation*.

5 The term "social capital" is often associated with Robert Putnam. For example, see Putnam, *Bowling Alone*.

6 Axelrod, *Evolution of Cooperation*, p.126.

7 See Axelrod, *Evolution of Cooperation*, p.76.

8 Brandenburger and Nalebuff, *Co-opetition*, p.170.

9 Ibid., p.184.

10 See Olson, *Power and Prosperity*.

11 See, for example, the writings of Matt Ridley in Ridley, *Origins of Virtue*; and Ridley and Low, "Can Selfishness Save the Environment?"

12 Olson, *Logic of Collective Action*, p.13.

13 Ostrom, *Governing the Commons*, p.14.

14 See Schelling, *Choice and Consequence*.

15 See Murray, *Wealth of Choices*, p.93.

16 Stephen R. Covey, *The 7 Habits of Highly Effective People: Powerful Lessons in Personal Change* (New York: Fireside, 1990). Richard Carlson has a series of books on the "don't sweat the small stuff" theme, plus a "Don't sweat" website. See, for instance, Carlson, *Don't Sweat the Small Stuff – and It's All Small Stuff: Simple Ways to Keep the Little Things from Taking over Your Life* (New York: Hyperion, 1997).

Six Divide and Conquer

1   Klein, *No Logo*, p.xxi.
2   See chapter 1, p.6.
3   Quoted in Sen, *Development as Freedom*, p.122.
4   Information in this section is taken from Tim Weiner, "Lockheed and the Future of Warfare," *The New York Times*, Nov. 28, 2004.
5   Ortega, *In Sam We Trust*, pp.248–56.
6   See Sen, *Development and Freedom*, p.6.
7   Kaul, Grunber, and Stern, *Global Public Goods*, p.xix.
8   Sen, *Development and Freedom*, p.262.
9   Stiglitz, "What I Learned at the Economic Crisis." Stiglitz discusses the Russian economic transition in more detail in Stiglitz, *Globalization and Its Discontents*.
10 For an example of this thinking, see the quote from Thomas Friedman, p.7 here.
11 See Rodrik, Subramanian, and Trebbi, "Institutions Rule."

Seven That Obscure Object of Desire

1   See Schelling, *Strategy of Conflict*.
2   This example is discussed in Surowiecki, *Wisdom of Crowds*.
3   See Myerson, "Justice, Institutions, and Multiple Equilibria."
4   Kingwell, *Better Living*, p 222.
5   Ibid.
6   See McQuaig, *All You Can Eat*, p.12.
7   Friedman, *Hidden Order*, p.166.
8   Krugman, "Talking about a Revolution."
9   Tirole, *Theory of Industrial Organization*, p.7.
10 See Culler, *Literary Theory*, pp.82–83.

Eight Join or Get Run Over

1   See Frank and Cook, *Winner-Take-All Society*.
2   The phrase was introduced by sociologists in the 1960s and popularized by Malcolm Gladwell in Gladwell, *Tipping Point*.
3   See Nielsen-Hayden, "Profitable Colors."
4   Ibid.
5   *The Portland Press*, March 6, 2005.
6   Hamilton's paper, "Geometry of the Selfish Herd," reached a wider audience when retold by Richard Dawkins in Dawkins, *Selfish Gene*.
7   See Maynard Smith, *Evolution and the Theory of Games* and *Did Darwin Get It Right?* for examples, as well as Dawkins, *Extended Phenotype* and *Selfish Gene*.
8   Grant and Wood, *Blockbusters and Trade Wars*, pp.31–32.
9   See Borsook, *Cyberselfish*.

10   Jacobs, *Cities and the Wealth of Nations*.

11   Shiva, *Biopiracy*, pp.69–70.

12   Ibid., p.72.

13   Madeleine Bunting, "The Profits That Kill," *The Guardian* (London), Feb.12, 2001.

14   Hepburn, "Introduction," in Hepburn, ed., *Can the Market Save Our Schools?* p.1.

15   Frank, "Higher Education," p.4.

16   The research was reported in Jesson, *Educational Outcomes and Value Added by Specialist Schools*.

17   Frank and Cook, *Winner-Take-All Society*.

18   Frank, "Higher Education," p.5.

19   Stein, *Cult of Efficiency*, p.103.

20   Ibid., p.104.

21   Brighouse, "How Lotteries Could Make School Admissions a Whole Lot Fairer."

22   Hepburn, "Can the Market Save Our Schools?" p.4.

23   Murray, *Wealth of Choices*, p.9.

24   Lewis, *New New Thing*, back cover blurb.

25   J.C. Ramo, "1999 Person of the Year," *Time*, Dec. 27, 1999.

26   Taleb, *Fooled By Randomness*, p.113.

27   Ibid., p.27.

28   Ibid., pp.120–21.

29   Quoted by Carol Goar, "We've Become a Market Society," *The Toronto Star*, July 27 2002; the second quotation is a paraphrase by Goar of Rubin's ideas.

Nine **The Devil You Know**

1   This tale is loosely based on Bikhchandani, Hirshleifer, and Welch, "Theory of Fads, Fashion, Custom, and Cultural Change."

2   Keynes, *General Theory of Employment, Interest and Money*, p.156.

3   Klein, *No Logo*, p.69.

4   Ibid., p.72.

5   Ibid., p.73.

6   Gladwell, *Tipping Point*, pp.3–5.

7   Grant and Wood, *Blockbusters and Trade Wars*, p.48.

8   Industry analyst Larry Gerbrant, quoted in Grant and Wood, *Blockbusters and Trade Wars*, p.84.

9   Jack Valenti, remarks before the Canadian Film and Television Production Association (CFTPA), Ottawa, Feb. 7, 2002.

10   Akerlof, "The Market for 'Lemons.'"

11   Akerlof, "Writing the 'Market for Lemons.'"

12   See Stiglitz, *Whither Socialism?* for a detailed discussion.

13   See Varian, *Intermediate Economics*, p.672.

14   The canonical statement of this point of view is Becker, *Economics of Discrimination*.

15 The case for minimum-quality standards in a variety of markets affected by asymmetric information was made by Leland, "Quacks, Lemons, and Licensing."

16 The Society of Independent Brewers website, "'Beer Revolution' as Number of New Breweries Soars," Sept. 14, 2005 <www.siba.co.uk/news/news_item.asp?NewsID=104>.

17 Krugman, "Talking about a Revolution."

Ten Free to Choose, but Exploited

1 See Dawkins, *Selfish Gene*, p.285.

2 This section is based on the work of Mancur Olson; especially Olson, *Power and Prosperity*.

3 See Olson, *Power and Prosperity*, p.7.

4 See Becker and Becker, *Economics of Real Life*, p.263.

5 *Dirty Pretty Things*, directed by Stephen Frears, script by Steven Knight, U.K., 2002.

6 Nasar, *Beautiful Mind*.

Eleven Beyond Whimsley

1 See Akerlof and Kranton, "Economics and Identity," "Identity and Schooling," and "Identity and the Economics of Organizations.

2 Nowak, Page, and Sigmund, "Fairness Versus Reason in the Ultimatum Game," p.1773.

3 Sigmund, Fehr, and Nowak, "Economics of Fair Play," p.83.

4 Elster, "Doing Our Level Best," pp.12–13.

5 See, for example, Rapoport and Chammah, *Prisoner's Dilemma*.

6 Pierson, *Gender Trials*, p.134, quoted in Akerlof and Kranton, "Economics and Identity."

7 Akerlof and Kranton, "Economics and Identity," pp.736–37, quote a U.S. Supreme Court decision: "an employer who objects to aggressive traits in women but whose positions require this trait places women in an intolerable and impermissible Catch 22."

8 See Akerlof and Kranton, "Economics and Identity."

9 Akerlof and Kranton, "Identity and Schooling," p.1182. The student is quoted in Douglas E. Foley, *Learning Capitalist Culture: Deep in the Heart of Texas* (Philadelphia: University of Philadelphia Press, 1990).

10 Jacobs, *Death and Life of Great American Cities*, p.447.

BIBLIOGRAPHY

Akerlof, G.A. "The Market for 'Lemons': Quality Uncertainty and the Market Mechanism." *Quarterly Journal of Economics* 84,3 (1970): 488–500.

____. "Behavioural Macroeconomics and Macroeconomic Behavior." Nobel Prize Lecture, 2001.

____. "Writing 'The Market for "Lemons"': A Personal and Interpretive Essay." Nobel Prize Organization website <http://nobelprize.org/economics/articles/akerlof/index.html>, 2001.

Akerlof, G.A. and R.E. Kranton. "Economics and Identity." *The Quarterly Journal of Economics* 115 (2000): 715–53.

____. "Identity and Schooling: Some Lessons for the Economics of Education." *Journal of Economic Literature* 40 (2002): 1167–1201.

____. "Identity and the Economics of Organizations." *Journal of Economic Perspectives* 19 (2005): 19–32.

Allingham, M. *Choice Theory: A Very Short Introduction.* Oxford: Oxford University Press, 2002.

Axelrod, R. *The Evolution of Cooperation.* New York: Basic Books, 1984.

Baird, D.G., R.H. Gertner, and R.C. Picker. *Game Theory and the Law.* Cambridge, Mass: Harvard University Press, 1994.

Ball, Philip. *Critical Mass: How One Thing Leads to Another.* London: Arrow Books, 2005.

Becker, G.S. *The Economics of Discrimination.* Chicago: University of Chicago Press, 1957.

Becker, G.S. and G.N. Becker. *The Economics of Life: From Baseball to Affirma-*

tive Action to Immigration, How Real-World Issues Affect Our Everyday Life. New York: McGraw-Hill, 1997.

Benbrook, C.M. "Troubled Times Amid Commercial Success for Roundup Ready Soybeans." Ag BioTech InfoNet Technical Paper, Idaho, 2001.

Bikhchandani, S., D. Hirshleifer, and I. Welch. "A Theory of Fads, Fashion, Custom, and Cultural Change as Informational Cascades." *Journal of Political Economy* 100 (1992): 992–1026.

Borsook, P. *Cyberselfish: A Critical Romp Through the Terribly Libertarian Culture of High Tech*. New York: Public Affairs Books, 2000.

Brandenburger, A.M. and B.J. Nalebuff. *Co-opetition: A Revolutionary Mindset That Combines Competition and Cooperation: The Game Theory Strategy That's Changing the Game of Business*. New York: Currency Doubleday, 1996.

Brighouse, H. "How Lotteries Could Make School Admissions a Whole Lot Fairer." *The Independent*, June 8, 2000 <http://education.independent.co.uk/news/article258775.ece>.

Chong, D. *Collective Action and the Civil Rights Movement*. Chicago: University of Chicago Press, 1991.

Culler, J. *Literary Theory: A Very Short Introduction*. Oxford: Oxford University Press, 1997.

David, P.A. "Clio and the Economics of QWERTY." *The American Economics Review* 75,2 (1985): 332–37.

Davis, M.D. *Game Theory: A Nontechnical Introduction*. New York: Basic Books, 1983.

Dawkins, R. *The Extended Phenotype: The Long Reach of the Gene*. New York: W.H. Freeman, 1983.

____. *The Selfish Gene*. 2nd ed. Oxford: Oxford University Press, 1989.

Dushoff, Jonathan. "A License to Pollute." *Multinational Monitor* 11,3 (March 1990).

Elster, J. *Ulysses Unbound: Studies in Rationality, Precommitment, and Constraints*. Cambridge: Cambridge University Press, 2000.

____."Doing Our Level Best." *The Times Literary Supplement* 29 (March 12–13, 1996): 12–13.

____. *Ulysses and the Sirens: Studies in Rationality and Irrationality*. Cambridge: Cambridge University Press, 1979.

Frank, R.H. "Higher Education: The Ultimate Winner-Take-All Market?" In *Forum Futures: Exploring the Future of Higher Education*, ed. M. Devlin and J. Meyerson. San Franciso: Jossey-Bass, 2001.

Frank, R.H. and P.J. Cook. *The Winner-Take-All Society: Why the Few at the Top Get So Much More Than the Rest of Us*. New York: Penguin Books, 1995.

Frank, T. *One Market under God: Extreme Capitalism, Market Populism, and the End of Economic Democracy*. New York, Anchor Books, 2000.

Friedman, D. *Hidden Order: The Economics of Everyday Life*. New York: HarperBusiness, 1996.

Friedman, T.L. *The Lexus and the Olive Tree: Understanding Globalization*. New York: Farrar, Straus and Giroux.

Fudenberg, D.J. and J. Tirole. *Game Theory*. Cambridge: MIT Press, 1991.

Fukuyama, F. *The Great Disruption: Human Nature and the Reconstitution of Social Order*. New York: Simon and Schuster, 1999.

Gibbons, R. *Game Theory for Applied Economists*. Princeton, N.J.: Princeton University Press, 1992.

Gilpin, R. *Global Political Economy: Understanding the International Economic Order*. Princeton, N.J.: Princeton University Press, 2001.

Gladwell, M. *The Tipping Point: How Little Things Can Make a Big Difference*. Boston: Little, Brown and Company, 2000.

Gordon, Peter. "Plan Obsolescence." *Reason Online* <hhtp://reason.com>, June 1998.

Grant, P.S. and C. Wood. *Blockbusters and Trade Wars: Popular Culture in a Globalized World*. Vancouver: Douglas and McIntyre, 2004.

Hardin, G. "The Tragedy of the Commons." *Science* 162 (1968): 1243–48.

Hardin, R. *Collective Action*. Baltimore: Johns Hopkins University Press, 1982.

Heath, J. and A. Potter. *The Rebel Sell: Why the Culture Can't Be Jammed*. Toronto: Harper Perennial, 2004.

Hepburn, C.R., ed. "Can the Market Save Our Schools?" Technical Report, The Fraser Institute, Vancouver, 2001.

Jacobs, J. *The Death and Life of Great American Cities*. New York: Random House, 1961.

_____. *Cities and the Wealth of Nations*. New York: Vintage Books, 1984.

Kaul, I., I. Grunber, and M.S. Stern, eds. *Global Public Goods: International Co-operation in the 21st Century*. Oxford: Oxford University Press, 1999.

Kerstetter, S. "Rags and Riches: Wealth Inequality in Canada." Technical Report, Canadian Centre for Policy Alternatives, Ottawa, 2002.

Keynes, J.M. *The General Theory of Employment, Interest and Money*. London: Macmillan, 1936.

Kingwell, M. *Better Living: In Pursuit of Happiness from Plato to Prozac*. Toronto: Penguin Books, 1998.

Klein, N. *No Logo: Taking Aim at the Brand Bullies*. Toronto: Knopf Canada, 2000.

Kreps, D., J. Milgrom, J. Roberts, and R. Wilson, R. "Rational Cooperation in the Finitely-Repeated Prisoner's Dilemma." *Journal of Economic Theory* 27 (1982): 245–252.

Krugman, P. *Development, Geography, and Economic Theory*. Cambridge: The MIT Press, 1995.

_____. *The Accidental Theorist and Other Dispatches from the Dismal Science*. New York: W.W. Norton and Company, 1998.

_____. "Talking about a Revolution." *Slate*, Sept. 27, 1999 <http://www.slate.com/id/33334>.

_____. "The Mercury Scandal." *The New York Times*, editorial page, April 6, 2004.

Laffont J-J. *The Economics of Uncertainty and Information*. Cambridge: The MIT Press, 1989.

Leland, H.E. "Quacks, Lemons, and Licensing." *Journal of Political Economy* 87 (1979): 1328–46.

Lewis, Michael. *The New New Thing: A Silicon Valley Story*. New York: W.W. Norton, 2000.

Lipsey, R.G., C.T.S. Ragan, and P.N. Courant. *Microeconomics*. 9th Canadian ed. Don Mills, Ont.: Addison Wesley, 1997.

Maital, S. and S. Maital. *Economic Games People Play*. New York: Basic Books, 1984.

Maynard Smith, J. *Evolution and the Theory of Games*. Cambridge: Cambridge University Press, 1982.

____. *Did Darwin Get It Right? Essays on Games, Sex and Evolution*. New York: Chapman and Hall, 1988.

McEwan, I. *Enduring Love*. Toronto: Knopf, 1997.

McQuaig, L. *All You Can Eat: Greed, Lust and the New Capitalism*. Toronto: Penguin, 2001.

Murray, A. *The Wealth of Choices: How the New Economy Puts Power in Your Hands and Money in Your Pocket*. New York: Crown Publishers, 2000.

Myerson, R. *Game Theory: Analysis of Conflict*. Cambridge, Mass.: Harvard University Press, 1991.

____. "Justice, Institutions, and Multiple Equilibria." *Chicago Journal of International Law* 5 (2004): 91–107.

Nasar, S. *A Beautiful Mind: The Life of Mathematical Genius and Nobel Laureate John Nash*. Waterville, Me.: Thorndike Press, 1999.

Nielsen-Hayden, T. "Profitable Colors." Making Light Weblog. <http://nielsenhayden.com/makinglight> (accessed Feb. 24, 2006).

Nowak, M.A., K.M. Page, and K. Sigmund. "Fairness Versus Reason in the Ultimatum Game." *Science* 289 (2000): 1773–75.

Olson, M. *The Logic of Collective Action: Public Goods and the Theory of Groups*. Cambridge, Mass.: Harvard University Press, 1965.

____. *Power and Prosperity: Outgrowing Communist and Capitalist Dictatorships*. New York: Basic Books, 2000.

Ortega, R. *In Sam We Trust: The Untold Story of Sam Walton and Wal-Mart, the World's Most Powerful Retailer*. New York: Times Business Books, 1998.

Ostrom, E. *Governing the Commons: The Evolution of Institutions for Collective Action*. Cambridge: Cambridge University Press, 1990.

Oswald, A. "Happiness and Economic Performance." *Economic Journal* 107 (1997).

Pierson, R.R. *Gender Trials: Emotional Lives in Contemporary Law Firms*. Berkeley: University of California Press, 1995.

Piketty, T. and E. Saez. "Income Inequality in the United States, 1913–1998." National Bureau of Economic Research (NBER) Working Paper no. 8467, Cambridge, Mass., 2001.

____. "The Evolution of Top Incomes: A Historical and International Perspective." NBER Working Paper no. 11955, Cambridge, Mass., 2006.

Poundstone, W. *Prisoner's Dilemma: John von Neumann, Game Theory, and the Puzzle of the Bomb*. New York: Doubleday, 1992.

Putnam, R. *Bowling Alone: The Collapse and Revival of American Community*. New York: Simon and Schuster, 2000.

Rapoport, A. *Strategy and Conscience*. New York: Harper and Row, 1964.

Rapoport, A. and A.M. Chammah. *Prisoner's Dilemma*. Ann Arbor: University of Michigan Press, 1965.

Ridley, M. *The Origins of Virtue: Human Instincts and the Evolution of Cooperation*. New York: Penguin, 1997.

Ridley, M. and B.S. Low. "Can Selfishness Save the Environment?" *The Atlantic Monthly*, September 1993: 76–86.

Rodrik, D., A. Subramanian, and F. Trebbi. "Institutions Rule: The Primacy of Institutions over Geography and Integration in Economic Development." National Bureau of Economic Research (NBER) Working Paper no. W9305, Cambridge, Mass., November 2002.

Royal Society of Canada. *Elements of Precaution: Recommendation for the Regulation of Food Biotechnology in Canada*. Ottawa, January 2001.

Sandler, T. *Collective Action: Theory and Applications*. Ann Arbor: University of Michigan Press, 1992.

Schelling, T.C. *The Strategy of Conflict*. Cambridge, Mass.: Harvard University Press, 1963.

____. *Micromotives and Macrobehaviour*. New York: W.W. Norton and Company, 1978.

____. *Choice and Consequence: Perspectives of an Errant Economist*. Cambridge, Mass.: Harvard University Press, 1984.

Schwartz, B. *The Paradox of Choice: Why More Is Less*. New York: HarperCollins, 2004.

Sen, A. *Choice, Welfare and Measurement*. Oxford: Basil Blackwell, 1982.

____. *Development as Freedom*. New York: Knopf, 1999.

Shiva, V. *Biopiracy: The Plunder of Nature and Knowledge*. Toronto: Between the Lines, 1997.

____. *Stolen Harvest: The Hijacking of the Global Food Supply*. Boston: South End Press, 2000.

Sigmund, K., E. Fehr, and M. Nowak. "The Economics of Fair Play." *Scientific American* 286 (2002):83–87.

Singer, P. *A Darwinian Left: Politics, Evolution and Cooperation*. London: Weidenfeld and Nicolson, 1999.

Stein, J.G. *The Cult of Efficiency*. Toronto: House of Anansi Press, 2001.

Stiglitz, J. *Whither Socialism?* Cambridge, Mass.: The MIT Press, 1994.

____. "What I Learned at the Economic Crisis." *The New Republic*, April 17, 2000.

____. *Globalization and Its Discontents*. New York: W.W. Norton and Company, 2002.

Surowiecki, J. *The Wisdom of Crowds: Why the Many Are Smarter Than the Few and How Collective Wisdom Shapes Business, Economies, Societies and Nations*. New York: Doubleday, 2004.

Taleb, N.N. *Fooled by Randomness: The Hidden Role of Chance in the Markets and in Life*. New York and London: Texere, 2001.

Tenner, E. *Why Things Bite Back: Technology and the Revenge of Unintended Consequences*. New York: Vintage Books, 1996.

Thaler, R.H. *The Winner's Curse: Paradoxes and Anomalies of Economic Life*. Princeton, N.J.: Princeton University Press, 1992.

Tirole, J. *The Theory of Industrial Organization*. Cambridge, Mass.: The MIT Press, 1988.

Varian, H.R. *Intermediate Economics*. 6th ed. New York: W.W. Norton and Company, 2003.

von Neumann, J. and O. Morgenstern. *Theory of Games and Economic Behavior*. Princeton, N.J.: Princeton University Press, 1944.

Weibull, J. *Evolutionary Game Theory*. Cambridge, Mass.: The MIT Press, 1995.

INDEX